# Learning Disabilities Spectrum

# LEARNING DISABILITIES SPECTRUM

## *ADD, ADHD, and LD*

**Edited by Arnold J. Capute, Pasquale J. Accardo, and Bruce K. Shapiro**

**York Press, Inc.**
Baltimore • Toronto • Sydney

This book was manufactured in the United States of America.
Typography by The Type Shoppe, Inc.
Printing and binding by BookCrafters.
Cover design by Joseph Dieter, Jr.
Book design by Sheila Stoneham.

**Library of Congress Cataloging-In-Publication Data**

Learning disabilities spectrum : ADD, ADHD, and LD / edited by Arnold
   J. Capute, Pasquale J. Accardo, and Bruce K. Shapiro.
     p. cm.
   Includes bibliographical references and index.
   ISBN 0-912752-33-5
   1. Learning disabilities—Congresses. 2. Attention-deficit
hyperactivity disorder—Congresses. 3. Learning disabled children—
Mental health—Congresses. I. Capute, Arnold J., 1923- .
II. Accardo, Pasquale J. III. Shapiro, Bruce K.
RJ496.L4L454   1994                       93-39701
618.92'8588—dc20                           CIP

# Contents

# Participants

*Pasquale J. Accardo, M.D.*
Director, Knights of Columbus
Development Center
Cardinal Glennon Children's
Hospital
Room 416, Glennon Hall
1465 South Grand Boulevard
St. Louis, MO 63104-1095

*Thomas Baumgardner, Ph.D.*
Research Coordinator,
Behavioral Neurogenetics
and Neuroimaging Research
Center
The Kennedy Krieger Institute
707 North Broadway
Baltimore, MD 21205

*Michael Bender, Ed.D.*
Vice President,
Educational Programs
The Kennedy Krieger Institute
and School
100 North Ann Street
Baltimore, MD 21231

*Arnold J. Capute, M.D.*
Director, Pediatric Training
The Kennedy Krieger Institute
707 North Broadway
Baltimore, MD 21205

*James C. Harris, M.D.*
Director, Developmental
Neuropsychiatry
The Johns Hopkins University
School of Medicine
600 North Wolfe Street
Baltimore, MD 21205

*Stephen R. Hooper, Ph.D.*
Assistant Professor of Psychiatry
Clinical Center for the Study of
Development and Learning
and the Department of
Psychiatry

CB #7255, BSRC University of
North Carolina
Chapel Hill, NC 27599

*Doris J. Johnson, Ph.D.*
Professor of Learning
Disabilities
Northwestern University
Frances Searle Building
2299 Sheridan Road
Evanston, IL 60208-3560

*Paramjit T. Joshi, M.D.*
Associate Professor, Division
of Child & Adolescent
Psychiatry
The Johns Hopkins University
School of Medicine
314 CMSC
600 North Wolfe Street
Baltimore, MD 21205

*Walter E. Kaufmann, M.D.*
Instructor in Neurology,
Department of Neurology
The Johns Hopkins University
School of Medicine
915 Hunterian Building
725 North Wolfe Street
Baltimore, MD 21205

*Herbert A. Lubs, M.D.*
Director, Division of Genetics
University of Miami School
of Medicine
PO Box 016820 (D-820)
Miami, FL 33101

*Allan L. Reiss, M.D.*
Director, Behavioral
Neurogenetics and
Neuroimaging
Research Center
The Kennedy Krieger Institute
707 North Broadway
Baltimore, MD 21205

*Bruce K. Shapiro, M.D.*
Assistant Vice President for
The Learning Center and
Family Center
The Kennedy Krieger Institute
707 North Broadway
Baltimore, MD 21205

*Bennett A. Shaywitz, M.D.*
Professor of Pediatrics and
Neurology
Director of Pediatric
Neurology
Yale University School of
Medicine
PO Box 3333
New Haven, CT 06510-8064

*Sally E. Shaywitz, M.D.*
Professor of Pediatrics
Director, Learning Disorders
Unit
Yale University School of
Medicine
PO Box 3333
New Haven, CT 06510-8064

*Wendy L. Stone, Ph.D.*
Assistant Professor of
Pediatrics and Psychology
& Human Development
Child Development Center
Vanderbilt University-Medical
Center South
Room 426
2100 Pierce Avenue
Nashville, TN 37232-3573

*Elisabeth H. Wiig, Ph.D.*
Professor Emerita, Sargent
College for Allied Health
Professions
7101 Lake Powell Drive
Arlington, TX 76016

# *Preface*

In this decade of the brain, teams of basic researchers and clinical investigators are attempting to correlate topographical brain dysfunction with clinical patterns of a wide variety of cognitive and neurobehavioral dysfunction syndromes. Such cerebral localizations would, we hope, result in the discovery of specific neurotransmitter and neural pathway problems, improved neuropharmacological management, gene localization for isolated deficits, and more specific delineation of the natural history of different neurocognitive syndromes. Although slow, but steady, progress has been made in these investigations, the prevalent "aspirin" therapy—Ritalin—continues to benefit selected neurobehavioral profiles. Only recently have professionals again come to the realization that neurobehavioral profiles in many of these learning and attention disorders mirror a single—if diffuse—neuromaturational deficit pattern.

Alfred A. Strauss originally described a neurobehavioral profile associated with nonspecific brain injury as the "brain-damaged child syndrome" or Strauss syndrome (Strauss and Lehtinen 1947). This milestone inaugurated an era of lumping that came to be accepted despite the nagging misgivings of many professionals that this profile was too heterogeneous to be diagnostic of "brain damage." In the past decade, splintering arose along with attempts to classify the various learning disability patterns better and to unravel their complex associations with differing attention deficit disorders and hyperactivity syndromes. Other nebulous psychiatric diagnostic entities, such as conduct disorder and oppositional defiant disorder, were incorporated into this confusing surfeit of pediatric conditions in need of clarification. This approach was significant to clinical investigators, but it may have added to the confusion of clinicians attempting to work with children with learning disabilities.

In the past decade, we came to the realization that most earlier research upon which much of our clinical practice was based was seriously flawed. Many measures did not meet the minimal standards for psychodiagnostic instruments (Berk 1984), and the effectiveness of many accepted and expensive interventions could not be validated (Kavale and Forness 1985). In response to this chaotic and contradictory mix of data and beliefs, the National Institutes of Health launched a national research effort in an attempt to create order from all the chaos.

One initial result of this effort is a draft neuropsychological framework that attempts to categorize the diverse phenomena according to research-validated localization studies. This nosology (Pennington 1991) proposes a five-item categorization system: (1) dyslexia, phonological processing disorders, or developmental language disorders (with localization of brain damage/dysfunction documented in the left perisylvian fissure); (2) executive function disorders of attentional deficits (with localization of brain damage/dysfunction documented in the prefrontal region); (3) right hemisphere learning disorders with problems in written language, mathematics, and spatial cognition (with localization of brain damage/dysfunction documented in the posterior right hemisphere); (4) autistic spectrum disorders or deficits in social cognition (with localization of brain damage/dysfunction documented in the limbic system, frontal lobe, and cerebellum); (5) acquired long-term memory disorders or amnesia (with localization of brain damage/dysfunction documented in the hippocampus and amygdala).

Although many controversial aspects of this proposed classification remain—such as the inclusion of attentional problems under learning disabilities and the separation of autism and Asperger syndrome under social cognition deficits, rather than placing autism under language disorders—it is the beginning of an attempt to constitute dialog between research neuroscience and the clinical practice of learning and attentional disorders. Zametkin et al. (1990) have reinforced the organic basis of what had been perceived as a more behavioral component of these syndromes. The correlation of topographical and clinical patterns of a wide variety of cognitive and neurobehavioral syndromes will enhance the understanding of the natural history of these disorders and the events that modify them. Other methods have bypassed the cerebral intermediary; recent research has been able to localize human gene segments associated with both dyslexia and attention deficit hyperactivity disorder (Hauser et al. 1993).

This volume, the conference proceedings from the Fifteenth Annual Spectrum of Developmental Disabilities Course presented at The Johns Hopkins Medical Institutions, March 16–18, 1992, is an attempt to begin to bridge some of the gaps between the lumping and splintering camps. Both lumpers and splitters have much to offer; both have a long way to go.

Arnold Capute, M.D.
Pasquale Accardo, M.D.
Bruce Shapiro, M.D.

### REFERENCES

Berk, R. A. 1984. *Screening and Diagnosis of Children with Learning Disabilities.* Springfield, IL: Charles C Thomas.

Hauser, P., Zamethkin, A. J., Martinez, P., Vitiello, B., Matochik, J. A., Mixson, J., and Weintraub, B. D. 1993. Attention deficit-hyperactivity disorder in people with generalized resistance to thyroid hormone. *New England Journal of Medicine* 328:997–1001

Kavale, K., and Forness, S. 1985. *The Science of Learning Disabilities.* Boston: Little, Brown and Company.

Pennington, B. F. 1991. *Diagnosing Learning Disorders: A Neuropsychological Framework.* New York: The Guilford Press.

Strauss, A., and Lehtinen, L. 1947. *Psychopathology and Education of the Brain Injured Child.* New York: Grune & Stratten.

Zametkin, A. J., Nordahl, T. E., Gross, M., King, A. C., Semple, W. E., Rumsey, J., Hamburger, S., and Cohen, R. 1990. Cerebral glucose metabolism in adults with hyperactivity of childhood onset. *New England Journal of Medicine* 323: 1361–1366.

# Chapter • 1

## A New Conceptual Model for Dyslexia

*Sally E. Shaywitz,
Jack M. Fletcher, and
Bennett A. Shaywitz*

For almost a century now, clinicians, investigators, and educators have been intrigued by the inability to learn to read in persons with otherwise adequate intelligence. Beginning with the description by the British physician, W. Pringle Morgan, in 1896 of a 14-year-old boy who was "bright and intelligent" but whose "great difficulty has been—and is now—his inability to read," this syndrome, in which words have "no meaning" in an otherwise normal patient (one who suffered no injury or illness), has continued both to puzzle and challenge generations of researchers interested in the workings of the nervous system. Hinshelwood (1896) described dyslexia as a "peculiar form of word blindness" (p. 1451). Reporting on an adult patient, Hinshelwood differentiated complete word blindness, *alexia*, from patients with partial impairment, or what he termed *dyslexia*, so that, by the end of the nineteenth century, a specific syndrome in children and adults, dyslexia, was defined, which involved the inability to read despite normal vision. Thus, in less than a quarter of a century, from the earliest reports beginning in 1877 with the description by Kussmaul (Hinshelwood 1896) of word blindness in adults with

Supported in part by Grant #PO1 HD21888 and #1P50 HD25802 from NICHD. Presented, in part, at the Ross Conference on School Function, September 9–11, 1992, Washington, DC.

acquired inability to read, to the first use of the term dyslexia in 1887 by Berlin (Hinshelwood 1896), who ascribed the problem to cerebral, not ocular, pathology, to the description by Morgan of dyslexia affecting a child with no known antecedent injury (1896), the basic foundation of our current notion of dyslexia was in place.

Once established as a clinical entity, the next important phase of inquiry into dyslexia was the important contributions of Samuel Torey Orton. Orton's 1925 report heralded the modern era of dyslexia, and several of his conclusions are still valid. He likened dyslexia to the aphasias, he postulated that the problem was at the symbolic level, and he warned that psychometric tests unfairly penalized persons with dyslexia and suggested special training as a remedial step in treating children with dyslexia. Orton speculated that, rather than a cerebral defect as suggested by Hinshelwood, the mechanism responsible for dyslexia was a dysfunction. His work presaged the modern concept of dyslexia as a disability—rather than a defect—which did not imply low intelligence.

Since Orton's seminal contributions, the field has been concerned both with understanding the basic biological mechanisms underlying dyslexia and with ensuring that affected individuals are first identified and then receive beneficial interventions. Results of recent investigations suggest that these two critical goals are interrelated and that a re-examination of conceptual models underlying the disorder are necessary in order to provide both the best strategies for understanding the basic neurobiology of dyslexia and for helping to assure that each child receives the help he or she requires for success in reading and in school.

## CONCEPTUAL MODELS AS THE CORNERSTONE OF INQUIRY

Although much attention and discussion is focused on learning more about dyslexia, what is often overlooked is the critical role of a conceptual model as the cornerstone of inquiry. How we choose to address the most critical questions necessary to characterize and understand dyslexia, including its epidemiology, identification, treatment, and prognosis will reflect the particular criteria used to define the disorder. How we define any disorder, including dyslexia, in turn, reflects the conceptual framework used to think about that disorder. Thus, the conceptual framework or model within which a disorder is considered will set the parameters for definition and will be inextricably linked both to the clinical care of affected individuals and to the strategies chosen to investigate the disorder itself.

## MODELS OF DYSLEXIA

### Traditional Model of Dyslexia

Traditionally, dyslexia has been viewed as a specific categorical entity that affects a small, circumscribed group of children and that is invariant over time (table I). Classically, this group of individuals, often referred to as having specific reading retardation (SRR) (Rutter, Tizard, and Whitmore 1970), has been envisioned as primarily male and as qualitatively distinct from other poor readers, readers variously referred to as having general reading backwardness (GRB) or as being garden variety poor readers (Stanovich 1988). Investigators, attempting to validate this notion of dyslexia as a separate entity, have concentrated their efforts on trying to demonstrate that persons with dyslexia are qualitatively distinct from other poor readers, that is, that there are boundaries separating the two groups. In such a conceptualization, there is a discontinuity between dyslexic readers and the so-called garden variety poor readers. Evidence for just such a discontinuity was interpreted as confirmed in the Isle of Wight series of studies of 1964 and 1965, which were published in the 1970s (Rutter, Tizard, and Whitmore 1970). Together, the statistical data from the Isle of Wight studies and the gender prevalence data that suggested that dyslexia somehow affected more boys than girls (Finucci and Childs 1981) were interpreted as evidence that dyslexia, rather than occurring along a continuum, was best represented as a categorical entity. This categorical conceptualization of dyslexia served as the basis for the definition of dyslexia and with it the identification and classification of affected individuals—both for the provision of educational services and for the construction of research samples to investigate the disorder itself.

**Statistical Support for the Categorical Model.** The Isle of Wight studies provided data that were interpreted as providing both a rationale and empirical support for the classification of SRR as a categorical entity (Rutter and Yule 1975; Yule and Rutter 1985). Two groups of readers were identified: (1) those with SRR, defined as a severe discrepancy between *observed* reading and *predicted* reading based on age

Table I.  Traditional Models of Dyslexia

| Categorical Models |
| --- |
| Specific categorical entity |
| Affects small circumscribed group |
| Affects predominantly males |
| Qualitatively distinct |
| Demarcated by boundaries |
| Discontinuities exist |

and short-WISC IQ; and (2) those with GRB, reading below age but not below ability. Children identified as SRR conform to traditional definitions of dyslexia: compared to the level of reading predicted by their intelligence, their observed reading scores represent an unexpected failure to learn to read (Critchley 1970). In contrast, in children identified as GRB, the reading difficulty is not unexpected; their relatively poor reading scores are consistent with their relatively low ability levels.

These definitions were then used to determine the prevalence rate of each type of reading impairment. Compared to the predicted prevalence rate, an overrepresentation of observed children with SRR was reported and interpreted as providing support for the notion that "children with (specific reading retardation) form a 'hump' at the bottom of the normal curve" (Yule and Rutter 1975, p. 447). Thus, Rutter and Yule used these findings to argue that reading ability is bimodally distributed, with SRR representing the extreme lower tail of the distribution (see figure 1).

**Influence of the Categorical Model.** As noted earlier, although not often discussed directly, the conceptual model describing a particular disorder will be reflected in how we think about that disorder and in how we operationalize the care of affected individuals, including both how we identify such individuals and how we go about treating them. Categorical disorders are characterized as highly discrete entities, entities that are discontinuous with, and sharply demarcated from the normal distribution (see table II). Such disorders typically occur as all-or-none phenomena and have distinct cut-points that separate affected individuals from the rest of the population. In such a model, the mechanisms responsible for the expression of the disorder are

Table II.  Models of Reading Disability—Categorical versus Dimensional

| Categorical | Dimensional |
|---|---|
| Discrete | On a continuum |
| Discontinuous | Blends into normal |
| Cut-points distinct | Cut-points arbitrary |
| All or none | By degrees |
| Qualitative differences | Quantitative differences |
| Mechanisms | |
| Characteristics | |
| Prognosis | |
| Interventions, treatments | |
| Diagnosis stable over time | Variability in diagnosis |
| e.g., Muscular dystrophy | Hypertension |
| Tay-Sachs Disease | Obesity |
| Achondroplasia | Short stature |
| Down syndrome | Mental retardation |

viewed as representing qualitative differences from the norm. These mechanisms are considered to be either absolutely different from the norm or so quantitatively different from the norm as to constitute a qualitative difference. The mechanisms underlying such categorical entities as muscular dystrophy, cystic fibrosis, or Down syndrome represent such qualitative departures from the norm. Often, sharply demarcated disorders in which affected individuals are categorically different from the norm represent the expression of a single or major genetic disturbance. Characteristics of affected individuals are viewed as qualitatively distinct from those of nonaffected persons. As we discuss below, our views of prognosis, stability of diagnosis, approaches to intervention, and interpretation of results of intervention studies all reflect the conceptual framework or model within which the disorder is considered (Shaywitz et al. 1992). The view of dyslexia or SRR as a discrete classification, as a categorical, rather than a dimensional disorder, has served as the basis for investigations into the neurobiology of dyslexia and for the identification and provision of services to individuals with the disorder.

### Dimensional Models

The need to refer to disorders, even those that occur along a continuum, by a specific diagnostic label often obscures the fact that many, if not most, disorders in nature occur in gradations and, thus, conform to a dimensional rather than a categorical model. Dimensional disorders occur along a continuum that blends into the normal distribution and requires the imposition of, often arbitrary, cut-off points for identification (see figure 1). Hypertension and obesity represent two of the most common of the dimensional disorders. Blood pressure, as most

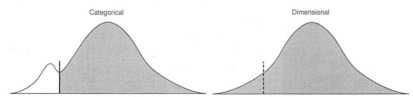

Categorical · Dimensional

Figure 1. Classification models. The categorical model posits that there is a bimodal distribution with a sharply demarcated lower mode. Within the categorical model of dyslexia, this second, lower mode is considered to represent the cases of dyslexia. In contrast, within a dimensional model there is a unimodal distribution and no obvious cutoff point to separate one group of children from another. Within such a dimensional model, children with dyslexia are represented as the extreme lower tail of the distribution; there are no "natural joints" serving as cut-points. While cut-points may be imposed, these are arbitrary and do not necessarily represent a natural break.

physiological parameters (heart rate, temperature), occurs along a continuum, somewhere along a gradient from low to high readings, a cut-point is arbitrarily imposed and individuals with values above that cut-point are considered to have hypertension. Such hypertensive individuals will differ in degree, but not necessarily in kind, from individuals on the other side of this cut-off point. Clearly, individuals just on the other side of the cut-point—although not labeled as hypertensive—will share many commonalities with those meeting clinical criteria for hypertension. Within such a dimensional model, we acknowledge that there will be quantitative rather than qualitative differences in the characteristics of individuals who may or may not meet these arbitrary criteria. Conversely, individuals at the more extreme poles of the blood pressure distribution may differ from one another in more significant ways. Furthermore, we assume that, rather than qualitative differences, there are quantitative differences in the mechanisms responsible for somewhat higher versus somewhat lower blood pressure readings. As a function of the normal distribution, there may be also variability in the diagnosis over time. Because individuals with the characteristic or quality in question are distributed along a continuum with no distinct or absolute boundary separating them, individuals may, from time to time, shift positions along the distribution and find themselves on one side or the other of an arbitrarily imposed boundary marker. If a dimensional disorder is clinically defined and treated as a categorical (all-or-none) entity, then small quantitative variations in scores may shift individuals to the other side of the cut-point, which then may be misinterpreted as qualitative changes in status (Shaywitz et al. 1992). Such intraindividual variation has recently been described for blood cholesterol levels in children, leading to the conclusion that "the magnitude of within-person variability of . . . limits the ability to classify children into risk categories recommended by the National Cholesterol Education Program" (Gillman et al. 1992, p. 342). This study emphasizes the limitations of trying to use dimensionally distributed variables, whether they be blood lipids or reading achievement, in order to assign children to categories.


## EMANATIVE INFLUENCES OF MODELS OF DYSLEXIA

For many years, dyslexia has been conceptualized within a categorical framework—either you have it or you do not. Such a conceptualization is dichotomous and does not account for gray areas. Children undergo clinical assessments, whereafter determination is made that they have or do not have dyslexia. Often, based on such categorical diagnoses, children will or will not receive special education services. Public policy for provision of such services is formulated on an absolute basis of the categorical model—either you meet criteria for dyslexia or you do not. Current conceptualizations of dyslexia do not have a provision for gradations of dyslexia. Dyslexia is viewed as a severe, specific, and unvarying deficit in reading in which the deficit is not explained by IQ score. The failure to learn to read is believed to represent a specific syndrome distinct from the normal distribution of readers.

An alternative hypothesis considers dyslexia to represent the lower tail of a continuum of reading disability in which dyslexia blends imperceptibly with normal reading ability. As Blashfield (1984) has noted, such a notion is in contradistinction to the categorical view that is based on the concept of discontinuity. Kendell (1975), as quoted by Blashfield (1984), perhaps best captures the inherent discontinuity intended by the categorical classification model: "Classification is the art of carving nature at the joints, it should indeed imply that there is a joint there, that one is not sawing through bone" (p.65). In contrast to the natural joints intended by the categorical classification model, the dimensional model of dyslexia posits that there is no natural break, no natural joint separating dyslexic children from children with GRB.

## INVESTIGATION OF THE CATEGORICAL/DIMENSIONAL HYPOTHESIS

### The Connecticut Longitudinal Study

To examine the categorical model and the dimensional model of dyslexia we used data from the Connecticut Longitudinal Study (CLS), a sample survey of Connecticut schoolchildren (Shaywitz et al. 1992). The research design—a population-based survey incorporated within a longitudinal study design framework—provided data that enabled us to investigate the definition, prevalence including gender ratio, distribution, and temporal stability of reading disability over time.

Reflecting the traditional concepts of dyslexia as an unexpected failure to learn to read (Critchley 1970), and conforming to the Isle of Wight survey definition of "reading difficulties not explicable in terms of the child's general intelligence," (Rutter and Yule 1975, p. 181) and to guidelines proposed by the Office of Education (U.S. Office of Education 1977), SRR was defined as a discrepancy between the level of reading achievement predicted on the basis of ability and the actual, observed level of reading achievement. Examination of the data from the CLS sample indicated that the normal-distribution model fitted the data extremely well. Availability of longitudinal data enabled us to examine the stability of the reading disability classification. We found that the *observed* degree of stability (or instability) of the diagnosis was reflected in the degree of stability *predicted* by the model. For example, the model predicted that in grades one and three there would be 28.3 children classified as dyslexic in each year, with 8.38 children classified as having dyslexia in both years. The actual data indicated that there were 25 children classified in grade one, 31 children classified in grade three, and 7 of these children classified as dyslexic in both grades. Similar findings between predicted and observed numbers of dyslexia classifications were found when we compared grade three and grade five data, confirming the adequacy of the normal distribution model.

## Differences Between the Isle of Wight and the Connecticut Studies

Several important differences between the Isle of Wight and the Connecticut studies may help explain the discrepant results obtained by the two surveys. Data from the Isle of Wight reflect group testing, whereas the Connecticut data were obtained by individual administration of both the ability and the achievement measures. A shortened ability measure was used in the former study, whereas the full WISC-R was given to all children in the latter survey. Furthermore—and more to the point—the measure of reading used in the English study was selected to identify the poorest readers; several investigators have hypothesized that the reading test itself imposed a ceiling on reading ability, and as a consequence, skewed the reading score causing the artifactual appearance of a hump or lower mode in the Isle of Wight data. Inspection of the distribution data from the Isle of Wight support the notion that, rather than an overrepresentation of poor readers, there is an underrepresentation of good readers (van der Wissel and Zegers 1985). The CLS data are consistent with data reported by investigators from around the world who, too, have been unable to replicate the Isle of Wight findings (Silva, McGee, and Williams 1985; Rodgers 1983).

## Further Support for the Normal Distribution Model of Dyslexia

Further support for the dimensional hypothesis has come from growth-curve models of the longitudinal data provided by the CLS and also from studies of a high-density disabled population of children with reading disabilities. Investigators have now used the technique of individual growth curve modeling to compare the educational progress of children meeting criteria for GRB versus those meeting SRR criteria. These data indicate that the shape of the growth curves for the two reading-disabled groups are similar, differing only in level of severity (Francis et al. 1993). Thus, when IQ is controlled, IQ-achievement discrepant children (SRR) perform at a lower level and have poorer expected reading outcomes than low achievers who are not IQ-discrepant (GRB), but the shape of the growth curves are not qualitatively different. These findings are consistent with the notion of reading disability representing extreme cases in an otherwise normal distribution of ability and achievement.

Data from cross-sectional studies of high-density reading-disabled samples add further support to the continuous nature of reading disability. In one of the largest studies of its kind, 140 extremely well-characterized children were selected from a sample of 227 children, ages 7.5 to 9.5 years; sample selection for this subset was based on two definitions of reading disability: a regression-based discrepancy (SRR) and a low-achievement (GRB) criterion. The performance of the two groups was compared on a series of tasks including phonologic, vocabulary, speech production, memory, visual-spatial, visual-motor, and attentional measures. Results of cluster analyses indicated that the two reading-disabled groups did not differ qualitatively in the shape of their profiles. These data further support the notion that there is a continuum of reading achievement, the most extreme end of the distribution representing reading disability. Interestingly, these data indicate that no matter which specific criterion (for example, SRR or GRB) is used to define reading disabled groups, deficits in phonological processing represent the most characteristic impairment and the most severely affected cognitive skill (Fletcher et al. in press). Taken together, the data provide a strong suggestion that phonological difficulties lie at the core of the reading problems experienced by both children with SRR and children with GRB, and that these groups of reading-disabled children differ only in degree, not in kind, from one another. These findings lead to the further supposition that it is the phonological processing ability that is normally distributed through the population, and that children with dyslexia represent the extreme tail-end of this distribution.

## Studies Examining Prevalence of Dyslexia in Boys vs. Girls

In addition to statistical support for the distinctiveness of SRR from GRB, support for the categorical model of dyslexia has come from studies reporting a higher prevalence of dyslexia in boys as compared to girls (Finucci and Childs 1981). In considering reports of prevalence rates for dyslexia, it is important to consider first the special circumstances relating to the identification of cases of dyslexia. Dyslexia is an unusual disorder, because although it is biologically based, it is expressed within the context of the classroom. As a result, selection of subjects for the scientific investigation of dyslexia frequently depends on school identification of the subject as having a reading disability.

Most research studies are based on children who have been identified by their schools as having a reading disability and who receive special education services. Thus, often the boundaries between the failure to read and the failure to be successful within the sociological context of the classroom are unclear. Theoretically, school identification procedures are based on the policies set forth in P.L. 94-142 (Education for All Handicapped Children Act 1975) and subsequently operationalized as an ability–achievement discrepancy (U.S. Department of Education 1977). If this were the case, then school- or system- identified (SI) children should be the same as children identified by objective measures that assess the presence of such a discrepancy. If, however, there is some form of systematic bias operating, then SI and research-identified (RI) samples will not be equivalent. Such biases that affect who is identified by schools as reading disabled could then impact on the composition of research samples, and ultimately the findings of such investigations.

We hypothesized that results indicating an increased prevalence of dyslexia in boys compared to girls reflect a bias in sample selection rather than a gender (biologic) difference in the prevalence of the disorder. We used the sample and the measures of the CLS to investigate this hypothesis. Our data, consistent with reports in the literature from other SI samples, indicated that schools identified over four times as many boys as girls as RD (13.6% versus 3.2% respectively, $p < .0001$) (Shaywitz et al. 1990). In contrast, there were no significant differences between the numbers of boys and girls identified as reading disabled on the basis of objective measures of reading and IQ (see figure 2). Behavioral problems—the same behavioral characteristics that differentiate normal boys from girls—significantly differentiated reading-disabled children who were and who were not identified by their schools. These findings suggest that teachers' perceptions of what constitutes inappropriate behavior enter into school identification decisions and that, in particular, overactivity and behavioral difficulties are likely to be disruptive in the classroom and to influence SI decisions.

## CONCLUSIONS

Reading difficulties occur along a continuum that blends imperceptibly with normal reading ability. Both the statistical and presumed biological data supporting the discontinuity of SRR from GRB are disputed. Although the etiology of dyslexia is indisputably biologic in nature, the current cut-points used to define dyslexia are arbitrarily imposed—such cut-points do not represent the expression of a natural biological phenomenon. The disorder is biologically based, the cut-

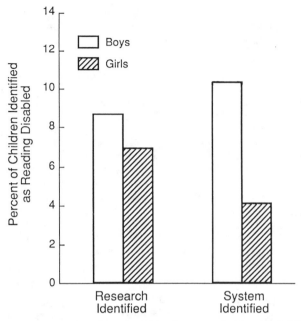

Figure 2.   Prevalence of reading disability in research-identified (RI) and system-identified (SI) boys and girls. RI boys compared to RI girls = *ns*. SI boys compared to SI girls = $X^2 = 5.7, p < .02$.

points are artificially imposed. Such a finding is consistent with the experience of many clinicians who feel constrained to make categorical decisions reflecting a diagnosis of dyslexia when many children fall somewhere in between performing at an acceptable level of reading and being at the extreme lower tail of the distribution. Finally, dyslexia should be conceptualized in the same framework within which we consider obesity and hypertension, that is, the disorder occurs in degrees or gradations (Stanovich 1988). Identification and intervention procedures should reflect this newer dimensional conceptualization.

## IMPLICATIONS

These results are of particular importance to the physician who must make decisions about school-aged patients. Awareness of newer findings supporting a dimensional model for dyslexia and of the bias in previous reports of an increased prevalence of dyslexia in boys increases a physicians's role and, we hope, effectiveness in both identifying and managing children with school failure. The results of these studies encourage the physician's active participation in the evaluation of patients with potential reading disability and provide guidelines for such evaluation. These results are particularly important for what they say about the appropriateness of current school identification procedures:

> The notion of dyslexia as a discrete entity has provided the basis for a special-education policy that provides services only to those who satisfy what are seen as specific, unvarying criteria for dyslexia. In contrast, our findings indicate that dyslexia is not an all-or-none phenomenon but, like obesity or hypertension occurs in varying degrees of severity. Although limitations on resources may necessitate the imposition of cut-points for the provision of services, physicians must recognize that such cutoffs may have no biological validity. Instead, children who do not meet these arbitrarily imposed criteria may still require and benefit from special help. (Shaywitz et al. 1992; p. 149)

The results of these studies should encourage physicians to advocate forcefully for special help for their patients, even if the school may indicate that a child does not meet a particular cutoff. Just as there is a continuum of reading ability and disability, there must also be a continuum of services to assist the struggling child so that no child will have to fail before he or she becomes eligible for help.

Furthermore, the absence of behavioral difficulties should not be taken as an indication that the child does not have a reading disability. In practical terms, our data indicate that physicians should not rely solely on schools for identification of reading disability in their patients. These data should encourage physicians to inquire directly about academic functioning, particularly in girls. If any question arises about a child's experiencing academic difficulty, even if not corroborated by the school, the physician should request tests of ability and achievement. Increased and active involvement of physicians in the care of patients with potential learning disability also carries with it additional responsibility—the responsibility to become more knowledgeable about important measures in assessing children for a possible learning disability. If physicians are to become effective, responsible advocates for children experiencing school learning problems, they must become as adept in using and interpreting the psychoeducational tools available to them as they are any other laboratory measure that could contribute to their ability to care for patients. Just as they do not personally perform blood chemistries or run hematological indices but are expert in interpreting the results of these studies, physicians must begin to gain competence in understanding and analyzing the results of cognitive studies.

Our data further indicate that, by following a categorical model in identifying children as dyslexic, schools may be under-identifying many children who will go on to experience significant reading problems. Thus, SI procedures are based on the notion that reading disability is a fixed, unvarying entity. Such a framework considers that if a small set of children is identified as reading disabled in grade one, the reading-disabled group will be the same in subsequent grades. On the contrary, our data indicate that only a small percentage of children meeting a categorical definition of reading disability in grade one will be meeting criteria in grade three (see figure 3). In fact only about one-third of the children classified as reading disabled in grade one will also be so classified in grade three. Reflecting the normal variability inherent in the normal distribution model, many of the children just outside the categorical boundaries delineating the reading disabled group in grade one, will now shift and exchange places with some children within the boundaries designated for reading disability in grade three. As the figure indicates, if help is reserved only for those meeting categorical criteria in an

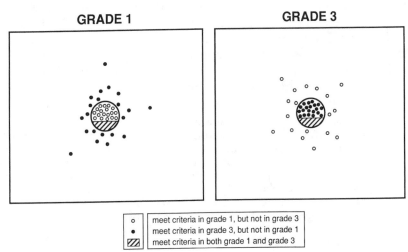

Figure 3.   Classification of reading disability (RD) in grade 1 and in grade 3. The figure, based on the results of the Connecticut Longitudinal Study, indicates which children meet criteria for (RD) in grade 1 and in grade 3. In each grade, children (dots and hatched lines) within the circle represent those meeting criteria for RD. However, only the cases ($n = 7$) represented by the hatched lines are also identified in the other year; children within the circle but represented by dots are classified as having RD for that year but not for the other year shown. For example, for Grade 1, children represented by hatched lines within the circle are classified as RD in both grades 1 and 3; children represented by open dots within the circle are identified in Grade 1 but not in Grade 3. Outside of the circle, dots represent children meeting criteria in the alternate year but not in the year shown. Thus, for Grade 1, children represented by black dots outside of the center circle are identified as RD in Grade 3 but not in Grade 1. Reprinted with permission from Shaywitz et al. 1992. Evidence that dyslexia may represent the lower tail of a normal distribution of reading disability. *New England Journal of Medicine* 326:145–50.

early grade, many children who will subsequently meet criteria for reading disability will be denied services based on an arbitrary categorical model. Provision must be made for the children who are at-risk, that is, the children who are just on the other side of the arbitrary cutoff point, also to receive reading help. The model predicts and our data indicate that these children, too, will require special help and eventually meet criteria for severe reading disability.

It is important to be aware that the finding that reading disability follows a continuum in no way detracts or minimizes its importance as a serious disorder warranting accurate identification and treatment. The data indicate that many more children may be affected and should not be denied help because of mistaken notions of arbitrary cutoff points and boundaries. Even if children who experience difficulty are not found to meet some arbitrary criterion or cut-point early on, they still should be considered as vulnerable to a serious reading disability requiring monitoring and possible intervention. The results of these investigations provide an opportunity for professionals, particularly physicians who see children from birth and monitor their developmental progress, to become more involved and to serve as informed advocates for their patients. As we have indicated previously:

> Physicians caring for children accept as their responsibility the fullest understanding of the factors affecting growth and development. As such, physicians are in a unique position to assume a leadership role in identifying and helping to manage children with school-related problems. Just as the physician has undertaken responsibility for understanding the interrelationships between the child and family as significant factors that influence the child's developmental progress, the physician now adds a new dimension—understanding the relationship with the school—as critical to providing optimal health care services to children. (Shaywitz et al. 1990, p. 1002).

## REFERENCES

Blashfield, R. K. 1984. The Classification of Psychopathology. New York: Plenum Press.

Critchley, M. 1970. The Dyslexic Child. Springfield, IL: Charles C Thomas.

Education for All Handicapped Children Act, PL No. 94–142. S.6, 94th Congress, 1st Sess (1975). Report No. 94-168.

Finucci, J. M., and Childs, B. 1981. Are there really more dyslexic boys than girls? In Sex Differences in Dyslexia, eds. A. Ansara, N. Geshwind, A. Galaburda, M. Albert, and N. Gartrell. Towson, MD: The Orton Dyslexia Society.

Fletcher, J. M., Shaywitz, S. E., Francis, D. J., Stuebing, K. K., Shankweiler, D. P., Katz, L., Liberman, I. Y., and Shaywitz, B. A. In press. Cognitive profiles of reading disability: Comparisons of discrepancy and low achievement definitions. Journal of Educational Psychology.

Francis, D. J., Shaywitz, S. E., Stuebing, K. K., Shaywitz, B. A., and Fletcher, J. M. 1993. The measurement of change: Assessing behavior over time and within a developmental context. In *Frames of Reference for the Assessment of Learning Disabilities: New Views on Measurement Issues*, ed. R. Lyon. Baltimore: Paul H. Brookes.

Gillman, M. W., Cupples, L. A., Moore, L. L., and Ellison, R. C. 1992. Impact of within-person variability on identifying children with hypercholesterolemia: Framingham Children's Study. *Journal of Pediatrics* 121:342–47.

Hinshelwood, J. 1896. A case of dyslexia: A peculiar form of word blindness. *Lancet* 1451–1454.

Kendell, R. E. 1975. *The Role of Diagnosis in Psychiatry*. London: Blackwell Scientific Publications.

Morgan, W. P. 1896. A case of congenital word blindness. *British Medical Journal* 1378.

Orton, S. T. 1925. "Word blindness" in school children. *Archives of Neurology and Psychiatry* 14:581–615.

Rodgers, B. 1983. The identification and prevalence of specific reading retardation. *British Journal of Educational Psychology* 53:369–73.

Rutter, M., Tizard, J., and Whitmore, K. 1970. *Education, Health and Behavior*. Huntington, NY: Robert E. Krieger.

Rutter, M., and Yule, W. 1975. The concept of specific reading retardation. *Journal of Child Psychology and Psychiatry* 16: 181–97.

Shaywitz, S. E., Shaywitz, B. A., Fletcher, J. M., and Escobar, M. D. 1990. Prevalence of reading disability in boys and girls: Results of the Connecticut Longitudinal Study. *Journal of the American Medical Association* 264:998–1002.

Shaywitz, S. E., Escobar, M. D., Shaywitz, B. A., Fletcher, J. M., and Makuch, R. 1992. Evidence that dyslexia may represent the lower tail of a normal distribution of reading disability. *New England Journal of Medicine* 326: 145–50.

Silva, P. A., McGee, R., and Williams, S. 1985. Some characteristics of 9-year-old boys with general reading backwardness or specific reading retardation. *Journal of Child Psychology and Psychiatry* 26:407–421.

Stanovich, K. 1988. Explaining the differences between the dyslexic and the garden variety poor reader: The phonological-core variable-difference model. *Journal of Learning Disabilities* 21:590–612.

van der Wissel, A., and Zegers, F. E. 1985. Reading retardation revisited. *British Journal of Educational Psychology* 44:1–12.

U.S. Office of Education. 1977. Assistance to states for education for handicapped children: Procedures for evaluating specific learning disabilities. *Federal Register 1977* 42:62082–62085.

Yule, W., and Rutter, M. 1985. Reading and other learning difficulties. In *Child and Adolescent Psychiatry: Modern Approaches*, eds. M. Rutter and L. Hersov. Oxford: Blackwell.

# Chapter • 2

# Experimental and Clinical Models of Attention Deficit Hyperactivity Disorder (ADHD)

*Walter E. Kaufmann*

The syndrome of attention deficit hyperactivity disorder (ADHD) is characterized by inattention, impulsiveness, and hyperactivity (Buttross 1988; American Psychiatric Association 1987). Although the disorder is quite prevalent and can lead to disturbed individual development and social interactions (Shaywitz and Shaywitz 1985), it is surprising how little is known about its pathogenesis (Voeller 1991). Several factors have operated against an easy elucidation of the mechanisms underlying ADHD. First, until recently, there has been an active controversy regarding its nosology (Buttross 1988; Voeller 1991). Having abandoned initial focuses on hyperactivity and minor brain dysfunction (Clements and Peters 1962; Anderson 1963; Buttross 1988), the current approach favors an attentional deficit as the central component of the disorder (Douglas 1972; Cantwell 1980; Buttross 1988; American Psychiatric Association 1987). Furthermore, because of the heterogeneity of the syndrome, the definition of subtypes, perhaps with different neurobiologic bases, remains incomplete (Voeller 1991). In addition, significant controversies regarding co-morbidity and differential diagnosis have not yet been settled (Brumback and Weinberg 1990; Shaywitz and Shaywitz 1991).

Other factors have also played an important role in the confusion about the pathophysiologic substrata of ADHD. The lack of a recognized neuropathology is not unique to ADHD but is also seen in other disorders that have relatively less severe impact on cognition and spare the rest of the organism. Postmortem examinations of patients with specific developmental cognitive disorders are unusual. In the case of classic neurologic disorders such as Parkinson's disease, pathologic descriptions showing affected structures and neural systems have traditionally provided an excellent orientation for functional studies (Hornykiewicz 1963).

A third critical issue, related to the problematic nosology of ADHD, is the absence of an animal model, such as a mutant mouse, that spontaneously presents anatomic and/or physiologic features characteristic of the condition. Changes over the years in the definition of cardinal symptoms of ADHD have led to experimental models featuring those selective expressions fashionable at a particular time (Shaywitz, Yager, and Klopper 1976; Clark, Geffen, and Geffen 1987). Indeed, the study of animals with genetic traits resembling human neurologic diseases has been crucial in advancing our understanding of neurologic disorders, such as neuromuscular diseases and epilepsy (Hogan and Greenfield 1984; Fisher 1989).

In summary, our current view of ADHD pathogenesis derives from a heterogeneous body of data including neuropathologic analyses of related developmental learning disorders, neuroimaging studies of subjects with ADHD, rodent models of specific features of ADHD, primate models, studies on the physiology of attention, and experiments with drugs that induce hyperactivity. In addition, neuropsychologic data focusing on cerebral lateralization have provided an interesting feedback for these experimental models and have helped to shape comprehensive models of neural networks affected in ADHD.

## NEUROPATHOLOGY AND NEUROIMAGING

Although ADHD was initially related to several perinatal and acquired pathologic processes such as prematurity, encephalitis, and head injury (Strecker and Ebaugh 1924; Strecker 1929; Lillienfeld, Pasamanick, and Rogers 1955), systematic studies have failed to show a significant contribution by these factors (Voeller 1991). The concept of "minimal brain damage" was re-explored with the advancement of imaging; however, brain lesions were not found on computed tomographic scans (Shaywitz et al. 1983). Formal neuropathologic studies on individuals suffering ADHD are not available. Nevertheless, some information can be inferred from postmortem investigations on people with related developmental learning disorders. Studies of severely dyslexic individuals have revealed the presence of many developmental lesions in the left perisylvian cortex and an unusual symmetry of the planum temporale (normally larger on the left side) (Galaburda et al. 1985; Galaburda et al. 1987). The predominant microscopic anomalies were of heterotopias and laminar disruptions in male subjects and myelinated scars in female individuals (Humphreys, Kaufmann, and Galaburda 1990) affecting the gray matter. Microdysgenetic lesions in the left temporal cortex as well as symmetry of the planum temporale have also been found in one case of developmental dysphasia (Cohen, Campbell, and Yaghmai 1989). Considering that developmental language disorders often precede dyslexia, the neuropathologic similarities between these conditions should not be surprising. However, if one considers that anomalous development of the left temporal/perisylvian cortex underlies disturbed language development, many additional lesions seen in the dyslexic brain still have poor behavioral correlation. Indeed, cortical microdysgenesis and scars are also observed in the right perisylvian regions and particularly in the frontal lobe. As a matter of fact, both dorsolateral and orbitofrontal areas may exhibit large numbers of microdysgenetic lesions (Galaburda et al. 1985; Humphreys, Kaufmann, and Galaburda 1990) in comparison with normative individuals (Kaufmann and Galaburda 1989). Based on current knowledge on the role of the frontal lobe in attention (Stuss and Benson 1986) and the coexistence of dyslexia and attentional disorder in many cases of dyslexia, one can speculate that abnormal frontal lobe development might contribute to attentional deficits, at least in severely dyslexic individuals.

This last proposal is supported by a recent magnetic resonance imaging (MRI) study looking at the patterns of brain asymmetry both in children with dyslexia and ADHD. Both dyslexic and ADHD subjects showed smaller right anterior-width measurements in comparison with the controls who had an asymmetry in favor of the right side (Hynd et al. 1990). However, most ADHD children exhibited the expected asymmetry of the planum temporale in favor of the left side whereas the majority of dyslexics evidenced symmetry or reversed asymmetry at that level (Hynd et al. 1990).

These data suggest that anomalous structural development of the frontal region of the cortex will predispose to attention deficits in the same way that temporal lobe anomalies predispose to language disorders (Galaburda et al. 1987). This involvement of the frontal lobe in ADHD is confirmed by functional data. Studies of cerebral blood flow have found decreased flow to the frontal regions, basal ganglia, and midbrain in children with ADHD. This situation is reversible only at the subcortical level after administration of methylphenidate (Lou, Henriksen, and Bruhn 1984). A second study confirmed the initial results and showed that the right striatum was more affected than the left side (Lou et al. 1989). Positron emission tomography (PET) studies in adults with residual ADHD have demonstrated a decrease in glucose utilization throughout the brain, a decrease more pronounced in the frontal lobe, particularly in the orbital aspects and on the right side (Zametkin et al. 1990). Both sets of studies indicate a hypometabolic pattern, predominantly in the frontal cortex and striatum, more on the right hemisphere. These findings correlate well with several behavioral investigations that imply a dysfunction of the frontal-striatal axis as the neuroanatomical basis of ADHD in children (Trommer et al. 1988; Heilman, Voeller, and Nadeau 1991).

**ANIMAL MODELS OF ADHD**

Numerous neuroanatomic and neurochemical studies have attempted to explain the symptoms of ADHD. Historically, these studies have been influenced both by the prevalent view of clinical manifestations of the syndrome and by the available neurobiologic techniques (Zametkin and Rapoport 1987; Voeller 1991). Two complementary approaches have been employed for this research. The first concentrates on a particular clinical expression of ADHD, tries to reproduce it, and to establish chemical and anatomic correlates. The second targets a particular structure and/or pathway based on behavioral information, disturbs it, and correlates the outcome with manifestations of ADHD. In the present review, investigations are presented according to the related clinical expression.

## Hyperactivity

Initial studies linking brain dysfunction to hyperactivity go back to the 1940s. Reports looked at the impact of lesions in different areas of the brain on spontaneous locomotor activity (Beach 1941a; Davis 1958). Lesions in the striatum produced hyperactivity in rats (Beach 1941b), a finding that was confirmed later in monkeys (Kennard, Spencer, and Fountan 1941). In rats, hyperactivity secondary to dysfunction of the mesial frontal cortex has been explained by monoamines depletion (Carter and Pycock 1980).

The frontal lobe was the second structure to which damage resulted in hyperactivity. Before describing these investigations, it is important to mention the different anatomic/functional regions that make up the frontal lobe. Anatomo-functionally, the frontal lobe can be divided into three main regions: primary motor cortex, premotor region, and prefrontal lobe. The primary motor cortex is the origin of the pyramidal tract that activates muscles or group of muscles that originate movements. By contrast, the premotor region, located anteriorly with respect to the motor region, coordinates different movements with a particular function as, for example, those involved in speech. Finally, the prefrontal area, the largest portion of the frontal lobe, is its most rostral. It is responsible for planning complex activities (usually called executive function domain).

To this simplified division of the frontal lobe, a dorsoventral axis can be superimposed. Dorsolateral aspects of the prefrontal region are more directly related to sensory areas and process information coming from outside the body. On the other hand, ventromedial areas receive dense projections from the limbic system, and as a consequence, their function involves mainly interoception (Baleydier and Mauguiere 1980; Stuss and Benson 1986; Fuster 1989).

Lesions in specific areas of the frontal lobes induce hyperactivity in primates (Kennard, Spence, and Fountan 1941). Ablations of the frontal association cortex (prefrontal areas 8–12 of Brodmann), but not of areas 6 and rostral 8 (premotor regions) result in increased total activity in monkeys and chimpanzees. There is a direct correlation between extension of the lesion and degree of hyperactivity. The abnormal behavior is characterized by purposeless and repetitive activity. This regional specificity of the frontal lobe in the control of locomotor activity was confirmed by the same authors when they noted that lesions of the rostral portions of areas 6 and 8 produced hypomotility.

These studies were essential in understanding circuits involved in modulation of activity and also helped to explain symptomatology in patients with frontal damage (Hebb and Penfield 1940). Interest in experimental modes of hyperactivity was greatly reactivated during the 60s and 70s by accumulating experience when pharmacologic interventions in children with ADHD used drugs that affect brain monoamine levels.

There emerged a new approach that focused on specific pathways and neurotransmitters. Kornetsky postulated a possible role for catecholamines in the genesis of hyperactivity in children with ADHD (Kornetsky 1970); efforts were then made to develop animal models to test this theory. In adult rats, Le Moal, Cardan, and Stinus 1969; Le Moal, Stinus and Galey 1976) used high frequency lesions of the ventral tegmental area (VTA) of the midbrain to produce a syndrome characterized by locomotor hyperactivity, hyper-reactivity, difficulties in tolerating frustration, disturbances in organized behaviors, and hypoemotivity. The characteristics of this syndrome mimic the motor restlessness (inability to remain still) observed in individuals with ADHD (Voeller 1991).

The VTA is an area of the mesencephalon containing the A10 group of dopaminergic cell bodies (Dahlstrom and Fuxe 1965) from which arise mesolimbic and mesocortical dopaminergic systems innervating frontal and cingulate cortices (Wang 1981). The VTA also contains serotoninergic fibers from the raphe nuclei that project to the forebrain. Therefore, the same research group that originally developed the VTA-lesioned animal model studied changes in all three central catecholamines and demonstrated that both dopamine and serotonin levels (but not norepinephrine levels) decreased in the forebrain after VTA lesions. Furthermore, they observed a good correlation between increase in locomotor activity and decrease in dopamine content in the frontal cortex (Tassin et al. 1978).

A second important model of hyperactivity was reported at about the same time. Based on clinical investigations revealing abnormal dopamine metabolism in children with ADHD, Shaywitz, Cohen, and Bowers (1977) induced dopamine depletion in neonatal rats. Six-hydroxydopamine was administered to rat pups and a marked decrease in brain dopamine was observed without changes in other monoamines (Shaywitz, Yager, and Klopper 1976). The treated animals exhibited an increase in total activity between 12 and 22 days of age. This anomalous behavior declined with the course of time, although some degree of learning impairment persisted. Moreover, as in the VTA model, the intensity and duration of the hyperactivity correlated with the magnitude of dopamine depletion (Miller et al. 1981). Although it is clear that a relationship exists between abnormal dopaminergic systems and some manifestations of ADHD, involvement of other monoamines cannot yet be excluded (Zametkin and Rapoport 1987).

Norepinephrine and dopamine exhibit an interesting complementary pattern of cortical innervation. Norepinephrine is more prominent in primary sensory and motor cortices, while dopamine innervates mainly associational cortices such as prefrontal and temporal regions (Brown, Crane, and Goldman 1979; Moore and Bloom 1978, 1979). Although both catecholamines modulate cortical activity, they seem to play different roles in terms of preferential cortical activation (Oades 1985). The involvement of both monoamines in the pathogenesis of ADHD has been suggested by experimental reduction in areas as the prefrontal cortex (Carter and Pycock 1980). The fact that hyperactivity has been induced by lesions and/or neurotransmitter depletion in the fronto-striatal-midbrain axis supports the notion that imbalances between these monoaminergic systems, at one or more levels, may underlie ADHD (Clark, Geffen, and Geffen 1987). Finally, clinical studies give additional evidence of multiple monoaminergic dysfunction (including probably also serotonin) as subjacent to different aspects of the ADHD syndrome (Garfinkel et al. 1983).

## Attention Deficit

Due to the relatively recent focus on attention disturbance and the intrinsic difficulties in studying it experimentally, this syndrome has not been explored as intensely as hyperactivity (Ferguson and Pappas 1979; Voeller 1991; Heilman, Voeller, and Nadeau 1991). The VTA-lesioned model mentioned above included elements of decreased attention and hyper-reactivity to stimuli, although they were combined with hyperactivity (Le Moal et al. 1976). So far, no animal model with an isolated deficit of attention has been developed. Analyses of patients with ADHD suggest that frontal and/or basal ganglia dysfunction could underlie this manifestation (Pontius 1973; Benson 1991). Difficulties in obtaining a model of pure attentional deficiency can be explained by the complexity of the attention processes per se. Nevertheless, some anatomic and physiologic information relevant to the understanding of ADHD has been accumulated in recent years.

Comprehensive approaches to attention have emerged in recent years integrating anatomic information (regarding connectivity) with physiological data, to understand attention. Data derived particularly from analyses of visual attention support the concept that attention is a distributed process (Colby 1991). Although attention seems to be a unitary phenomenon, it seems to involve many regions of the brain. Almost all cortical areas are involved, and several discrete subcortical circuits may be critical for it. In terms of mechanisms, some basic principles can be deduced. The operation of discrete neural networks depends on the source of the stimulus—external (a sensory stimulus) or internal (the representation of stimulus) (Albano et al. 1982; Braun and Breitmeyer 1988). A critical balance is established between responses to sensory stimuli and responses to internal representation of previous information. The complexity of the relations between different brain regions involved in attention makes a systematic conceptualization of the mechanism involved difficult.

Using the neural circuit patterns underlying visual attention, the following scheme is suggested. The supracontrol of attention and related responses is at the level of the entire cortex. Association (suprasensory modality) areas such as the prefrontal cortex and other regions of the temporal, parietal, and limbic cortices project, in a nonoverlapping pattern, mainly to the caudate portion of the striatum. Premotor and sensory areas project somatotopically, on the other hand, to the putamen. The two mentioned divisions of the striatum also receive independent information from the thalamus and other subcortical structures. The caudate innervates the substantia nigra, that by direct projections to the putamen, and by indirect connections through the thalamus, closes a critical loop involved in visual attention. In fact, multiple loops of this sort are present at all cortical and subcortical levels of these attentional systems. Structures located at a central situation of these loops are particularly well equipped to serve as gating or multichannel distributors of information. This seems to be precisely the role of the striatum in terms of cortical-subcortical interactions (Alexander, De Long, and Strick 1986; Fuster 1989; Colby 1991).

Some basic principles of attentional control have been derived from the study of visual attention. At different levels (subcortical nuclei, cortical areas) of these networks there is an *enhancement*—an increase in the cellular firing rate—associated with visual attention (Goldberg and Wurtz 1972). This response is independent of the level of arousal (global attention) and can represent, in some instances, a sensorimotor filtering mechanism, as in the superior colliculus or a purer attentional phenomenon, as in the parietal cortex (Goldberg and Bruce 1985). A second important observation is the tonic firing found in delayed matching tasks. Interpretations of this phenomenon include associating it with short-term memory and receptive field contraction (Funahashi, Bruce, and Goldman-Rakic 1989). A third issue relates to attentional shifts. The Posner task was developed to dissociate changes in attention from eye movements. While the subject is fixating on the center of a screen, a peripheral visual stimulus is presented. Providing a cue shortly before the stimulus permits one to observe changes in reaction time. The direction of this change depends on the validity of the prediction; a correct prediction leads to a faster reaction time and the opposite situation vice versa. The test has been useful for the study of structures involved in visual attention and eye movements in monkeys: caudate nucleus, substantia nigra pars reticulata, superior colliculus (intermediate layers) and thalamus (mainly pulvinar nucleus) (Colby 1991). The Posner paradigm has been applied to both animals and humans for the study of balance in attention between both sides or hemispheres (Posner and Cohen 1984). In general, lesions to any of the structures mentioned above result in decreased responses to contralateral stimuli. The circuit assessed by the Posner paradigm seems to be affected in ADHD (Heilman, Voeller, and Nadeau 1991).

## Other Cognitive Disorders

Hyperkinesis and inattention are not the only symptoms of ADHD. Most of the additional manifestations, including impulsiveness and executive domain dysfunctions, have also been associated with frontal lobe disturbances (Mesulam 1985). In fact, the frontal lobe has been the brain region most frequently implicated in the pathogenesis of ADHD (Gualtieri and Hicks 1985; Chelune et al. 1986). Several lines of evidence support this association. First, some of the cognitive impairments seen in children with ADHD resemble those seen in adult subjects with acquired damage to the frontal lobe (Pontius 1973; Zametkin and Rapoport 1987). Second, studies of animals, particularly primates, with frontal lobe lesions show disorders with striking similarities to the cognitive dysfunctions in ADHD (Roeltgen and Schneider 1991). As references to frontal lobe involvement in hyperkinesis and inattention have already been described, this section concentrates on other cognitive disorders.

Impulsiveness can be explained partially by deficient inhibition of inappropriate responses. Trommer et al. (1988) confirmed observations in monkeys, showing that children with ADHD fail in response inhibition. The test employed in these investigations, the go-no go task, consists of producing a simple motor response to one cue (go stimulus) and then inhibition of the same response when a different cue is presented (no go stimulus) (Leimkuhler and Mesulam 1985). This test has become a useful tool not only for the assessment of attentional dysfunction but also for therapy evaluation, because of the measurable influence on test results by methylphenidate administration (Trommer, Hoeppner, and Zecker 1991). In experimental animals, the neuroanatomical sites underlying the go-no go paradigm have been localized to ventral aspects of the prefrontal cortex, although other subcortical structures related to the fronto-striatal axis, such as the pulvinar, may be important. Furthermore, studies have demonstrated association between frontal lesions and go-no go test failures in humans (Drewe 1975; Leimkuhler and Mesulam 1985). Nevertheless, it is still unclear which frontal region is responsible for this response inhibition task. Iversen and Mishkin (1970) showed perseverative interference in monkeys after lesions were induced in the inferior (orbital aspect) of the prefrontal region. On the other hand, disruptions by cooling of the medial premotor area, which connects prefrontal and primary motor cortices, also affects response initiation and inhibition in monkeys (Tanji, Kurata, and Okano 1985). Moreover, Dabrowska (1972) found deficient go-no go performance after lesions involving more dorsal and medial aspects of the prefrontal areas in dogs. This last observation has been confirmed recently in patients with different lesions involving mesial frontal cortex including the nondominant supplementary motor area (a region of the premotor cortex located medially) (Leimkuhler and Mesulam 1985; Verfaellie and Heilman 1987).

Similarly to what has been found in hyperkinesis, striatal dysfunction could be implicated in failure to inhibit a motor response. Nadeau and collaborators (1987) trained rats to turn to the side contralateral to a tactile stimulus in order to receive a reward. This paradigm is similar to those used to evaluate response inhibition in patients with lesions involving medial frontal cortex as well as dorsolateral aspects of the prefrontal lobe (Butter et al. 1988). When the rats suffered a unilateral chemical ablation of the striatal dopaminergic innervation, they failed to inhibit the spontaneous orienting response toward the touched limb (Nadeau, Watson, and Heilman 1987). These studies do not have a counterpart in human subjects, and inferences regarding striatal dysfunction can only be speculative (Johnson, Palmer, and Freedman 1983).

Motor impersistence is another cognitive disturbance in children with ADHD. It is defined as inability to sustain a simple motor task, and motor impersistence improves after methylphenidate administration in children with ADHD (Voeller and Heilman 1988a, 1989). Motor impersistence has also been observed in adult patients after cortical and striatal lesions (Kertesz et al. 1985; Roeltgen, Roeltgen, and Heilman 1989), and has been reported in a child with caudate damage (Roeltgen and Schneider 1991). These observations led to the analysis of animal models with striatal lesions and analogous cognitive anomalies.

An interesting experimental situation involves monkeys treated with $N$-methyl-4-phenyl-1,2,3,6-tetrahydropyridine (MPTP) (Schneider et al. 1988). This toxic substance was accidentally created during the production of an illicit drug (Ballard, Teturd, and Longston 1985). Animals exposed to MPTP developed symptoms similar to those seen in human Parkinson's disease. These behavioral features are dose-dependent. In fact, chronic low-dose administration of MPTP produces cognitive rather than motor deficit (Schneider and Kovelowski 1990), with behavioral disturbances resembling those seen in children with ADHD. As expected, the pattern of cognitive disturbances in monkeys exposed to MPTP suggests a disruption of the fronto-striatal axis. The animals, like those with frontal damage, fail in delayed response and alternation tests (Battig, Rosvold, and Mishkin 1960). Although these tasks are related to immaturity in children, it is unclear if they are anomalous in patients with ADHD (Diamond 1988); therefore, the interpretation of this animal model should be considered with caution until more clinical data are available. Hemispatial neglect has been shown to result from contralateral carotid injection of MPTP similar to that observed in monkeys after chronic low-dose treatment (Roeltgen and Schneider 1989). Neglect, in fact, has been demonstrated in children with ADHD (Voeller and Heilman 1988b), as described in the next section. A final point about this promising animal model is the finding that after injection of dopamine D2 receptor agonists, monkeys develop hyperactivity that resembles akathisia (Roeltgen and Schneider 1991). This behavioral anomaly is characterized by self-aware restlessness with fidgety movements, and seems to reflect dysfunction of the mesocortical dopaminergic system without relation to nigrostriatal dysfunction (Lang and Johnson 1987). After low-dose MPTP exposure, monkeys show monoaminergic imbalances consisting of decrease in striatal dopamine, cortical norepinephrine, and no changes in cortical serotonin (Roeltgen and Schneider 1991).

## Disturbances of Eye Movements

Children with ADHD can exhibit several disturbances in visual attention and eye movements. They have decreased capacity to maintain fixation on targets, irregular pursuit to slowly moving targets, and deficits in attending contiguous stimuli (Shapira, Jones, and Sherman 1980; Rasmussen et al. 1983). Anomalies in saccades, consisting of more frequent and wider scanning eye movements, are also found in such children (Bala et al. 1981). The cortical and subcortical structures potentially dysfunctional in these individuals are described below.

The difficulties in pursuit of moving targets that are observed in children with ADHD are probably secondary in nature, are more pronounced at slower speeds, and occur in monkeys after frontal and parietal lesions. Specifically, lesions in a region of the prefrontal cortex that projects heavily to the caudate and influences activity of the superior colliculus, the frontal eye fields, may be the main substrate for these problems. However, combined lesions of parieto-occipital areas (that connect with the superior colliculus ) and frontal eye fields can evoke irregular pursuit (Keating, Godey, and Kenney 1985; Lynch et al. 1986).

On the other hand, saccades can also result from lesions at different levels of the pathways described above: these include damage to the frontal eye field and substantia nigra in monkeys (Colby 1991; Hikosaka and Wurtz 1985), and to the frontal lobe and striatum in humans (Guitton, Buchtel, and Douglas 1985; Colby 1991). Square wave jerks (microsaccades) are observed after different types of corticial lesions in adults, with and without learning disabilities, and in children with ADHD (Sharpe, Herishanu, and White 1982). Symptoms and signs associated with ADHD and seen in animal models are summarized in table I.

### CEREBRAL LATERALIZATION AND ADHD

Cooperation between the left- and right-cerebral structures is essential for normal attention as well as for other integrative functions (Colby 1991). The possibility that at least some of the expressions of ADHD are the consequence of abnormal integration between hemispheres has been raised. One of the neuropsychologic abnormalities that best reflects this integration is the neglect syndrome. Neglect is a primary failure to recognize stimuli contralateral to a hemispheric lesion or dysfunction (Heilman, Voeller, and Nadeau 1991). It has been suggested that this syndrome could represent right hemisphere dysfunction because its high association with right side lesions (Gainotti, Messerli, and Tissof 1972). These observations gave rise to the hypothesis that arousal and attention would be lateralized in the right hemisphere (Heilman and Van Den Abell 1979; Mesulam 1981; Voeller and

Table I.  Signs Associated with ADHD in Animal Models

| Sign | Dysfunctional Structure | Species |
|------|-------------------------|---------|
| Hyperactivity | Prefrontal cortex (lateral) | Monkey |
|  | Medial frontal cortex | Rat |
|  | Striatum | Rat, Monkey |
|  | Midbrain | Rat |
| Attentional deficit | Midbrain | Rat |
| (mainly visual) | Superior colliculus | Monkey |
|  | Substantia nigra | Monkey |
|  | Pulvinar | Monkey |
|  | Striatum | Monkey |
|  | Frontal cortex | Monkey |
|  | Cingulate cortex | Monkey |
|  | Temporal cortex | Monkey |
|  | Parietal cortex | Monkey |
|  | Occipital cortex | Monkey |
| Impulsiveness | Prefrontal cortex | Monkey, dog |
|  | Premotor cortex | Monkey |
| Motor impersistence | Frontal cortex | Monkey |
|  | Inferotemporal cortex | Monkey |
|  | Striatum | Monkey |
| Increased frustration | Midbrain | Rat |
|  | Frontal cortex | Monkey |
|  | Inferotemporal cortex | Monkey |
|  | Striatum | Monkey |
| Neglect | Frontal cortex | Monkey |
|  | Striatum | Monkey |
| Defective pursuit | Prefrontal cortex | Monkey |
|  | Parietal cortex | Monkey |
| Saccades | Prefrontal cortex | Monkey |
|  | Substantia nigra | Monkey |

Heilman 1988a). More recent normative studies have supported this hemispheric specialization (Reivich, Alavi, and Gur 1984).

Using standard tests for evaluation of neglect, Voeller and Heilman investigated right hemispheric dysfunction in patients with ADHD. The ADHD subjects performed in a fashion similar to adult individuals with neglect syndrome due to right-side brain damage. In a cancellation task, deficit in cancelling lines on both halves of the page with a predominance on the left side was observed (Voeller and Heilman 1988b). Finally, it is important to note an association between the neglect syndrome and those deficits in eye movements already mentioned. These preliminary observations supporting right hemispheric dysfunction are strengthened by the observation of more frequent motor impersistence in ADHD patients (Voeller and Heilman 1988b). Descriptions of adult individuals with focal lesions suggest a strong association between more impersistence and right hemisphere dysfunction (Kertesz et al. 1985). Unfortunately, these neuropsychologic data do not point to any specific region of the right hemisphere. And animal studies demonstrating anomalous hemispheric cooperation in the context of deficient attention and/or activity are not yet available.

There is some indirect evidence of abnormal dominance at the subcortical level in ADHD. Lou et al. (1989) demonstrated involvement of the right basal ganglia in the pathogenesis of ADHD, manifested as decreased cerebral blood flow in the striatum, more dramatic on the right side. These findings suggest a decreased metabolic activity in this region; however, no neuropsychological information is available to confirm these functional implications. Nevertheless, Heilman, Voeller, and Nadeau (1991) have suggested that at least some aspects of ADHD could be explained by dysfunction of the right-sided striatum-frontal axis. They ground this hypothesis on the data mentioned above as well as other evidence of frontal dysfunction in children with ADHD. They stress the role of disruption of the supplementary motor area (SMA) in impaired motor response initiation and inhibition. The fronto-striatal axis would be responsible for filtering motor responses, receiving an important contribution of brainstem dopaminergic innervation. The latter would be responsible for the attentive components. Although this theory is intriguing, and receives some support from experimental and clinical data, insufficient knowledge of lateralized subcortical pathways makes for difficulty in unifying our concepts of cortico-subcortical interactions with hemispheric cooperation. Unquestionably, neuropathologic and imaging studies showing lesions and dysfunction lateralized to the right side support the desirability of further search for evidences of early abnormal lateral brain organization in the context of ADHD.

## PERSPECTIVES

Several drugs known to influence dopaminergic systems are also able to produce some symptoms of ADHD. The most important, because of its social implications, is cocaine. Cocaine inhibits the uptake of all three main monoamines: norepinephrine, dopamine, and serotonin, and reinforces the mesolimbic and mesocortical dopaminergic pathways. This action seems to be responsible for the reinforcement and withdrawal syndromes (Volpe 1992). Considering that the pathogenesis of ADHD suggests a developmental process, the study of infants and animals exposed in utero to cocaine is relevant. One of the outcomes in rats born to females injected with cocaine during pregnancy has been an increase in activity (Dow-Edwards 1991). However, other studies have shown decreased overall and stereotypic activity in these animals (Haller et al. 1990). Therefore, the issue remains uncertain and needs further investigation. A new line of evidence is provided by recent data showing that infants exposed to cocaine as fetuses not only have disturbances of neuronal proliferation and migration but also of cytodifferentiation. These anomalies are located in just those cortical areas presumably implicated in the pathogenesis of ADHD such as the dorsolateral and orbitofrontal cortices (Kaufmann and Cuello 1991; Volpe 1992). These findings reaffirm the hypothesized association between frontal lobe anomalies and some of the clinical manifestations of ADHD.

## CONCLUSIONS

Both experimental and clinical studies suggest an involvement in ADHD of the striatum-frontal cortex axis, and their monoaminergic neurotransmitters. This dysfunction is reflected mainly in defective attentive and activity-modulating mechanisms, and probably involves anomalous cerebral dominance; it can also have a structural dimension, such as developmental lesions in the frontal cortex. Although dopamine remains the best characterized neurotransmitter, the constellation of neurobehavioral manifestations can only be explained by multiple monamine dysfunctions or imbalances. Finally, our emerging knowledge about parallel subcortical-cortical pathways, via the basal ganglia, raises the possibility that different subtypes of ADHD can eventually be explained by selective disturbance of certain of these projections.

The future understanding of ADHD depends on the integration of multiple sources of data ranging from biochemical analyses in animals to neuropsychologic studies, as well as observations on similar findings in other conditions in patients. This route should be successful in providing new preventive and therapeutic approaches founded on solid neurobiological bases.

## REFERENCES

Albano, J. E., Mishkin, M., Westbrook, L. E., and Wurtz, F. H. 1982. Visuomotor deficits following ablation of monkey superior colliculus. *Journal of Neurophysiology* 48:338–51.

Alexander, G. E., De Long, M. R., and Strick, P. L. 1986. Parallel organization of functionally segregated circuits linking basal ganglia and cortex. *Annual Review of Neuroscience* 9:357–81.

American Psychiatric Association. 1987. *Diagnostic and Statistical Manual of Mental Disorders*, 3rd ed., Revised. Washington, DC: American Psychiatric Association.

Anderson, W. W. 1963. The hyperkinetic child: A neurological appraisal. *Neurology* 13:968–73.

Bala, S. P., Cohen, B., Morris, A. G., Atkin, A., Gittelman, R., and Kates, W. 1981. Saccades of hyperactive and normal boys during ocular pursuit.

*Developmental Medicine and Child Neurology* 23:323–36.

Baleydier, C., and Mauguiere, F. 1980. The duality of the cingulate gyrus in the monkey: Neuroanatomical study and functional hypothesis. *Brain* 103: 525–54.

Ballard, P. A., Teturd, J. W., and Longston, J. W. 1985. Permanent human parkinsonism due to 1-methyl-4-phenyl-1,2,3,6-tetrahydropyridine (MPTP): Seven cases. *Neurology* 35:949–56.

Battig, K., Rosvold, H. E., and Mishkin, M. 1960. Comparison of the effects of frontal and caudate lesions in delayed response and alternation in monkeys. *Journal of Comparative Psychology* 53:400–404.

Beach, F. A. 1941a. Effects of brain lesions upon running activity in the male rat. *Journal of Comparative Psychology* 31:145–78.

Beach, F. A. 1941b. Effects of lesions to corpus striatum upon spontaneous activity in the male rat. *Journal of Neurophysiology* 4:191–95.

Benson, F. D. 1991. The role of frontal dysfunction in attention deficit hyperactivity disorder. *Journal of Child Neurology* 6:S9–S12.

Braun, D., and Breitmeyer, B. G. 1988. Relationship between directed visual attention and saccadic reaction times. *Experimental Brain Research* 73:546–52.

Brown, R. M., Crane, A. M., and Goldman, P. S. 1979. Regional distribution of monoamines in the cerebral cortex and subcortical structures of the rhesus monkey: Concentrations and in vivo synthesis rates. *Brain Research* 168:133–50.

Brumback, R. A., and Weinberg, W. A. 1990. Pediatric behavioral neurology: An update on the neurologic aspects of depression, hyperactivity and learning disabilities. *Neurologic Clinics* 8:677–703.

Butter, C. M., Rapcsak, S. Z., Watson, R. T., and Heilman, K. M. 1988. Changes in sensory attention, directional hypokinesia and release of the fixation-reflex following unilateral frontal lesion: A case report. *Neuropsychologia* 26:533–45.

Buttross, S. 1988. Disorders of attention and vigilance. *Seminars in Neurology* 8:97–107.

Cantwell, D. P. 1980. Diagnostic validity of the hyperactive child (attention deficit disorder with hyperactivity) syndrome. *Psychiatric Developments* 3:277–300.

Carter, C. J., and Pycock, C. J. 1980. Behavioral and biochemical effects of dopamine and nonadrenaline depletion within the medial prefrontal cortex of the rat. *Brain Research* 192:163–76.

Chelune, G. J., Ferguson, W., Koon, R., and Dickey, T. O. 1986. Frontal lobe disinhibition in attention deficit disorder. *Child Psychiatry and Human Development* 16:221–32.

Clark, C. R., Geffen, G. M, and Geffen, L. B. 1987. Catecholamines and attention I. Animal and clinical studies. *Neuroscience and Biobehavioral Research* 11:341–52.

Clements, S. D., and Peters, J. E. 1962. Minimal brain dysfunctions in the school-aged child. *Archives of General Psychiatry* 6:185–87.

Cohen, M., Campbell, R., and Yaghmai, F. 1989. Neuropathological abnormalities in developmental dysphasia. *Annals of Neurology* 25:567–70.

Colby, C. L. 1991. The neuroanatomy and neurophysiology of attention. *Journal of Child Neurology* 6:S90–S118.

Dabrowska, J. 1972. On the mechanism of go-no go symmetrically reinforced tasks in dogs. *Acta Neurobiologica* (Warsz) 32:345–59.

Dahlstrom, A., and Fuxe, K. 1965. Evidence for the existence of monoamine-containing neurons in the central nervous system I. Demonstration of monoamines in the cell bodies of brain stem neurons. *Acta Physiologica Sandinavica* 62:1–55.

Davis, G. D. 1958. Effects of control, excitant and depressant drugs on locomotor activity in the monkeys. *American Journal of Physiology* 188:619–23.

Diamond, A. 1988. Abilities and neural mechanisms underlying AB performance. *Child Development* 59:523–27.

Douglas, V. I. 1972. Stop, look and listen: The problem of sustained attention and impulse control in hyperactivity and normal children. *Canadian Journal of Behavioral Sciences* 4:259–82.

Dow-Edwards, D. L. 1991. Cocaine effects on fetal development: A comparison of clinical and animal research findings. *Neurotoxicology and Teratology* 163:1525–1542.

Drewe, E. A. 1975. Go-no go learning after frontal lobe lesions in humans. *Cortex* 11:8–16.

Ferguson, H. B., and Pappas, B. A. 1979. Evaluation of psychophysiological, neurochemical and animal models of hyperactivity. In *Hyperactivity in Children. Etiology, Measurement and Treatment Implications*, ed. R. L. Trites. Baltimore: University Park Press.

Fisher, R. S. 1989. Animal model of the epilepsies. *Brain Research Reviews* 14:245–78.

Funahashi, B., Bruce, C. J., and Goldman-Rakic, P. S. 1989. Mnemonic coding of visual space in the monkey's dorsolateral prefrontal cortex. *Journal of Neurophysiology* 61:331–49.

Fuster, J. M. 1989. *The Prefrontal Cortex*. New York: Raven Press.

Gainotti, G., Messerli, P., and Tissot, R. T. 1972. Qualitative analysis of unilateral spatial neglect in relation to laterality of cerebral lesions. *Journal of Neurology, Neurosurgery and Psychiatry* 35:545–50.

Galaburda, A. M., Sherman, G. F., Rosen, G. D., Aboitiz, F., and Geschwind, N. 1985. Developmental dyslexia: Four consecutive patients with cortical anomalies. *Annals of Neurology* 18:222–33.

Galaburda, A. M., Sherman, G. F., Rosen, G. D., and Kaufmann, W. E. 1987. Neuropathologic findings and neurodevelopmental hypothesis in dyslexia. *Neuroscience* 22S:2017W.

Garfinkel, B., Wender, P. H., Sloman, L, and O'Neill, I. 1983. Tricyclic antidepressant and methylphenidate treatment of attention deficit disorder in children. *Journal of the American Academy of Child Psychiatry* 22:343–48.

Goldberg, M. E., and Bruce, C. J. 1985. Cerebral cortical activity associated with the orientation of visual attention in the rhesus monkey. *Vision Research* 25:471–81.

Goldberg, M. E., and Wurtz, R. H. 1972. Activity of superior colliculus in behaving monkey: II. The effect of attention on neuronal responses. *Journal of Neurophysiology* 35:560–74.

Gualtieri, C. T., and Hicks, R. E. 1985. Neuropharmacology of methylphenidate and a neural substrate for childhood hyperactivity. *Psychiatric Clinics of North America* 8:875–92.

Guitton, D., Buchtel, H. A., and Douglas, R. M. 1985. Frontal lobe lesions in man cause difficulties in suppressing reflexive glances and generating goal-directed saccades. *Experimental Brain Research* 58:455–72.

Haller, E. W., Hoffman, R. G., Eisenberg, R. M., and Vainio, A. 1990. Cocaine in pregnancy and development. *Society for Neuroscience Abstracts* 16:750.

Hebb, D. O., and Penfield, W. 1940. Human behavior after extensive bilateral removal from the frontal lobes. *Archives of Neurology and Psychiatry* 44:421–38.

Heilman, K. M., and Van Den Abell, T. 1979. Right hemisphere dominance for mediating cerebral activation. *Neuropsychologia* 17:315–21.

Heilman, K. M., Voeller, K. K. S., and Nadeau, S. E. 1991. A possible pathophysiologic substrate of attention deficit hyperactivity disorder. *Journal of Child Neurology* 6:S76–S81.

Hikosaka, O., and Wurtz, R. H. 1985. Modification of saccadic eye movements by GABA-related substances. I. Effect of muscimol and bicuculline in monkey superior colliculus. *Journal of Neurophysiology* 53:266–91.

Hogan, E. L., and Greenfield, S. 1984. Animal models of genetic disorders of myelin. In *Myelin*, ed. P. Morell. New York: Plenum Press.

Hornykiewicz, O. 1963. Die topische Lokalisation und das Verhalten von Noradrenalin und Dopamin (3-Hydroxytyramin) in der Sustantia nigra des normalen und Parkinson kranken Meschen. *Wiener Klinische Wochenschrift* 75:309–312.

Humphreys, P., Kaufmann, W. E., and Galaburda, A. M. 1990. Developmental dyslexia in women: Neuropathological findings in three cases. *Annals of Neurology* 28:727–38.

Hynd, G. W., Semrud-Clikeman, M., Lorys, A. R., Novey, E. S., and Eliopulos, D. 1990. Brain morphology in developmental dyslexia and attention deficit disorder. *Archives of Neurology* 47:919–26.

Iversen, S. D., and Mishkin, M. 1970. Perseverative interference in monkeys following selective lesions of the inferior prefrontal convexity. *Experimental Brain Research* 11:376–86.

Johnson, S. W., Palmer, M. R., and Freedman, R. 1983. Effects of dopamine on spontaneous and evoked activity of the caudate neurons. *Neuropharmacology* 22:843–51.

Kaufmann, W. E, and Galaburda, A. M. 1989. Cerebrocortical microdysgenesis in neurologically normal subjects: A histopathologic study. *Neurology* 39:238–44.

Kaufmann, W. E., and Cuello, N. 1991. Prenatal exposure to cocaine in humans. *Teratology* 43:486.

Keating, E. G., Gooley, S. G., and Kenney, D. V. 1985. Impaired tracking and loss of predictive eye movements after removal of the frontal eye fields. *Society for Neuroscience Abstracts* 11:472.

Kennard, M. A., Spencer, S., and Fountan, G. 1941. Hyperactivity in monkeys following lesions of the frontal lobes. *Journal of Neurophysiology* 4:512–24.

Kertesz, A., Nicholson, I., Cancelliere, A., Kassa, K., and Black, S. E. 1985. Motor impersistence: A right hemisphere syndrome. *Neurology* 35:662–66.

Kornetsky, C. 1970. Psychoactive drugs in the immature organism. *Psychopharmacologia* 17:105–136.

Lang, A. E., and Johnson, K. 1987. Akathisia in idiopathic Parkinson's disease. *Neurology* 37:477–80.

Le Moal, M., Cardo, B., and Stinus, L. 1969. Influence of ventral mesencephalic lesions on various spontaneous and conditional behaviours in the rat. *Physiology and Behavior* 4:567–74.

Le Moal, M., Stinus, L., and Galey, D. 1976. Radiofrequency lesions of the ventral mesencephalic tegmnentum: Neurological and behavioral considerations. *Experimental Neurology* 50:521–35.

Leimkuhler, M. E., and Mesulam, M. M. 1985. Reversible go-no go deficits in a case of frontal lobe tumor. *Annals of Neurology* 18:617–19.

Lillienfeld, A. M., Pasamanick, B., and Rogers, M. 1955. Relationship between pregnancy experience and development of certain neuropsychiatric disorders in childhood. *American Journal of Public Health* 45:637–43.

Lou, H. C., Henriksen,L., and Bruhn, P. 1984. Focal cerebral hypoperfusion in children with dysphasia and/or attention deficit disorder. *Archives of Neurology* 41:825–29.

Lou, H. C., Henriksen, L., Bruhn, P., Borner, H., and Nielsen, J. B. 1989. Striatal dysfunction in attention deficit disorder. *Archives of Neurology* 465:48–52.

Lynch, J. C., Allison, J. C., Hines, R. S., and Roark, R. L. 1986. Oculomotor impairment following combined lesions of parieto-occipital cortex and frontal eye fields in rhesus monkeys. *Society for Neuroscience Abstracts* 12:1086.

Mesulam, M.-M. 1981. A cortical network for directed attention and unilateral neglect. *Annals of Neurology* 10:309–325.

Mesulam, M.-M. 1985. *Principles of Behavioral Neurology.* Philadelphia: F.A. Davis.

Miller, F. E., Heffner, T. G., Kotake, C., and Seiden, L. S. 1981. Magnitude and duration of hyperactivity following neonatal 6-hydroxydopamine is related to the extent of dopamine depletion. *Brain Research* 229:123–32.

Moore, R. Y., and Bloom, F. E. 1978. Central catecholamine neuron systems: Anatomy and physiology of the dopamine systems. *Annual Review of Neuroscience* 1:129–69.

Moore, R. Y., and Bloom, F. E. 1979. Central catecholamine neuron systems: Anatomy and physiology of the norepinephrine and epinephrine systems. *Annual Review of Neuroscience* 2:113–68.

Nadeau, S. E., Watson, R. T., and Heilman, K. M. 1987. Defects of motor gating: A tentative explanation of neglect due to unilateral lesions of the nigrostriatal pathway. *Neurology* 37:178.

Oades, R. D. 1985. The role of noradrenaline in tuning and dopamine in switching between signals in the CNS. *Neuroscience and Biobehavioral Reviews* 9:261–82.

Pontius, A. A. 1973. Dysfunction patterns analogous to frontal lobe system and caudate nucleus syndromes in some groups of minimal brain dysfunction. *Journal of the American Medical Women Association* 28:285–92.

Posner, M. I., and Cohen, Y. 1984. Components of visual orienting. In *Attention and Performance*, Vol X, eds. H. Bouma and D. Bowhuis. Hillsdale, NJ: Lawrence Erlbaum Associates.

Rasmussen, P., Gillberg, C., Waldenstrom, E., and Svenson, B. 1983. Perceptual, motor and attentional deficits in seven-year-old children: Neurological and neurodevelopmental aspects. *Developmental Medicine and Child Neurology* 25:315–33.

Reivich, M., Alavi, A., and Gur, C. 1984. Positron emission tomographic studies of perceptual tasks. *Annals of Neurology* 38:806–808.

Roeltgen, D. P., and Schneider, J. S. 1989. Hemispatial neglect in hemiparkinsonian monkeys. *Annals of Neurology* 26:126.

Roeltgen, D. P., and Schneider, J. S. 1991. Chronic low-dose MPTP in nonhuman primates: A possible model for attention deficit disorder. *Journal of Child Neurology* 6:S82–S89.

Roeltgen, M.G., Roeltgen, D. P., and Heilman, K. M. 1989. Unilateral motor impersistence and hemispatial neglect from a right striatal lesion. *Neuropsychology, Neuropsychiatry and Behavioral Neurology* 2:125–35.

Schneider, J. S., Unquez, G., Yuwiler, A., Berg, S. C., and Markham, C. H. 1988. Deficits in operant behavior in monkeys treated with N-methyl-4-phenyl-1,2,3,6-tetrahydropyridine (MPTP). *Brain* 111:1265–1285.

Schneider, J. S., and Kovelowski, C. J. 1990. Chronic exposure to low doses of MPTP I. Cognitive deficits in motor asymptomatic monkeys. *Brain Research*

519:122–28.

Shapira, Y. A., Jones, M. H., and Sherman, S. P. 1980. Abnormal eye movements in hyperkinetic children with learning disability. *Neuropediatrie* 11:36–44.

Sharpe, J. A., Herishanu, Y. O., and White, O. B. 1982. Cerebral square wave jerks. *Neurology* 32:57–62.

Shaywitz, B. A., and Shaywitz, S. E. 1991. Comorbidity: A critical issue in attention deficit disorder. *Journal of Child Neurology* 6:S13–S22.

Shaywitz, B. A., Cohen, D. J., and Bowers, M. D. 1977. CSF monoamine metabolites in children with minimal brain dysfunction: Evidence for alteration of brain dopamine. *Journal of Pediatrics* 90:67–71.

Shaywitz, B. A., Shaywitz, S. E, Byrne, T., Cohen, D. J., and Rothman, S. 1983. Attention deficit disorder: Quantitative analysis of CT. *Neurology* 33: 1500–1503.

Shaywitz, B. A., Yager, R. D., and Klopper, J. H. 1976. Selective brain dopamine depletion in developing rats: An experimental model of minimal brain dysfunction. *Science* 191:305–308.

Shaywitz, S. E., and Shaywitz, B. A. 1985. Diagnosis and management of attention deficit disorder: A pediatric perspective. *Pediatric Clinics of North America* 31:429–57.

Strecker, E. A. 1929. Behavior problems in encephalitis: Clinical study of relationship between behavior and acute and chronic phenomena of encephalitis. *Archives of Neurology and Psychiatry* 21:137–44.

Strecker, E. A., and Ebaugh, F. H. 1924. Neuropsychiatric sequelae of cerebral trauma in children. *Archives of Neurology and Psychiatry* 12:443–53.

Stuss, D. T., and Benson, D. F. 1986. *The Frontal Lobes.* New York: Raven Press.

Tanji, J., Kurata, K., and Okano, K. 1985. The effect of cooling of the supplementary motor cortex and adjacent cortical areas. *Experimental Brain Research* 60:423–26.

Tassin, J., Stinus, L., Simon, H., Blanc, G., Thierry, A.-M., Le Moal, M., Cardo, B., and Glowinski, J. 1978. Relationship between the locomotor hyperactivity induced by A10 lesions and the destruction of the frontocortical dopaminergic innervation in the rat. *Brain Research* 141:267–81.

Trommer, B. L., Hoeppner, J. B., and Zecker, S. G. 1991. The go-no go test in attention deficit disorder is sensitive to methylphenidate. *Journal of Child Neurology* 6:S128–S131.

Trommer, B. L., Hoeppner, J. B., Lorber, R., and Armstrong, K. J. 1988. The go-no go paradigm in attention deficit disorder. *Annals of Neurology* 24:610–14.

Verfaellie, M., and Heilman, K. M. 1987. Response preparation and response inhibition after lesions of the medial frontal lobe. *Archives of Neurology* 44:1265–1271.

Voeller, K. K. S. 1991. Toward a neurobiologic nosology of attention deficit hyperactivity disorder. *Journal of Child Neurology* 6:S2–S8.

Voeller, K. K. S., and Heilman, K. M. 1988a. Motor impersistence in children with attention deficit hyperactivity disorder: Evidence for right hemisphere dysfunction. *Annals of Neurology* 24:323.

Voeller, K. K. S., and Heilman, K. M. 1988b. Attention deficit disorder in children: A neglect syndrome? *Neurology* 38:806–808.

Voeller, K. K. S., and Heilman, K. M. 1989. Motor impersistence in children with attention deficit hyperactivity disorder: Decreases in response to treatment with methylphenidate. *Neurology* 39:S276.

Volpe, J. J. 1992. Effect of cocaine use on the fetus. *New England Journal of Medicine* 327:399–407.

Wang, R. Y. 1981. Dopaminergic neurons in the rat ventral tegmental area. I. Identification and characterization. *Brain Research Reviews* 3:123–40.

Zametkin, A. J., and Rapoport, J. L. 1987. Neurobiology of attention deficit disorder with hyperactivity: Where have we come in 50 years? *Journal of the American Academy of Child and Adolescent Psychiatry* 26:676–86.

Zametkin, A. J., Nordahl, T., Gross, M., King, C., Semple, W. E., Rumsey, J., Hamburger, S., and Cohen, R. M. 1990. Cerebral glucose metabolism in adults with hyperactivity of childhood onset. *New England Journal of Medicine* 323:1361–1366.

# Chapter • 3

# Learning Disability Subtypes
## *Splitting Versus Lumping Revisited*

*Stephen R. Hooper*
*Carl Swartz*

Over two decades ago Denckla (1972) published her study advocating increased emphasis on syndrome analysis and detailed functional descriptions in the field of learning disabilities. In that paper, Denckla addressed a broad array of issues confronting the field at that time. For example, she suggested that the field had moved beyond "lumping" children into a single diagnostic category (e.g., minimal brain dysfunction(s), learning disability) and using unitary conceptualizations of learning problems (e.g., organicity). She implied that with "controlled compulsiveness" (i.e., the observation and recording of behavioral detail with some basic organization in mind), professionals working with children with learning problems should be able to "split" children into different kinds of learning profiles or syndromes that more accurately reflected their unique abilities and disabilities. She noted that this controlled compulsiveness also should avoid the "endless and indecisive hair-splitting . . . that can only lead to the cliché that every individual is different" (Denckla 1972).

Denckla then presented three syndromes she had observed via this multidimensional conceptualization (i.e., Specific Language Dis-

This chapter was completed with support from grants from Maternal Child Health (#MCJ–379154–02–0) and the Administration of Developmental Disabilities (#90DD0207) awarded to the Center for Development and Learning.

abilities, Specific Visuo-Spatial Disabilities, Dyscontrol Syndrome), and called for combining the strengths of neurology and psychology to continue investigating issues of etiology, prognosis, and treatment for children with learning problems. Since that seminal paper, which appeared about the time when research into learning disability sub-typing was beginning to emerge, there have been significant efforts and energies devoted to examining the heterogeneity of this group of learning disorders.

This chapter provides an overview of this multidimensional conceptualization of learning disabilities. In addition to discussing historical foundations, specific subtyping models are discussed, with a particular emphasis on representative efforts to date. Several key issues in establishing subtyping models are outlined as well. The chapter concludes with general directions for the future.

## HISTORICAL FOUNDATIONS FOR SUBTYPING

Nearly ten years prior to Denckla's paper, Kirk (1963) coined the term *learning disability*; however, the study of children with specific learning difficulties has a clinical and research history dating back over 100 years. This history has included work devoted to case studies describing learning problems as well as single factor theories attempting to account for learning problems.

With respect to early case studies, Kussmaul (1877) was among the first scientists to report a patient who, although having no visual impairment, was unable to read words. Kussmaul used the term *word blindness* to describe this condition, and thus began the legacy of the study of specific learning problems.

While other adult cases continued to surface (e.g., Hinshelwood 1895), Morgan (1896) was among the first to describe an adolescent with specific learning problems. He reported that after seven years of instruction, a 14-year-old male could read only letters and single syllables. The adolescent's transcribing from dictation also was poor. Morgan called this set of symptoms, *pure word blindness*. In 1898 Bastian described another adolescent with similar symptoms. Despite adequate speech and language skills, athletic prowess, and good arithmetic skills, an 18-year-old male consistently manifested word reversals in reading and severe deficiencies in spelling.

Other cases reported during this time further emphasized the heterogeneous nature of specific learning deficits (e.g., Hinshelwood 1900, 1902). Several of these case reports postulated that a familial component might be contributing to learning difficulties (Fisher 1905; Hinshelwood 1909). Stephenson (1905), for example, described a case of congenital word blindness affecting three generations. Jackson

(1906) contributed to this literature, noting a greater frequency of specific reading problems among males than females.

Given these early case reports, a knowledge base with respect to specific learning problems (i.e., reading) was beginning to build by the early 1900s. By this time, accumulated data suggested that learning disabilities: (1) were present in children, adolescents, and adults with relatively intact cognitive functions; (2) occurred more frequently among males than females; (3) were heterogeneous in terms of symptom manifestation, differentially affecting reading, spelling, and higher-order cognitive functioning; (4) were generally unresponsive to traditional learning opportunities and instructional settings; (5) seemed to have a familial component; and (6) required a comprehensive clinical assessment for accurate diagnosis.

Although most of the early case studies suggested that learning problems were heterogeneous, nearly all the ensuing research focused primarily on single-factor conceptualizations. These conceptualizations sought to identify a single deficient process that contributed to the learning problem. These studies contributed to many often disparate single-factor theories. Although entire volumes have been devoted to single-factor explanations (e.g., Satz, Rardin, and Ross 1971), five of the more prominent conceptualizations include: (1) delayed development in cerebral dominance (Orton 1928, 1937; Satz, Rardin, and Ross 1971); (2) visual perceptual deficits (Frostig 1964; Kephart 1971; Lyle and Goyen 1968, 1975); (3) auditory perceptual deficits and associated language inefficiencies (de Hirsch, Jansky, and Langford 1966); (4) deficits in intersensory integration (Birch and Belmont 1964, 1965; Senf 1969); and (5) attention/memory deficits (Lyle and Goyen 1968, 1975; Thomson and Wilsher 1979).

Despite apparent support for many of these single-factor concepts, none of them could account for the multitude of deficits manifested by children and adolescents with learning problems. It remained for theorists to begin to hypothesize a multidimensional conceptualization for these problems.

Taken together, the early case studies and the single-factor models provided a foundation for conceptualizing learning disabilities in a multidimensional manner. Each of the single-factor models gained limited support during its existence, but none could explain satisfactorily the full range of problems presented by children with learning impediments. It is likely that each of the single-factor models addressed a specific dysfunctional component or, perhaps, neurologic substrate in the learning process and, from that perspective, contributed to improved understanding of that functional system and its interactive complexities. Although none of the models has been able to account for all behavioral variance manifested within the learning disabled population, the clinical presentation of many of the early case studies and the prevalence of single-factor models together provided a good foundation for investigations of the multidimensional nature of learning disabilities. This foundation began with the emergence, through case studies, of syndromes directly related to specific learning problems, and continues to be acknowledged in the most recent definitions of learning disabilities.

## LEARNING DISABILITY SUBTYPING MODELS

A number of subtype models for learning disabilities have been proposed. Given the high frequency of reading problems as compared to other learning difficulties, many models have focused on identifying reading disability subtypes. More recent studies, however, have begun to address other academic areas as well (e.g., math, written language). The search for homogeneous types of learning disabilities is well illustrated by the appearance of nearly 100 subtyping studies in the literature since the early 1960s. Even more studies have used subtyping models in related research endeavors. Approximately half these studies have used clinical-inferential models to provide an acceptable classification system, and the other half have employed empirical techniques in their subtyping efforts.

### Clinical-Inferential Models

Clinical-inferential models of subtype derivation represent attempts to group children into homogeneous clusters by identifying similarities in their performance profiles. These are largely post hoc models in which the investigator typically uses measures of achievement and cognition as the basis for group separation. Prior to the emergence of high-speed technological assistance, clinical-inferential models were the prototypes for subtype derivation studies. Clinical-inferential models for subtyping waned during the 1980s in favor of empirical computerized counterparts. Even so, these models are seminal in the subtyping literature. Although space does not permit a thorough discussion of the many clinical-inferential models presented to date, representative studies are highlighted. A thorough review of the multitude of subtyping studies presented to date can be seen in works by Rourke (1985), Hooper and Willis (1989), and Feagans, Short, and Meltzer (1991).

*Representative Studies.* Perhaps one of the most widely cited clinical-inferential classification models is the early subtyping efforts of Boder (1970, 1971, 1973). Her subtype model was based on an individual's performance on simple word recognition and spelling tasks. Boder predicted that because the processes involved in reading and spelling likely are interrelated, these performance tasks would discriminate effectively among normal, retarded, and dyslexic readers. These tasks also were predicted to discriminate among subtypes of dyslexia. Boder reasoned that if dyslexia were due to neurological factors, then these factors would manifest specific and differential reading-spelling patterns.

Using a screening tool designed to detect qualitative as well as quantitative reading and spelling errors, Boder proposed five distinct reading patterns. These included a normal pattern, a retarded reading pattern, and three different dyslexic patterns. *Dysphonetic* readers were characterized by deficient phonetic decoding strategies, poor letter-sound integration, and weak auditory memory. These children tended to be global, gestalt readers who were unable to decipher unfamiliar words. These children showed frequent misspellings in their written work with specific errors characterized by nonphonetic attempts, semantic substitutions (e.g., "car" for "automobile") and unintelligible letter strings. Boder estimated the prevalence rate of this subtype as about 62%, making it the largest single group of dyslexics within her sample.

In contrast, *dyseidetic* readers were characterized by poor visual-perceptual abilities and weak visual memory skills. These children employed phonetic decoding strategies almost exclusively and had limited sight-word vocabularies. Their over-reliance on phonetic decoding strategies tended to interfere with the flow and rate of the reading task and, consequently, also tended to interfere with reading comprehension. Although general spelling skills were less appropriate than expected for age, errors tended to be phonetically accurate (e.g., "biznes" for "business"). Boder estimated the prevalence rate of this subtype as about 9% making it the smallest single group of dyslexics within her sample.

The *alexic* readers, Boder's third subtype, were characterized as a combination of deficits. These children demonstrated primary processing deficiencies in both visual perceptual and phonetic decoding strategies. Boder contended that this subtype was the most severely impaired of the three subtypes and that without aggressive intervention these children would probably not learn to read. Boder estimated the prevalence rate of the alexic subtype to be about 22% of her disabled reader sample.

Mattis, French, and Rapin (1975) reported the existence of at least three independent learning disability subtypes. Employing neuropsychological techniques, Mattis, French, and Rapin classified children (*n* = 113), ranging in age from 11 to 12, into a brain-damaged reader group, a brain-damaged dyslexic group, and a nonbrain-damaged dyslexic group. All of the children had an IQ score of 80 or greater, and none showed evidence of severe psychopathology. The reading-disabled children scored at least two years below grade level on WRAT Reading (i.e., recognition).

After the three groups were formed, a comprehensive neuropsychological battery was administered that included the WISC or WAIS, the Benton Test of Visual Retention, Raven's Colored or Standard Progressive Matrices, Illinois Test of Psycholinguistic Abilities (ITPA) Sound Blending Subtest, Purdue Pegboard, and other related measures of language and motor abilities. The results of these tests were used to identify three relatively homogeneous subtypes. These subtypes were a *language disorder syndrome*, an *articulatory and graphomotor dyscoordination syndrome*, and a *visual-perceptual disorder syndrome*. These three subtypes accounted for approximately 39%, 37%, and 16% of the sample, respectively. Taken together, these three syndromes accounted for over 93% of the total reading-disabled sample. Based on these findings, Mattis, French, and Rapin provided quantitative guidelines for determining each of the subtypes based on the neuropsychological battery.

Still other subtype models were presented by Pirozzolo (1979) and Bakker (1979a). Pirozzolo (1979) proposed two subtypes of developmental dyslexia, one having distinct *auditory-linguistic* deficits relative to visual-perceptual strengths, and the other having *visual-spatial* deficits relative to intact verbal abilities. Using a comprehensive neuropsychological battery that included the WISC-R, Raven's Progressive Matrices, and neurolinguistic analyses of reading and writing errors, Pirozzolo was able to describe these two subtypes in an operational fashion. Specifically, the auditory-linguistic dyslexic subtype showed deficits in language processing characterized by expressive and receptive language difficulties, and grapheme-to-morpheme problems. The visual-spatial dyslexic subtype showed processing deficiencies in the visual-perceptual domain. These processing problems included right-left discrimination problems, finger agnosia, visual-spatial deficits, and visual encoding problems.

Bakker (1979a) also proposed a clinical-inferential model with two subtypes of learning disabilities. This particular conceptualization is noteworthy because of its developmental perspective. Concentrating largely on reading-disabled children, Bakker reviewed evidence suggesting that the right cerebral hemisphere is the primary mediator in the beginning stages of learning to read. This was based largely on the assumption that reading seems to be more visual-perceptual and less linguistic during these early stages of the reading process. As the demands of learning to read begin to become more linguistically complex, however, the reading process begins to be mediated more by left cerebral hemisphere strategies. Consequently, as the reading process develops from single letters, to monosyllabic and multisyllabic words, to simple and more complex sentences, there should be a normal shift from right to left hemisphere mediated reading strategies, although a developmental increase in hemispheric asymmetry may not be seen. This has been called the *balance model*.

When learning to read, some children may show an overuse of right hemisphere strategies (i.e., perceptual) and poor emergence of left hemisphere strategies. Bakker labeled these children *P-Type dyslexics* because they learn to read using visual-perceptual strategies, and continue to show an over-reliance on these strategies as reading progresses. Conversely, *L-Type dyslexics* show an over-reliance on left hemisphere strategies and poor emergence of right hemisphere functioning. These children demonstrate an over-reliance on linguistic-semantic strategies throughout the development of reading.

Subsequent hemispheric dominance studies have begun to provide support for Bakker's conceptualization (Bakker 1979b, 1981; Bakker et al. 1980; Bakker, Moerland, and Goekoop-Hoefkens 1981; Keefe and Swinney 1979). Tomlinson-Keasey and Kelly (1979a, 1979b) also have demonstrated this conceptualization with respect to spelling and arithmetic. Although Pirozzolo and Bakker's models began to show empirical linkages of learning problems to assumed brain functions, Bakker's model also provided support for viewing learning problems from a developmental perspective, as well as from a treatment perspective (e.g., Bakker and Vinke 1985).

Other investigators have targeted selected aspects of reading in their subtyping efforts. For example, Lovett (1983a, 1983b, 1984) described a classification model for specific reading dysfunction based on accuracy and rate dimensions. Although these dimensions are not novel to the reading literature, they do represent relatively new concepts in the subtyping literature, particularly the rate dimension. *Accuracy*-disabled readers, of course, evidenced significant difficulties in reading accuracy, whereas *rate*-disabled readers evidenced significant difficulties in reading rate despite relatively intact reading accuracy. Although no reading comprehension differences were noted between these subtypes, the accuracy-disabled readers showed poorer spelling achievement and greater difficulty with manipulation of language structures as well as possible reading-acquisition deviancies. Although rate-disabled readers showed relatively intact language comprehension skills, these children may account for a significant number of special education referrals. One reason for this phenomenon is that their cognitive deficits may not be manifested until learning materials increase in length and complexity.

Some investigators have begun to explore the language-based underpinning of learning problems. For example, Wilson and Risucci (1986) offered a well-developed conceptualization for the classification of language disabled preschool children. Drawing largely on neuropsychological assessment methods, Wilson and Risucci (1986) clinically identified five subtypes. These were an *Expressive Language Subtype*, a *Receptive Language Subtype*, and a *Globally Deficient Language Subtype*. Two additional subtypes included children who exhibited *Memory and Retrieval* problems and *No Deficits*.

This classification model is important because of its use of quantified rules for subtype membership and its reliance on a neuropsychological assessment battery. Moreover, Wilson and Risucci (1986) have begun to establish internal and external validity for this classification model. For example, good comparative results were obtained when the clinical subtypes were evaluated against a stringently applied cluster analysis. Clearly, this study provides an excellent example of carefully considered research in learning disability subtyping and classification.

Similarly, Curtiss and Tallal (1988) classified 100 language-impaired preschool children into three subtypes. One subtype showed expressive language deficits, the second showed receptive language deficits, and the third showed deficits in both processing domains. Curtiss and Tallal, however, found performance differences among each clinical subtype only in linguistic processing skills and not linguistic competence (e.g., grammatical skills). These data document the importance of task, as opposed to modality, parameters in language-impaired preschoolers. They also illustrate the qualitative nature of this particular clinical-inferential model.

Along with the more traditional model for grouping language disorders in a homogeneous fashion, neurolinguists also have made progress in subtyping reading disabilities. Marshall (1984) provided a classification model based largely on the adult literature on acquired alexia. This classification model encompassed four basic subtypes of reading disabilities. These included *surface dyslexia, deep dyslexia, phonological dyslexia*, and *direct dyslexia*.

*Surface dyslexia* was characterized by difficulty with the visual aspects of word recognition. Despite good phonological capabilities for regular and irregular words, whole word recognition and reading comprehension were impaired. Individuals with surface dyslexia also showed an inability to use context clues in deciphering written text. Given these deficits in accessing the visual modality in the reading process, individuals showing surface dyslexia usually read better aloud than silently. Deloche, Andreewsky, and Desi (1982) described these same characteristics in their surface dyslexia subtype.

The second subtype described by Marshall (1984) was *deep dyslexia*. This subtype was characterized by adequate reading of familiar words in an adequate manner, but frequent semantic paralexias when reading aloud (e.g., substituting "car" for "automobile"). Reading errors also were characterized by visual confusion and a dependence on concrete problem solving strategies. Despite these inherent deficits, these individuals are able to employ context clues adequately and, consequently, tend to show satisfactory reading comprehension. Some investigators have speculated that deep dyslexia is related to anomia. Specifically, it seems that these individuals can access the correct semantic category, but an incorrect visual-semantic association occurs resulting in the paralexic response. Other researchers have suggested that the deep dyslexic reading pattern is mediated primarily by the right cerebral hemisphere (Coltheart 1980; Saffran et al. 1980) as opposed to the neurolinguistic processes associated with the left cerebral hemisphere (Hynd and Hynd 1984). Siegel (1985) provided case study data to support the existence of this subtype of dyslexia in childhood.

The third neurolinguistic subtype that Marshall (1984) described was *phonological dyslexia*. This subtype was characterized by severe deficiencies in efficiently accessing the phoneme-to-grapheme system. These individuals typically will add or delete prefixes and suffixes in their reading, although this finding is equivocal (Funnell 1983). In contrast to deep dyslexia, phonological dyslexia is characterized by an average oral vocabulary. In a case study of developmental phonological dyslexia, oral reading errors tend to be orthographically similar to the target word or derivational forms of the target word. Beauvois and Derouesne (1979) similarly described this neurolinguistic subtype.

The *direct dyslexia* subtype described by Marshall (1984) was characterized by adequate or accelerated oral reading capabilities for regular and irregular words. Comprehension skills, however, typically were poorly developed and dysfunctional. Direct dyslexia also has been called hyperlexia (McClure and Hynd 1983).

Clinical-inferential models have provided a great deal of evidence to support the multidimensional nature of learning disabilities. We have reviewed a number of representative studies that provided clinical classification schemes based on a variety of academic and neurodevelopmental variables. Although these models fall short of establishing a definitive classification methodology, they do exemplify the complexities of learning disorders and serve to underscore the need for a valid differential nosology.

From the clinical-inferential models proposed to date, one could deduce the presence of at least three broad-band subtypes. The most commonly reported subtype is characterized by auditory-linguistic deficits. The other two comprise a subtype showing visual-perceptual deficits and one showing a combination of deficits. Other clinical-inferential subtypes have been proposed, such as those with motor deficiencies or memory problems, but most of these clinically derived subtypes represent modifications of the three broad-band descriptions.

The clinical-inferential subtyping models have provided a foundation for the acceptance of the concept of heterogeneity of learning disabilities. Not only have the efforts provided a clinical classification model, but each has assisted the clinician and researcher by also suggesting an assessment model that includes specific guidelines for subtype membership. In addition, Bakker (1979a) has provided a developmental paradigm from which to understand the neurodevelopmental parameters of learning disability subtyping, and a subtype-to-treatment paradigm as well.

## Empirical Subtyping Models

Although many of the clinical-inferential classification models make intuitive sense and, in fact, may represent broad-band descriptions for a learning disability nosology, there also are inherent problems with these models. Generally, the clinical-inferential models suffer from methodological weaknesses, limited data reduction strategies, and questionable validity. Consequently, the clinical utility of these methods is limited, especially when used to build classification systems that comprise numerous interacting variables.

With the ready availability of advanced computer technologies, many of the problems manifested by clinical-inferential models can be addressed effectively by empirical classification techniques (e.g., cluster analysis). Generally, the methods used to develop these models are designed to group *subjects* on the basis of profile similarities. One major advantage is that these methods can be used to generate classification schemes and, consequently, contribute to the validation of the classification model. These complex methods are not new to the biological sciences, but they only recently have been applied to the behavioral sciences.

Given the complexities involved in using these techniques, they require rapid data management capabilities afforded by computerized technology. It is important to note, however, that these methods are not truly statistical in nature because they are not based on probabilistic models. Further, they serve to organize any data set, even random numbers, into relatively homogeneous groupings. Consequently, the number of clusters derived and their interpretive significance require sound clinical judgment on the part of the investigator. As can be surmised, clustering techniques are relatively complex and require statistical sophistication for proper use. More detailed information about these strategies can be found in sources by Skinner (1978), Everitt (1980), and Morris, Blashfield, and Satz (1981).

***Representative Studies.*** Satz and Morris (1981) used achievement variables to begin their subtyping investigations. In addition, however, this study is important because these investigators did not define the population a priori; instead, they used clustering techniques with large numbers of subjects to establish groups of learning-disabled persons and comparison groups. This strategy allowed for a more objective classification of probands and avoided the use of exclusionary criteria in the selection of learning-disabled subjects (Satz and Morris 1981).

Using data from the Wide Range Achievement Test (WRAT), Satz and Morris (1981) identified nine viable achievement clusters in a sample of 236 white males (mean age = 11 years). Seven of these clusters represented variants of a normal learning profile. Two of the clusters, however, showed significantly low achievement in reading (i.e., deficit > 2 years) and warranted the designation of learning problem groups. External validation of the groups was demonstrated using Peabody Picture Vocabulary Test (PPVT) standard scores, neuropsychological performance, socioeconomic status, and neurological "soft" signs. These two subtypes were combined and a second clustering technique was performed on four neuropsychological measures administered at the end of the fifth grade. This clustering technique identified five reliable subtypes: *global language impaired, specific language impaired, visual-perceptual deficit, mixed deficit,* and *neuropsychologically intact with low achievement*. These subtypes were validated across neurological variables, socioeconomic status, and parental reading levels. Additionally, they were replicated across samples (Johnston, Fennell, and Satz 1987) as well as across cultures with Dutch children (Van der Vlugt and Satz 1985).

Other subtyping approaches have used psychoeducational, intellectual, and neuropsychologic variables in identifying learning disability subtypes. Empirical subtyping models developed by Rourke (Del Dotto and Rourke 1985; Fisk and Rourke 1979; Joshko and Rourke 1985; Petrauskas and Rourke 1979) and Lyon (Lyon, Stewart, and Freedman 1982; Lyon and Watson 1981) nicely illustrate these subtyping efforts. The impact of these studies has created a theoretic basis for the subtyping models. In this sense, they have suggested putative brain-behavior relationships and have linked multidimensional conceptualizations of learning disabilities to neuropsychological theory.

For example, Petrauskas and Rourke (1979) identified four subtype patterns of performance on a neuropsychologic battery. This battery comprised 44 measures classified into six categories as outlined by Reitan (1974). These were tactile-perceptual, sequencing, motoric, visual-spatial, auditory-verbal, and abstract-conceptual domains. The sample included 160 children, ages seven and eight, of which 133 were retarded readers (i.e., WRAT Reading percentile < 26) and 27 normal readers (i.e., WRAT percentile > 44). The overall sample initially was divided into two equal subsamples and Q-type factor analysis was performed on each subsample. Profiles that correlated significantly across samples were retained in the final subtype solution, and the Q-factor analysis then was performed on the entire sample of 160 children.

The first subtype contained the largest grouping of subjects. It was characterized by auditory-verbal and language related deficits. Reading and spelling achievement were lower than arithmetic functioning. The second subtype demonstrated deficits in visual sequencing, bilateral finger agnosia, and global achievement problems. This subtype also evidenced ipsative weaknesses on WISC Arithmetic, Coding, Information, and Digit Span subtests (i.e., the ACID pattern). The third reliable subtype showed right unilateral sensory and motor deficits. Specific impairment was observed in expressive speech and visual-motor coordination. The fourth subtype was not a reliable one, but generally reflected a normal neuropsychological profile. Petrauskas and Rourke speculated that, respectively, these subtypes were consistent with dysfunction involving: (1) the temporal lobe of the left hemisphere; (2) the temporo-parieto-occipital regions of the left hemisphere; and (3) the frontal regions of the left hemisphere.

Lyon and associates (Lyon 1985; Lyon et al. 1981; Lyon, Stewart, and Freedman 1982; Lyon and Watson 1981) also have made a significant contribution to the subtyping literature. Using the Mattis, French, and Rapin (1975) clinical-inferential subtyping model and clustering techniques, Lyon and Watson (1981) empirically identified six independent subtypes from a population of 11- to 12-year-old learning-disabled youngsters ($n = 100$) and a matched group of normal achievers ($n = 50$). In addition to a normal learner subtype, Lyon and Watson found five disabled-reader subtypes.

*Subtype 1* was characterized by mixed deficits in auditory processing, receptive language, visual memory, and visual-perceptual abilities. This subtype performed the poorest on academic tasks. *Subtype 2* demonstrated a similar, but less impaired, neuropsychological profile. *Subtype 3* was characterized by expressive and receptive language deficits, whereas *Subtype 5* seemed to be more severely impaired with respect to overall language functioning. Subtype 5 also manifested global achievement deficits. *Subtype 4* exhibited significant visual-perceptual impairment and surprisingly, given the reported low prevalence of this kind of subtype (Boder 1970; Mattis, French, and Rapin 1975), comprised the largest number of children.

This subtyping model subsequently was replicated by Lyon, Stewart, and Freedman (1982) with six- through nine-year-old disabled readers. The replication of these subtypes with a younger population suggested some degree of age-related stability for subtypes, albeit not necessarily for individuals. Evidence for external validity of these subtypes also has accrued. Specifically, both qualitative and quantitative differences among the subtypes have been noted on tasks of reading recognition, reading comprehension, oral reading, and spelling (Lyon et al. 1981; Lyon, Stewart, and Freedman 1982).

Many of the studies conducted to date have tended to focus on reading functions. However, other studies have begun to emerge that address other academic functions. For example, DeLuca, Del Dotto, and Rourke (1987) used clustering techniques to group children with arithmetic deficiencies into homogeneous subtypes. These investigators used 156 children, ages 9 to 14, with WRAT Arithmetic percentile scores less than 27 and Reading percentile scores greater than 40. All children were referred for evaluation of suspected neuropsychologic impairment. Intellectual functioning for the sample was within an average range (i.e., Full Scale WISC IQ = 85 to 115). Hierarchical cluster analytic techniques were used on WRAT Reading, Spelling, and Arithmetic standard scores. Four stable subtypes of arithmetic-disabled children were identified.

The first subtype was characterized by mild deficits in tactile-perception, conceptual flexibility, and some aspects of expressive language. This group also showed inconsistent performance on tasks measuring attention, short-term auditory memory, and visual-spatial output. These children evidenced intact functioning, however, in nonverbal problem solving, motor skills, visual-perceptual organization, and selected aspects of language. The second subtype was characterized by significant deficiencies in higher order tactile perception, visual-motor speed and coordination, verbal fluency, verbal memory, and conceptual flexibility. This subtype also experienced difficulties in the efficient use of verbal mediation strategies.

The third subtype showed deficiencies in nonverbal problem solving and processing. Basic language abilities were relatively intact, but there were selective deficits in psychomotor skills, conceptual flexibility, and finger localization. This subtype evidenced average to above average reading skills in the presence of poor arithmetic calculation skills. The final subtype manifested mild difficulties in verbal expression, conceptual flexibility, finger graphesthesia, and manipulation of visual-symbolic materials. This subtype experienced intact reading abilities despite significant deficits in spelling and arithmetic. Organizational deficiencies and poor work-study habits also were characteristic of this subtype.

The DeLuca, Del Dotto, and Rourke (1987) study is unique because the sample selected for study evidenced a specific area of deficit, thus allowing for examination of different profile patterns within the area of arithmetic achievement. This kind of investigation has potential to facilitate the development of more detailed intervention approaches and to provide prognostic information about particular subtypes. This study also is noteworthy because it highlights the heterogeneous nature of learning problems *within* as well as *among* specific achievement domains.

Another longitudinal study conducted in Finland addressed the derivation of motor subtypes. Using a sample of motorically impaired ($n = 106$) and normal ($n = 40$) seven-year-old children, Lyytinen and Ahonen (1988) used cluster analysis on scores from a battery of motor tasks to identify six motorically impaired subtypes. These included subtypes with: (1) general developmental delay; (2) specific motor problems; (3) motor control problems; (4) spatial constructive problems; (5) mild spatial constructive problems; and (6) kinesthetic problems. Follow-up of these children at age 11 revealed that nearly half of the motorically impaired subjects continued to show significant motor difficulties. In addition, many of the children in the motorically impaired subtypes manifested significant lags in basic academic skills.

Some of the empirical studies also have begun to elucidate the developmental course of particular learning disability subtypes. For example, Fisk and Rourke (1979) used Q-factor analysis in a cross-sectional fashion in their investigation of potential subtypes at three different ages, 9 to 10 years, 11 to 12 years, and 13 to 14 years ($n = 264$). In contrast to the Petrauskas and Rourke (1979) study, this investigation used children deficient in all achievement domains (i.e., WRAT Reading, Spelling, and Arithmetic percentiles $< 31$). Results of Q-factor analysis revealed two basic subtype patterns for all three age levels. A third subtype appeared only at the youngest and oldest age levels. Subtype 1 was characterized by poor auditory-verbal processing with marked impairment in tactile perception. Subtype 2 also was characterized by auditory-verbal deficiencies, but also showed motor deficits and impaired shifting of attentional sets. Subtype 3 demonstrated auditory-verbal, memory, and tactile perceptual problems. Given this cross-sectional design, developmental interpretations are tenuous, but the findings do suggest the importance of considering age-related factors in learning disability subtyping efforts. The results of this study also underscored the importance of psycholinguistic processes in generic learning problems.

In an innovative study using longitudinal clustering techniques, Morris, Blashfield, and Satz (1986) presented a developmental classification model based on a sample of reading-disabled children. Morris, Blashfield, and Satz classified 200 nonclinical normal and reading-disordered males based on patterns of performance on eight neuropsychologic measures. Four of these measures tapped verbal-conceptual abilities (e.g., verbal fluency) and four tested sensorimotor-perceptual skills (e.g., Embedded Figures Test). All 200 children were tested with all measures at the start of kindergarten, and again at the end of the second and fifth grades. Clustering techniques and subsequent internal and external validation procedures identified two reliable broad-band subtypes: namely, good readers and poor readers.

This two-group classification was further differentiated into five subtypes. These included two good reader subtypes and three poor reader subtypes. *Subtype A* evidenced deficient verbal abilities and poor achievement. These children, however, showed a trend toward improving their visual-perceptual abilities over time. Teacher ratings also suggested that this group of boys was more physically active than their peers. *Subtype B* demonstrated increasingly poorer performance with age, particularly in verbal-conceptual abilities. This subtype was characterized by parental history of learning problems and a greater frequency of significant neurological findings and birth history events. *Subtype C* members and their families manifested below average performance on all neuropsychologic measures over time. *Subtypes D and E* showed average to above average performance, and a lower incidence of significant neurologic anomalies and birth difficulties. The performances of these subtypes were relatively stable over time. Although the results were obfuscated somewhat by limitations in the sample (e.g., all white males) and the use of an unvalidated clustering technique (i.e., longitudinal cluster analysis), this study was the first to address the issue of continuity of subtype topography.

From still another perspective, Spreen and Haaf (1986) presented an eloquent study that addressed many reliability and validity issues in empirical classification models. The initial phase of this study examined the classification patterns derived from an extensive battery measuring a wide array of cognitive abilities in two groups of learning-disabled children. In the second phase of this study, a subgroup of these children and a matched control group were followed into adulthood and reevaluated in an effort to investigate the continuity of particular learning disability patterns. This study is important because of its focus on long-term outcome of particular subtypes. Similar to other research (e.g., Morris, Blashfield, and Satz 1986; Rourke and Orr 1977; Satz et al. 1978), this study used a longitudinal design, but it is the only study to date that has followed specific subtype patterns into adulthood.

Children included in this study were referred to the University of Victoria Neuropsychology Clinic because of learning problems. The subjects (*n* = 63) were between the ages of 8 and 12 (mean age = 10.14 years), had a VIQ or PIQ greater than 69, showed no acquired brain damage, and evidenced no primary psychopathology. A second group of referred subjects ($n$ = 96) was selected directly from clinic files according to similar criteria, except that the IQ cutoff was more stringent (i.e., VIQ or PIQ > 79). This group was included to assess the possible effects of intelligence on the learning-disabled profiles. Approximately 92% of the first sample and about 84% of the second sample performed significantly below expected levels (i.e., one standard deviation below age and grade) on reading, arithmetic, or both.

Cluster analysis identified six subtypes for the first sample (i.e., project referral group) and eight subtypes for the second sample (e.g., restricted IQ referral group) accounting for about 86% and 92% of the subjects, respectively. Subtypes in the first sample were two severity-specific subtypes (i.e., minimal and pervasive), two specific learning disability subtypes (i.e., arithmetic and reading), and two subtypes showing global impairments in achievement and specific cognitive functions (i.e., linguistic and visual-perceptual). The eight subtypes generated in the second sample were similar. They were two severity subtypes, three specific achievement deficit subtypes (i.e., one arithmetic and two reading), two global achievement deficit subtypes, again implicating cognitive and linguistic deficiencies, respectively, and a mildly impaired global achievement subtype with specific problems in right-left orientation. None of these subtypes, however, was noted to differ in terms of degree of neurological impairment.

During a second phase of this study, 170 subjects were retested at age 24. This sample included 86% of the initial referred subjects and 46 normal controls. Clustering techniques classified 100% of the subjects. Nine subtypes were identified (probably reflecting the larger sample size and the inclusion of normal controls) as compared to six and eight subtypes at younger age levels. Specifically, there seemed to be three groups of normal learners, with one perhaps having greater difficulty with arithmetic, three specific achievement subtypes, two globally impaired subtypes, and one visual-motor coordination subtype.

Although these subtypes seemed to resemble the child subtypes in terms of topography, subtype membership at the two age levels showed little correspondence. Only about 36% of the subjects were classified into similar clusters at both age levels, perhaps because of treatment or neurodevelopmental effects that occurred over the years. Subjects who, at childhood, were classified on the basis of visual-perceptual deficits, specific reading or arithmetic impairment, or severity continued to show these problems into adulthood. The linguistic deficient subtype found during middle childhood, however, was curiously absent during adulthood, with most of these subjects moving into adult clusters reflecting more global deficits. This may suggest a poor long-term prognosis for this subtype. These findings challenge the continuity of specific subtypes (Lyon, Stewart, and Freedman 1982;

Morris, Blashfield, and Satz 1986; Rourke and Orr 1977) and the primary ascendant-skill hypothesis postulated by Satz et al. (1978); however, they do underscore the importance of developmental parameters in learning disability subtypes.

This section presented a brief discussion of pertinent issues related to empirical classification methods. While newer studies continue to emerge (e.g., Batchelor and Dean 1992; Bender and Golden 1990; Sandler et al. 1992), efforts using empirical classification models suggest that the identification of two, three, or even four broad-band learning disability subtypes is not as simple as it seemed to be with the clinical-inferential models. The sophistication of the empirical classification methodology has enabled researchers to explore the complexities associated with degree of severity and specificity of impairment across, as well as within, a wide array of functional domains. A number of methodological improvements have characterized the empirical classification literature (e.g., Morris, Blashfield, and Satz 1986). These improvements have provided a basis for understanding learning disability subtypes from a longitudinal perspective. Studies by Morris, Blashfield, and Satz (1986) and Spreen and Haaf (1986) represent important attempts to begin examining these issues.

Finally, given the homogeneous subtypes that now have been identified by various clustering techniques, initial attempts to describe and validate relationships among etiological factors, assessment, and treatment have begun to be explored. These kinds of relationships may be among the most important reasons to develop an adequate subtyping nosology. Even so, despite the rapid advancement in learning disability subtyping illustrated by the models presented, a universally accepted clinical classification model has not yet been adopted. Perhaps this is because, as Satz and Morris (1981) noted, classification models are probably best considered to be preliminary. As such, they require further refinement, especially in terms of validity and clinical applicability.

## ISSUES IN THE DEVELOPMENT OF SUBTYPES

The clinically and empirically based studies addressing the heterogeneous nature of this group of disorders attest to the remarkable progress made in the field of learning disability subtyping in a relatively brief amount of time. This progress has been impeded, however, by a number of fundamental issues related to the field. In 1983 Rourke presented issues that faced the learning disability field in general (e.g., definitional concerns, methodological issues, the determination of reliable subtypes, prediction, treatment issues), and many of these issues continue to plague the field. Several of the more pertinent issues are mentioned here.

## Definitional Problems

A major obstacle that has impeded progress in learning disability research is the lack of a universally accepted, operational definition. Definitions of learning disabilities, for example, have been controversial since the introduction of the term. As early as 1972, Cruikshank published a list of 40 different terms used to describe these disorders, and Vaughan and Hodges (1973) subsequently compiled a collection of 38 different definitions. Definitions have continued to proliferate, including the most recent definition proposed by the Interagency Committee on Learning Disabilities (ICLD 1987), but none has been universally embraced by researchers and clinicians. This has led to confusion even about what issues and factors are comprised by the domain of learning disabilities, as well as a variety of assessment and identification problems.

Definitional problems have led some investigators to question the clinical utility and, ultimately, the existence of learning disabilities (Algozzine and Ysseldyke 1986), while others (e.g., Adelman and Taylor 1986) have argued that a learning disability actually may represent one point on a continuum of learning problems. In this sense, a learning disability is conceptualized as only one of many different kinds of learning problems. This conceptualization serves to establish a learning disability as a diagnostic entity that is part of a broader scheme, yet separate from other learning problems. As such, explorations of distinct subtypes of a variety of learning problems is not precluded. Learning disabilities research, therefore, can focus on different levels, such as on the continuum level, or the subtype level, or on the severity level. Indeed, some investigators have noted the clear lack of differentiation between children showing only low achievement and those with ability-achievement discrepancies (Fletcher et al. 1992; Siegel and Metsala 1992).

Given these definitional and conceptual problems, it is not surprising that currently there is no generally accepted learning disability classification model. The growing body of literature addressing the subtyping question, however, indicates that the field is moving, albeit slowly, toward that goal. Keogh (1983) advanced three reasons why such a classification model should be developed: advocacy, research, and intervention. A clearly delineated homogeneous group of disorders provides a basis for advocacy on behalf of individuals with differential risk factors and prognoses. Advocacy is important in order to obtain the support and resources needed to study particular problems. Such research leads to understanding, and understanding is prerequisite to intervention and treatment progress. Thus, a generally accepted classification model clearly is fundamental to efforts designed to improve service delivery.

## Lack of a Conceptual Framework

From the subtype models described previously, it is clear that many different learning disability classification models have been proposed. Much of this apparent progress, however, has been hampered by definitional issues and a poorly articulated conceptual framework for subtype development. With several notable exceptions (e.g., Lyon et al. 1981; Mattis, French, and Rapin 1975; Rourke 1983, 1989; Satz and Morris 1981) most of the proposed classification models lack the conceptual frameworks from which to evaluate their respective subtyping schemes.

Skinner (1981) advanced one such conceptual framework to formulate and evaluate proposed classification models. This framework comprises three fundamental components that, according to Skinner, should characterize any classification model. These include: (1) theory formulation; (2) internal validation; and (3) external validation.

The first component, theory formulation, involves decisions regarding the theory upon which the subtyping model is based. These decisions include selecting a set of measures that coincide with the theoretical orientation of the model. Additionally, a priori hypotheses are proposed to assess the clinical and theoretical validities of identified subtypes (e.g., response to treatment, differences on variables, and tasks not included in the subtype derivation). Other hypotheses address the relationships among the subtypes, and the relationship of the overall model to other learning parameters.

The second component, internal validation, refers to the reliability and validity of the identified subtypes. These psychometric issues involve selecting an appropriate classification technique to identify homogeneous subtypes of disabled learners (e.g., hierarchical cluster analysis). Currently, given the status of many classification techniques, there are few explicit rules for determining the reliability of a classification model (Blashfield 1980; Morris, Blashfield, and Satz 1981). Fletcher and Morris (1986), however, suggested that internally valid typologies should: (1) result in the classification of the majority of the sample into the identified subtypes; (2) result in homogeneous subtypes; (3) be replicable across samples and techniques (e.g., clinical groupings versus Q-factor analysis); and (4) be based on reliable variables that are appropriate to a variety of samples. In particular, most subtyping models proffered to date fail to address the latter two points in a substantive manner.

Finally, the third component, external validation, is important independent of internal reliability and validity. Here, the obtained model is evaluated against external criteria (e.g., achievement) not used in the original derivation of the subtypes. Fletcher and Morris (1986) suggested that simple comparisons on external variables only partially addressed this component; moreover, results should be hypothesized a priori so that the utility of the subtyping model can be properly assessed in terms of specific parameters.

It is common to evaluate the validity of a typology via clinical comparisons of the subtypes with previously identified subtypes. For example, Lyon and Watson's specific language impaired subtypes are remarkably similar to Boder's dysphonetic subtype, Mattis, French, and Rapin's language subtype, and Satz and Morris's naming deficit subtype. Satz and Morris (1981), however, cautioned that, although many of the independently derived subtypes seem to be similar, these similarities do not truly provide valid evidence for a specific subtype. The validities of specific subtypes and subtyping models are more appropriately evaluated with other methods, such as those outlined by Skinner. Skinner's framework for developing and evaluating learning disability subtyping models is useful because it emphasizes the conceptual or theoretical basis absent from many current models, and models such as Skinner's should be employed in any subtyping effort.

## Developmental Considerations

Brain-behavior relationships are dynamic and developmental changes in those relationships are characterized by both continuities and discontinuities. These developmental changes, however, are only beginning to be investigated. Effects of childhood central nervous system trauma and neurodevelopmental anomalies also have been poorly understood. It is essential for neurodevelopmental issues to be considered in any learning disability subtyping model. Furthermore, it is reasonable to expect that these models be characterized by dynamic neurodevelopmental continuities and discontinuities.

In contrast to these expectations, many of the models presented suggest that variables are considered equally important at all age levels. As Adams (1985) noted, however, the actual "neurological weighting" of a particular variable may be greater at one time in a child's development than at another time. For example, in the Boder (1970) model, based on reading and spelling skills, the same kinds of tasks are used to determine the various subtypes at all age levels, despite evidence that the neurodevelopmental parameters associated with reading (e.g., Satz et al. 1978) and spelling (e.g., Frith 1983) change with age. Another example comes from the Florida Longitudinal Project. Here, Satz et al. (1978) asserted that visual-perceptual abilities were in primary ascendancy during the preschool and early elementary school years. Thus, they hypothesized that at this particular point in development, tasks assessing these skills would be better predictors of later learning problems than other tasks. Although this has been debated (Vellutino 1978), this series of studies does emphasize the importance of developmental considerations in establishing learning disability typologies.

Related to these neurodevelopmental considerations, are concerns about subtype continuity. To date few studies have addressed these concerns longitudinally (Morris, Blashfield, and Satz 1986; Spreen and Haaf 1986). Several others have addressed these concerns cross-sectionally (e.g., Lyon, Stewart, and Freedman 1982; Rourke and Orr 1977). Generally, data have provided relative support for the existence of particular subtypes over time, but not overwhelming support for continuity of subtype membership. For example, in their longitudinal investigation, Spreen and Haaf (1986) noted that many subjects changed classifications over time. A similar observation was reported by Morris, Blashfield, and Satz (1986). These findings suggest that children manifest different learning symptoms over time, even into adulthood (Spreen and Haaf 1986). This is not unexpected, given the plethora of variables that can impinge on a child's learning efficiency (e.g., social-emotional factors), but how these variables interact over time (e.g., student-teacher-environment-materials interaction) and the issue of subtype continuity require further examination.

Finally, it is important for investigators to examine factors potentially related to the early identification of specific subtypes of learning-disabled children. A great deal of research has been conducted on the early identification of generic learning disabilities, but none of these studies has addressed the subtype issue. For example, a recent review (Tramontana, Hooper, and Selzer 1988) suggested a multitude of variables related to the early prediction of learning disabilities. Similar to the literature on single-factor theories of learning disabilities noted earlier, this suggests that learning disabilities should be conceived multidimensionally, even during the preschool years. Two studies have attempted to address this concern with language-disordered preschool children (Aram and Nation 1975; Wilson and Risucci 1986), but other investigations also should be pursued, particularly given the subtyping concerns outlined by others (e.g., Rourke 1985).

## Social-Emotional Factors

Although researchers have investigated the social-emotional concomitants of heterogeneous groups of learning-disabled individuals (e.g., Bruck 1986), it was not until the 1980s that they began to explore possible social-emotional issues in homogeneous subtypes of learning disabilities. Consequently, the history of research exploring social-emotional issues in learning disability subtypes is brief, and definitive conclusions are premature. Some interesting hypotheses, however, already are beginning to emerge.

For example, Rourke (1989) has proposed what seems to be one of the first truly neuropsychologically based models for conceptualizing learning disabilities. In addition to a specific profile of academic and neuropsychologic strengths and weaknesses, perhaps one of the most interesting aspects associated with this syndrome is that there seems to be a strong relationship with social-emotional and adaptive behavior deficits. Affected individuals present great difficulty adapting to novel situations and manifest poor social perception and judgment which, in turn, results in poor social interaction skills. There seems to be a marked tendency for these individuals to engage in social withdrawal and social isolation as age increases and, consequently, they are at risk for internalized forms of psychopathology. In fact, Rourke, Young, and Leenaars (1989), Bigler (1989), and Kowalchuck and King (1989) all noted the increased risk that these individuals have for depression and suicide.

Although these behaviors previously have been documented among children with learning disabilities (e.g., Gerber and Zinkgraf 1982), their relationship with specific neuropsychologic findings only recently has been asserted. The emphasis placed on social-emotional functioning by this model also serves to accentuate the need for these issues to be addressed and, perhaps, enveloped in any clinical or research activity involving children with specific learning disabilities.

## Subtype-to-Treatment Linkages

Perhaps one of the most important reasons for determining homogeneous subtypes of learning-disabled individuals and, ultimately, developing a classification system, is the potential for specific intervention plans to be developed. Conceptually, given the support for specific subtypes, it makes sense that these subtypes would respond differently to selected treatment interventions.

To date, most of the subtyping studies investigating educational parameters have focused on the external validation of their respective models. Although this kind of external validation begins to address the specific treatment needs of these subtypes, it only suggests that a specific treatment approach might be useful. For greater assurance, specific treatment plans need to be developed and statistically evaluated in order to determine the effectiveness of a particular approach with a particular subtype in a valid manner. Only in this way can assessment-treatment linkages become validated and classification models useful to both clinicians and researchers.

From a neuropsychologic perspective, some investigators have noted that the power of subtyping models in relation to treatment lies in the clear and reliable delineation of a profile of strengths and weaknesses, the relationship of these cognitive processing variables to specific patterns of recovery/remediation, and the direct linkages that can be made from assessment to specific intervention plans (Alfano and Finlayson 1987; Lyon, Moats, and Flynn 1988; Newby, Recht, and Caldwell in press). At the present time, however, few studies exist to confirm these assessment-to-subtype-to-treatment connections.

Although the literature on subtype-to-treatment models is sparse, it is clear that direct and accurate matching of subtypes to specific treatment regimens has tremendous instructional potential for learning-disabled individuals (e.g., Newby, Recht, and Caldwell in press). The few research studies conducted, however, also suggest that this simple matching probably will not account for all of the variability in treatment response. Undoubtedly, other variables also play important roles in shaping treatment response. Conceptually, it seems that if learning problems are multidimensional, then treatment initiatives also should be multidimensional. The subtype-to-treatment match actually may represent one of many components of a comprehensive intervention for an individual with a specific learning disability. Other issues that should be considered in developing a comprehensive treatment intervention include the contribution of related variables (e.g., family factors, school variables, psychosocial issues, teacher-student issues), specific assessment-to-treatment linkages, and prognosis.

## CONCLUSIONS

It is clear from the preceding discussion that the conceptualization of learning disabilities as a multisyndrome group of disorders has replaced unidimensional thinking in this area. Over the past three decades, there have been rapid advances with respect to the development of a learning disability classification model, but the area still has far to go before a particular subtyping model will be accepted routinely by researchers and clinicians. Many critical issues remain unresolved, not the least of which are definitional in nature.

The bulk of evidence suggests that questions pertaining to "lumping versus splitting" have been changed to "How many different subtypes and/or dimensions are there?" At this time, the answer remains elusive; however, it is safe to say that the number of subtypes undoubtedly exceeds the numbers initially suggested by many of the clinical-inferential models. Although consistent with neurodevelopmental theory, this question requires continued exploration.

It remains important, however, for such explorations to be pursued in a logical, theoretical manner. The data presented suggest that the empirical classification techniques provide the most power and flexibility for identifying classification models. Researchers using these techniques, however, should move toward providing guidelines for their appropriate use for learning disability classification. It also will be important for researchers to invoke clear theoretical propositions for their subtyping scheme (e.g., Nonverbal Learning Disability Model, Rourke 1989; Wernicke-Geschwind Model, Mayeaux and Kandel 1985). Although these methods are strengthened by their flexibility, it is important for guidelines and an a priori theory to be suggested. This also will promote improved comparisons among studies and the various classification models derived.

Another important area to explore further concerns the continuity of learning disability subtypes. Although this chapter concentrates largely on learning disabilities in children and adolescents, there is a rapidly advancing literature dealing with adult learning disabilities (e.g., Reiff and Gerber 1992). To date, several longitudinal studies have been reported investigating the issue of subtype continuity, but only one of these has followed subjects into the adult years. It is important for additional studies to investigate this concern, particularly in terms of prognostic issues germane to treatment.

Finally, the efficacy of subtype-to-treatment paradigms requires further examination. It is important for research endeavors directed at treatment to attempt to adhere to methodological constraints and to move away from anecdotal reports and case study claims of improvement. Success in the treatment arena for a specific subtype model may be among the best tests for determining the ecological validity of that classification model, but it is important that a multidimensional focus be retained with respect to planning a comprehensive treatment program.

This chapter provides an overview of the literature of learning disability subtyping. As the literature presented will attest, however, classification of learning disabilities is only beginning to be clarified, with related areas, such as social-emotional functioning and treatment, following suit. Given the information generated at the present time, investigators might well heed the advice of Kavale and Nye (1986) and Lyon (1985), who urged investigators to begin to direct their measurement and methodology toward the development of a single nosology that has merit from theoretical, developmental, and treatment perspectives.

## REFERENCES

Adams, K. M. 1985. Theoretical, methodological, and statistical issues. In *Neuropsychology of Learning Disabilities: Essentials of Subtype Analysis*, ed. B. P. Rourke. New York: Guilford Press.

Adelman, H. S., and Taylor, L. 1986. The problems of definition and differentiation and the need for a classification schema. *Journal of Learning Disabilities* 19:514–20.

Alfano, D. P., and Finlayson, M. A. J. 1987. Clinical neuropsychology in rehabilitation. *The Clinical Neuropsychologist* 1:105–123.

Algozzine, B., and Ysseldyke, J. E. 1986. The future of the LD field: Screening and diagnosis. *Journal of Learning Disabilities* 19:394–98.

Aram, D. M., and Nation, J. E. 1975. Patterns of language behavior in children with developmental language disorders. *Journal of Speech and Hearing Research* 18:229–41.

Bakker, D. J. 1979a. Perceptual asymmetries and reading proficiency. In *Cognitive Growth and Development*, ed. M. Bortner. New York: Brunner/ Mazel.

Bakker, D. J. 1979b. Hemispheric differences and reading strategies: Two dyslexias? *Bulletin of The Orton Society* 29:84–100.

Bakker, D. J. 1981. Cognitive deficits and cerebral asymmetry. *Journal of Research and Development in Education* 15:48–54.

Bakker, D. J., Licht, R., Kok, A., and Bouma, A. 1980. Cortical responses to word reading by right and left eared normal and reading disturbed children. *Journal of Clinical Neuropsychology* 2:1–12.

Bakker, D. J., Moerland, R., and Goekoop-Hoefkens, M. 1981. Effects of hemisphere-specific stimulation on the reading performance of dyslexic boys: A pilot study. *Journal of Clinical and Experimental Neuropsychology* 3:155–59.

Bakker, D., and Vinke, J. 1985. Effects of hemisphere specific stimulation on brain activity and reading in dyslexics. *Journal of Clinical and Experimental Neuropsychology* 7:505–525.

Bastian, H. C. 1898. *A Treatise on Aphasia and Other Speech Defects*. London: H. K. Lewis.

Batchelor, E. S., and Dean, R. S. 1992. Empirical derivation and classification of subgroups of children with learning disorders at separate age levels. *Archives of Clinical Neuropsychology* 8:1–15.

Beauvois, M. F., and Derouesne, J. 1979. Phonological alexia: Three dissociations. *Journal of Neurology, Neurosurgery, and Psychiatry* 42:1115–1124.

Bender, W. N., and Golden, L. B. 1990. Subtypes of students with learning disabilities as derived from cognitive, academic, behavioral, and self-concept measures. *Learning Disability Quarterly* 13:183–94.

Bigler, E. D. 1989. On the neuropsychology of suicide. *Journal of Learning Disabilities* 22:180–85.

Birch, H. G., and Belmont, S. 1964. Auditory-visual integration in normal and retarded readers. *American Journal of Orthopsychiatry* 34:852–61.

Birch, H. G., and Belmont, L. 1965. Auditory-visual integration, intelligence, and reading ability in school children. *Perceptual and Motor Skills* 20: 295–305.

Blashfield, R. K. 1980. Propositions regarding the use of cluster analysis in clinical research. *Journal of Consulting and Clinical Psychology* 3:456–59.

Boder, E. 1970. Developmental dyslexia: A new diagnostic approach based on the identification of three subtypes. *The Journal of School Health* 40:289–90.

Boder, E. 1971. Developmental dyslexia: A diagnostic screening procedure based on three characteristic patterns of reading and spelling. In *Learning Disorders 4*, ed. B. Bateman. Washington: Special Child Publications.

Boder, E. 1973. Developmental dyslexia: A diagnostic approach based on three atypical reading-spelling patterns. *Developmental Medicine and Child Neurology* 15:663–87.

Bruck, M. 1986. Social and emotional adjustments of learning-disabled children: A review of the issues. In *Handbook of Cognitive, Social, and Neuropsychological Aspects of Learning Disabilities* (vol. 1), ed. S. J. Ceci. Hillsdale, NJ: Lawrence Erlbaum Associates.

Coltheart, M. 1980. Deep dyslexia: A review of the syndrome. In *Deep Dyslexia,* ed. M. Coltheart, K., Patterson, and J. C. Marshall. Boston, MA: Routledge & Kegan Paul.

Cruickshank, W. W. 1972. Some issues facing the field of learning disability. *Journal of Learning Disabilities* 5:380–88.

Curtiss, S., and Tallal, P. 1988. Neurolinguistic correlates of specific developmental language impairment. Paper presented at the Sixteenth Annual International Neuropsychological Society Meeting, January 1988, New Orleans.

de Hirsch, K., Jansky, J., and Langford, W. 1966. *Predicting Reading Failure.* New York: Harper & Row.

Del Dotto, J. E., and Rourke, B. P. 1985. Subtypes of left-handed learning-disabled children. In *Neuropsychology of Learning Disabilities. Essentials of Subtypes Analysis*, ed. B. P. Rourke. New York: Guilford Press.

Deloche, G., Andreewsky, E., and Desi, M. 1982. Surface dyslexia: A case report and some theoretical implications to reading models. *Brain and Language* 15:12–31.

DeLuca, J., Del Dotto, J., and Rourke, B. 1987. Subtypes of arithmetic disabled children: A neuropsychological, taxonomic approach. Paper presented at the Fifteenth Annual Meeting of the International Neuropsychological Society, February 1987, Washington, DC.

Denckla, M. B. 1972. Clinical syndromes in learning disabilities: The case for "splitting" versus "lumping." *Journal of Learning Disabilities* 5:401–406.

Everitt, B. 1980. *Cluster Analysis.* London: Heineman Educational Books.

Feagans, L. V., Short, E. J., and Meltzer, L. J. (eds.) 1991. *Subtypes of Learning Disabilities. Theoretical Perspectives and Research.* Hillsdale, NJ: Lawrence Erlbaum Associates.

Fisher, J. H. 1905. Case of congenital word-blindness (inability to learn to read). *Ophthalmic Review* 24:315–18.

Fisk, J. L., and Rourke, B. P. 1979. Identification of subtypes of learning disabled children at three age levels: A neuropsychological multivariate approach. *Journal of Clinical Neuropsychology* 1:289–310.

Fletcher, J. M., Francis, D. J., Rourke, B. P., Shaywitz, S. E., and Shaywitz, B. A. 1992. The validity of discrepancy-based definitions of reading disabilities. *Journal of Learning Disabilities* 25:555–61, 573.

Fletcher, J. M., and Morris, R. 1986. Classification of disabled learners: Beyond exclusionary definitions. In *Handbook of Cognitive, Social, and Neuropsychological Aspects of Learning Disabilities* (vol. 1), ed. S. J. Ceci. Hillsdale, NJ: Lawrence Erlbaum Associates.

Frith, U. 1983. The similarities and differences between reading and spelling problems. In *Developmental Neuropsychiatry*, ed. M. Rutter. New York: Guilford Press.

Frostig, M. 1964. *Frostig Developmental Test of Visual Perception.* Palo Alto, CA: Consulting Psychologists Press.

Funnell, E. 1983. Phonological processes in reading: New evidence from acquired dyslexia. *British Journal Psychology* 2:159–80.

Gerber, P. J., and Zinkgraf, S. A. 1982. A comparative study of social-perceptual ability in learning disabled and nonhandicapped students. *Learning Disability Quarterly* 5:374–78.

Hinshelwood, J. 1895. Congenital word-blindness. *Lancet* 1:1506–1508.

Hinshelwood, J. 1900. Word-blindness and visual memory. *Lancet* 2:1564–1570.

Hinshelwood, J. 1902. Congenital word-blindness with reports of two cases. *Ophthalmic Review* 21:91–99.

Hinshelwood, J. 1909. Four cases of congenital word-blindness occurring in the same family. *British Medical Journal* 2:1229–1232.

Hooper, S. R., and Willis, W. G. 1989. *Learning Disability Subtyping. Neuropsychological Foundations, Conceptual Models, and Issues in Clinical Differentiation.* New York: Springer-Verlag.

Hynd, G. W., and Hynd, C. R. 1984. Dyslexia: Neuroanatomical/neurolinguistic perspectives. *Reading Research Quarterly* 19:482–98.

Interagency Committee on Learning Disabilities 1987. *Learning Disabilities: A Report to the U.S. Congress.* Washington, DC: Author.

Jackson, E. 1906. Developmental alexia (congenital word-blindness). *American Journal of Medical Science* 131:843–49.

Johnston, C. S., Fennell, E. B., and Satz, P. 1987. Learning disability subtypes: A cross-validation. Paper presented at the Fifteenth Annual Meeting of the International Neuropsychological Society, February 1987, Washington, DC.

Joschko, M., and Rourke, B. P. 1985. Neuropsychological subtypes of learning-disabled children who exhibit the ACID pattern on the WISC. In *Neuropsychology of Learning Disabilities: Essentials of Subtype Analysis*, ed. B. P. Rourke. New York: Guilford Press.

Kavale, K. A., and Nye, C. 1986. Parameters of learning disabilities in achievement, linguistic, neuropsychological, and social/behavioral domains. *Journal of Special Education* 19:443–58.

Keefe, B., and Swinney, D. 1979. On the relationship of hemispheric specialization and developmental dyslexia. *Cortex* 15:471–81.

Keogh, B. K. 1983. Classification, compliance, and confusion. *Journal of Learning Disabilities* 16:25.

Kephart, N. C. 1971. *The Slow Learner in the Classroom* (2nd ed.). Columbus, OH: Charles E. Merrill.

Kirk, S. A. 1963. Behavioral diagnosis and remediation of learning disabilities. In *Proceedings of the Conference on Exploration into the Problems of the Perceptually Handicapped Child.* Chicago: Perceptually Handicapped Children.

Kowalchuck, B., and King, J. D. 1989. Adult suicide versus coping with nonverbal learning disorder. *Journal of Learning Disabilities* 22:177–79.

Kussmaul, A. 1877. Disturbance of speech. *Cyclopedia of Practical Medicine* 14:581.

Lovett, M. W. 1983a. The search for subtypes of specific reading disability: Reflections from a cognitive perspective. Unpublished manuscript.

Lovett, M. W. 1983b. Sentential structure and the perceptual spans of two subtypes of reading disabled children. Unpublished manuscript.

Lovett, M. W. 1984. A developmental perspective on reading dysfunction: Accuracy and rate criteria in the subtyping of dyslexic children. *Brain and Language* 22:67–91.

Lyle, J. G., and Goyen, J. 1975. Effects of speed of exposure and difficulty of discrimination on visual recognition of retarded readers. *Journal of Abnormal Psychology* 84:673–76.

Lyle, J. G., and Goyen, J. 1968. Visual recognition development lag and strephosymbolia in reading retardation. *Journal of Abnormal Psychology* 73:25–29.

Lyon, G. R. 1985. Identification and remediation of learning disability subtypes: Preliminary findings. *Learning Disabilities Focus* 1:21–35.

Lyon, G. R., Moats, L., and Flynn, J. M. 1988. From assessment to treatment: Linkage to interventions with children. In *Assessment Issues in Child Neuropsychology*, eds. M. G. Tramontana and S. R. Hooper. New York: Plenum.

Lyon, R., Stewart, N., and Freedman, D. 1982. Neuropsychological characteristics of empirically derived subgroups of learning disabled readers. *Journal of Clinical Neuropsychology* 4:343–65.

Lyon, R., and Watson, B. 1981. Empirically derived subgroups of learning disabled readers: Diagnostic characteristics. *Journal of Learning Disabilities* 14:256–61.

Lyon, R., Rietta, S., Watson, B., Porch, B., and Rhodes, J. 1981. Selected linguistic and perceptual abilities of empirically derived subgroups of learning disabled readers. *Journal of School Psychology* 19:152–66.

Lyytinen, H., and Ahonen, T. 1988. Developmental motor problems in children: A 6-year longitudinal study. Paper presented at the Sixteenth Annual Meeting of the International Neuropsychological Society, January 1988, New Orleans.

Marshall, J. C. 1984. Toward a rational taxonomy of the developmental dyslexias. In *Dyslexia: A Global Issue*, eds. R. N. Malatesha and H. A. Whitaker. The Hague: Nijhoff.

Mattis, S., French, J. H., and Rapin, I. 1975. Dyslexia in children and young adults: Three independent neuropsychological syndromes. *Developmental Medicine and Child Neurology* 17:150–63.

Mayeux, R., and Kandel, E. R. 1985. Natural language, disorders of language, and other localizable disorders of cognitive functioning. In *Principles of Neural Science* (2nd ed.), eds. E. R. Kandel and J. H. Schwartz. New York: Elsevier.

McClure, P., and Hynd, G. W. 1983. Is hyperlexia a severe reading disorder or a symptom of psychiatric disturbance? *Clinical Neuropsychology* 5:145–49.

Morgan, W. P. 1896. A case of congenital word-blindness. *British Medical Journal* 2:1978.

Morris, R., Blashfield, R., and Satz, P. 1981. Neuropsychology and cluster analysis: Potential and problems. *Journal of Clinical Neuropsychology* 3:79–99.

Morris, R., Blashfield, R., and Satz, P. 1986. Developmental classification of reading-disabled children. *Journal of Clinical and Experimental Neuropsychology* 8:371–92.

Newby, R. F., Recht, D., and Caldwell, J. In press. Empirically tested interventions for subtypes of reading disabilities. In *Advances in Child Neuropsychology* (Vol. 2), eds. M. G. Tramontana and S. R. Hooper. New York: Springer-Verlag.

Orton, S. T. 1937. *Reading, Writing, and Speech Problems in Children*. New York: Norton.

Orton, S. T. 1928. Specific reading disability-strephosymbolia. *Journal of the American Medical Association* 90:1095–1009.

Petrauskas, R., and Rourke, B. 1979. Identification of subgroups of retarded readers: A neuropsychological multivariate approach. *Journal of Clinical Neuropsychology* 1:17–37.

Pirozzolo, F. J. 1979. *The Neuropsychology of Developmental Reading Disorders*. New York: Praeger Press.

Reiff, H. B., and Gerber, P. J. 1992. Adults with learning disabilities. In *Learning Disabilities. Nature, Theory, and Treatment*, eds. N. N. Singh and I. L. Beale. New York: Springer-Verlag.

Reitan, R. M. 1974. Psychological effects of cerebral lesions in children of early school age. In *Clinical Neuropsychology: Current Status and Applications*, eds. R. M. Reitan and L. A. Davison. Washington, DC: Winston.

Rourke, B. P. 1983. Outstanding issues in research on learning disabilities. In *Developmental Neuropsychiatry*, ed. M. Rutter. New York: Guilford Press.

Rourke, B. P. (ed.) 1985. *Neuropsychology of Learning Disabilities: Essentials of Subtype Analysis*. New York: Guilford Press.

Rourke, B. P. 1989. *Nonverbal Learning Disabilities: The Syndrome and the Model.* New York: Guilford Press.

Rourke, B. P., Young, G. C., and Leenaars, A.A. 1989. A childhood learning disability that predisposes those afflicted to adolescent and adult depression and suicide risk. *Journal of Learning Disabilities* 22:169–75.

Rourke, B. P., and Orr, R. R. 1977. Prediction of the reading and spelling performance of normal and retarded readers: A four-year follow-up. *Journal of Abnormal Child Psychology* 5:9–20.

Saffran, E. M., Bogyo, L. C., Schwartz, M. F., and Martin, O. S. M. 1980. Does deep dyslexia reflect right hemisphere reading? In *Deep Dyslexia*, eds. M. Coltheart, K. Patterson, and J. C. Marshall. Boston: Routledge & Kegan Paul.

Sandler, A. D., Watson, T. E., Footo, M., Levine, M. D., Coleman, W. L., and Hooper, S. R. 1992. Neurodevelopmental study of writing disorders in middle childhood. *Developmental and Behavioral Pediatrics* 13:17–23.

Satz, P., and Morris, R. 1981. Learning disabilities subtypes: A review. In *Neuropsychological and Cognitive Processes in Reading*, eds. F. J. Pirozzolo and M. C. Wittrock. New York: Academic Press.

Satz, P., Rardin, D., and Ross, J. 1971. An evaluation of a theory of specific developmental dyslexia. *Child Development* 42:2009–2021.

Satz, P., Taylor, H. G., Friel, J., and Fletcher, J. M. 1978. Some developmental and predictive precursors of reading disabilities: A six year follow-up. In *Dyslexia: An Appraisal of Current Knowledge*, eds. A. L. Benton and D. Pearl. New York: Oxford University Press.

Senf, G. M. 1969. Development of immediate memory of bisensory stimuli in normal children and children with learning disabilities. *Developmental Psychology* 6:28.

Siegel, L.S. 1985. Deep dyslexia in childhood? *Brain and Language* 26:16–27.

Siegel, L. S., and Metsala, J. 1992. An alternative to the food processor approach to subtypes of learning disabilities. In *Learning Disabilities. Nature, Theory, and Treatment*, eds. N. N. Singh and I. L. Beale. New York: Springer-Verlag.

Skinner, H. A. 1978. Differentiating the contribution of elevation, scatter, and shape in profile similarity. *Educational and Psychological Measurement* 38: 297–308.

Skinner, H. A. 1981. Toward the integration of classification theory and methods. *Journal of Abnormal Psychology* 90:68–87.

Spreen, O., and Haaf, R. G. 1986. Empirically derived learning disability subtypes: A replication attempt and longitudinal patterns over 15 years. *Journal of Learning Disabilities* 19:197–80.

Stephenson, S. 1905. Six cases of congenital word-blindness affecting three generations of one family. *Ophthalmoscope* 5:482–84.

Thomson, M. E., and Wilsher, C. 1979. Some aspects of memory in dyslexics and controls. In *Practical Aspects of Memory*, eds. M. M. Grunebert, P. E. Morris, and R. N. Sykes. New York: Academic Press.

Tomlinson-Keasey, C., and Kelly, R. R. 1979a. Is hemispheric specialization important to scholastic achievement? *Cortex* 15:97–107.

Tomlinson-Keasey, C., and Kelly, R. R. 1979b. A task analysis of hemispheric functioning. *Neuropsychologia* 17:345–51.

Tramontana, M. G., Hooper, S. R., and Selzer, C. S. 1988. Research on the preschool prediction of later academic achievement. *Developmental Review* 8:89–146.

Van der Vlugt, H., and Satz, P. 1985. Subgroups and subtypes of learning-disabled and normal children: A cross-cultural replication. In *Neuropsychology of Learning Disabilities: Essentials of Subtype Analysis*, ed. B. P. Rourke. New York: Guilford Press.

Vaughan, R. W., and Hodges, L. A. 1973. A statistical survey into a definition of learning disabilities. *Journal of Learning Disabilities* 6:658–64.

Vellutino, F. F. 1978. Toward an understanding of dyslexia: Psychological factors in specific reading disabilities. In *Dyslexia: An Appraisal of Current Knowledge*, eds. A. L. Benton and D. Pearl. New York: Oxford University Press.

Wilson, B. C., and Risucci, D. A. 1986. A model for clinical-quantitative classification. Generation I: Application to language-disordered preschool children. *Brain and Language* 27:281–309.

# Chapter • 4

## Fragile X Syndrome
### *A Behavioral Genetics' Window into Understanding Social Emotional Learning Disability*

*Thomas Baumgardner*
*Allan L. Reiss*

In this chapter, the term *behavioral genetics* combines the fields of genetics and behavioral science with the objective of discovering associations between genotype and behavioral phenotype. Through the identification of neurobehavioral phenotypes associated with known genetic factors, behavioral genetics research can improve our understanding of the neurodevelopmental pathways along which both normal and abnormal behavior develop. Improving our understanding of these neurodevelopmental pathways may, in turn, add to the validity of behavioral syndrome classification by demonstrating the causal links between genetic etiology, brain development, neuropsychology, and symptoms.

This chapter focuses on the neurobehavioral characteristics of fragile X syndrome (fraX) and its similarities to two behaviorally defined syndromes—nonverbal learning disability (NLD) and autistic spectrum disorder (ASD). Recent authors have recognized these similarities (Denckla 1991; Voeller 1991). NLD is marked by primary neu-

Supported by grants HD25806 and MH50047-01 from the National Institutes of Mental Health, Bethesda, MD.

ropsychological deficits in processing spatial information, leading to academic problems in math and handwriting (Pennington 1991). A subtype of NLD that may be more relevant to fraX has been labeled *social-emotional learning disability* (SELD) (Denckla 1983; Voeller 1991). Deficits in processing emotional cues (Johnson and Myklebust 1971; Ozols and Rourke 1985) and deployment of attention to socially relevant information (Denckla 1991) are possible underlying mechanisms for social disability in SELD. Other features of SELD include deficits in emotional/interpersonal functioning, shyness, and inadequate paralinguistic communication skills, (e.g., poor eye contact) (Denckla 1983; Weintraub and Mesulam 1983). The primary symptom pattern associated with autistic spectrum disorder, another behaviorally defined syndrome associated with fraX, is composed of deficient social contact and understanding of social meaning.

Because many of the neurobehavioral components of SELD and ASD have also been identified as part of the fraX phenotype, the fraX syndrome seems to be a potential prototype condition through which to investigate the neurobiology and neurobehavior of these behaviorally defined syndromes. Specifically, mapping fundamental molecular events associated with fraX to a specific neurobehavioral profile opens the possibility of establishing direct links between genetic etiology and psychiatric outcome and the biologic pathways through which these events occur. Although this chapter focuses attention upon the social and emotional sequelae of the mutation, the full syndrome is expressed across domains of cognition, behavior, and emotion. In this regard, fraX may be able to clarify the intersection of these domains as they may contribute in combination to psychiatric disability.

In this chapter we present details regarding the molecular/genetic characteristics and transmission pattern of the fragile X mutation and the associated neurobehavioral profile thus far identified. We then discuss whether fraX can provide support for the construct validity of NLD, SELD, and ASD.

## THE FRAGILE X PHENOTYPE

FraX syndrome is an important genetic etiology for a broad spectrum of developmental disabilities in children. It is the most common heritable cause of mental retardation, with prevalence rates estimated at 0.5 to 1.0 per 1000 live male births and 0.2 to 0.6 per 1000 female births (Sherman 1991). It is second only to Down syndrome as a specific genetic cause of developmental disability. Transmitted on the X chromosome, diagnosis is made via a DNA probe that detects a characteristic amplification of a trinucleotide repeat sequence at the Xq27.3 site

(Oberle et al. 1991). Current prevalence rates of fraX are based on cytogenetic testing; rates based on DNA testing are not yet available.

## Genetics of Fragile X Syndrome

Recent advances aimed at uncovering the molecular basis of the fragile X syndrome have shown that there are at least two distinct *categories* of DNA variation at the fragile X locus. The *premutation* consists of a 50- to 600-base pair insertion or amplification (i.e., additional material) within the (FMR-1) gene. Males and females with the premutation do not seem to suffer the most deleterious features of the clinical syndrome such as overt mental retardation. In the case of the *full mutation*, an insertion of 600 to 3000 base pairs or more is typically present in the target fragment. Information compiled thus far suggests that males carrying the full mutation have the developmental, behavioral, and physical effects that we know as the fragile X syndrome and have a high percentage of Xq27.3 fragile sites in the karyotype, usually $\geq 4\%$ (Oberle et al. 1991; Rousseau et al. 1991). Females with the full mutation also have a higher percent fragility in the karyotype and are more likely to be affected than females carrying the premutation (Rousseau et al. 1991).

The unusual molecular characteristics associated with the fraX mutation have brought to light a new pattern of inheritance of genetic disease. A male who has the premutation on his only X chromosome passes it to each of his daughters relatively *unchanged* in size (Oberle et al. 1991). If a female who has the premutation present on one of her two X chromosomes passes the affected chromosome to her children, either sons or daughters can have the premutation *or* the full mutation. Children inheriting an X chromosome with the full mutation from their mother will also have the full mutation, usually increased in size. Therefore, the only condition in which the premutation increases in size and potentially converts from a premutation to a full mutation is when it *passes through a female* (Oberle et al. 1991; Rousseau et al. 1991).

In addition to the *category* of mutation present, two other factors are likely to influence the expression of the fragile X mutation. First, there are individuals who have been shown to have *both* the premutation and the full mutation present in their blood cells (Rousseau et al. 1991). This *mosaic* pattern provides a potential genetic mechanism for individuals to have less severe neurobehavioral effects than those associated with the nonmosaic, full mutation state. Second, because of the process of random X chromosome inactivation (Lyon 1991), normal somatic tissue in females heterozygous for the fraX mutation consists of two populations of cells, one in which the fragile X chromosome retains full capacity for genetic expression and one population in which the unaffected X chromosome is active. Accordingly, the proportion of cells having the fragile X versus the normal X activated may also be associated with phenotypic expression in females heterozygous for fraX.

## Ascertainment Bias in Determination of the Fragile X Phenotype

Because the size and category of the mutation can change when passed through a female, the severity of the syndrome can potentially increase with successive generations (Fu et al. 1991). This finding has relevance to the hypothesis that the current method of identifying families with fraX syndrome has created an ascertainment bias favoring families with more severely affected relatives. Most families are currently identified by the presence of a mentally retarded male proband. In this case, the mutation has already progressed to a stage where the proband's effects are of sufficient severity to bring this individual and his family to the attention of a medical professional. Thus, the research conducted to date considers children and adults ascertained under this bias. An additional confounding factor to precise phenotype identification, especially in the study of females with fraX, has been the inclusion of individuals carrying the premutation together with those carrying the full mutation.

The majority of adult males with the fraX full mutation are mentally retarded, usually in the moderate to severe range, while affected females are generally less impaired cognitively. The molecular events mentioned above are implicated in this differential expressivity in males and females.

## Cognitive Profile

Males with fraX are typically diagnosed in early to middle childhood. Cognitive disability is usually in the mild to moderate range of mental retardation. Borderline to average IQ is not uncommon in boys diagnosed at five years of age or younger. Therefore, because of a plateau or deceleration in cognitive development, IQ course appears to be downward and, by adulthood, the majority of males test in the moderate to severe range of mental retardation. Several longitudinal studies of fraX males have demonstrated this developmental decline in intellectual functioning (Hagerman and Smith 1983; Lachiewicz et al. 1987; Dykens et al. 1989). Some reports suggest that the decline in IQ trajectory, beginning at approximately 10 years of age, may be more prominent in certain areas of cognitive functioning such as sequential processing(Hodapp et al. 1991). As another explanation for cognitive decline in males with fraX, Fisch et al. (1992) reported a two-group solution in a cluster analytic study, with only one fraX group demonstrating the intellectual decline. The authors hypothesize an association between this two-cluster solution and the size of the base-pair insertion at the fragile X gene locus.

Males with idiopathic mental retardation typically display a flat cognitive profile, whereas mentally retarded males with fraX show strengths in verbal long-term memory and weaknesses in short-term memory and arithmetic (Pennington, Schreiner, and Sudhalter 1991). Males with fraX also show a characteristic profile on the Stanford-Binet, 4th edition. This profile includes deficits in visual short-term memory, visual-motor coordination and spatial awareness, and relative strength in verbal long-term memory (Freund and Reiss 1991).

Most females with fraX have normal IQ and show no decline in functioning with age as seen in some males. However, results from some studies suggest that despite overall cognitive function in the average range, females with fraX are at risk for learning disabilities (Wolff et al. 1988). Studies utilizing the Wechsler Intelligence Scales indicate a possible fraX-specific pattern of weakness on Arithmetic, Digit Span, and Block Design subtests in females (Miezejeski et al. 1986; Kemper et al. 1986). Significantly lower scores have also been observed on the WISC-R subtests of Block Design, Arithmetic, and Coding among fraX girls when compared to controls matched for verbal IQ (Freund and Baumgardner 1992). Girls carrying the fraX full mutation demonstrate relative strengths in verbal learning (selective reminding test) and verbal long-term memory (WAIS-R Vocabulary)(Freund and Reiss 1991; Freund and Baumgardner 1992). Hinton et al. (1992) found that fraX positive women displayed deficits on the WAIS-R third factor, a factor analytically derived summary score that includes the arithmetic, digit span, and coding subtests. Low scores on the WAIS-R third factor are associated with deficits in attention and short-term (working) memory. These results are consistent with the findings of deficient visual short-term memory, visual-motor coordination, spatial perception, and strengths in verbal long-term memory in fraX boys noted above.

Findings from cognitive assessments of individuals with fraX also suggest that there may be a specific neuropsychological component of the phenotype as well. In support of this hypothesis are the findings of deficits in spatial awareness (judgment of line orientation), spatial organization (Rey Osterreith complex figure), and visual attention (computerized continuous performance test) observed in neuropsychological testing of fraX girls (Freund and Baumgardner 1992).

***Executive functions.*** Pennington, Schreiner, and Sudhalter (1991) hypothesized that executive dysfunction may explain the cognitive profile of individuals with the fraX mutation. Executive functions refer to cognitive regulatory processes such as deploying and maintaining attention, planning, organizing, maintaining mental flexibility in problem-solving strategy, and performance monitoring. Although executive functioning has not been well studied in individuals with fraX, attention problems have been frequently observed in boys (Hagerman and Sobesky 1989; Reiss and Freund 1990a; Reiss and Freund 1992) and girls with fraX (Hagerman et al. 1992; Lachiewicz 1992). In a study comparing women with fraX to controls, Mazzocco et al. (1992) reported that women with fraX demonstrate more perseverative thinking and greater difficulty with abstract concept formation and planning. These results are consistent with those reported for girls with fraX (Freund and Baumgardner 1992) who show deficits on the Wisconsin Card Sorting test, a measure of mental flexibility and nonverbal problem solving, and in organizational ability on the Complex Figure drawing task. Mazzocco et al. (1992) have hypothesized that executive dysfunction may be responsible for many features of cognitive impairment in fraX males as well as language and behavior perseveration, attention deficits, distractibility, auditory processing problems, and difficulty with social/environmental transitions.

*Language.* Sudhalter, Maranion, and Brooks (1992), have described linguistic features in males with fraX that may to be related to executive and attentional dysfunction. Sudhalter, Maranion, and Brooks found that although pragmatic use of language was more deviant among fraX males than controls (e.g., increased perseverative speech), syntactic development was best described as delayed. Syntactic deficits did not correlate with the production of perseverative language but was associated with a deficit in expressive semantics (i.e., the ability to choose correct words during speech). This deficit in semantics was manifested as: (1) a failure to block words and ideas with high associative value during speech production; and (2) poor word-finding ability.

High levels of anxiety and tangential thought processes may also interfere with language production in fraX males. Sudhalter (1992) reported that production of repetitive speech was increased by forced eye contact in fraX males and was assumed to be related to anxiety or over-arousal. Ferrier et al.(1991) qualitatively analyzed conversational skills of IQ matched subjects with fragile X, autistic, and Down syndrome. They found males with fraX to display significantly more partial self-repetitions than either of the other groups and significantly fewer inappropriate responses than the autistic individuals. The authors suggest that males with fraX have a better grasp of conversational requirements than autistic individuals and employ partial self-repetitions in order to maintain participation in conversation.

*Memory.* Little has been written about memory functioning in females with fraX. Preliminary investigations have shown relative weakness in short-term verbal memory (Wolff et al. 1988; Brainard, Schreiner, and Hagerman 1991). Freund and Reiss (1991) found a relative deficit in short-term memory for sequenced, abstract-visual stimuli and a strength in memory for sequenced, meaningful-visual stimuli for both fraX-positive girls and boys. Miezejeski et al. (1986) reported impaired performance in females with fraX on the recall portion of the Benton Visual Retention Test, although they attributed this finding to visual-spatial deficits. Grigsby, Kemper, and Hagerman (1992) reported that fraX-positive females display deficits on measures of short-term semantic verbal memory compared to female carriers of the fraX pre-mutation and a combined group of head-injured and learning-disabled women. Results were interpreted as indicating deficits in short-term memory and learning efficiency in the fraX group. However, these results would also support an interpretation of deficits in visual attention or in memory retrieval in females with fraX.

## Social and Emotional Profile

The behavioral component of the fraX phenotype in males includes deficits in understanding social cues, qualitative abnormalities in communication, unusual responses to sensory stimuli, stereotypic behavior, self-injurious behaviors, hyperactivity, and attention deficits (Cohen et al. 1989; Reiss and Freund 1990; Sudhalter et al. 1990; Cohen et al. 1991a; Hagerman 1991; Reiss and Freund 1992). All of these areas of dysfunction have implications for adequate social and emotional functioning. Investigators have emphasized the similarity between the severe deficits found in males and the qualitatively similar but less severe disabilities proposed to be present in females (Reiss and Freund 1990; Crowe and Hay 1990; Hagerman and Sobesky 1989).

*Fragile X and Autism.* An important feature of the communicative profile in males with fraX is the predominance of gaze aversion. A recent study by Cohen et al. (1991) found that poor eye contact in males with fraX does not improve with age or communication level, as has been reported for non-fraX autistic males. Cohen et al. (1991a) conclude that the behavior of males with fraX is consistent with a specific, socially mediated gaze aversion rather than with an attentional deficit for socially relevant stimuli. On the other hand, there seems to be considerable overlap between the descriptive behaviors comprising the diagnosis of autism and the profile of behavioral features observed in affected fraX males such that fraX has been hypothesized to be one genetic etiology for autism (Brown et al. 1982a, 1982b; Wisniewski et al. 1985; Reiss and Freund 1990a). A recent editorial by Einfeld and Hall (1992) refuted the association of fraX and autism on the basis that most studies (e.g., Dykens et al. 1988; Einfeld, Molony, and Hall 1989) thus far have failed to conclude that fraX is a strong predictor of a diagnosis of autism. Counter-arguments by Cohen et al. (1991b) indicate several possible pathogenic sequences through which the relationship may be explained and assert that an association between a genetic syndrome and a behavioral disorder does not require that the association be unique. Reiss and Freund (1992) found that males with fraX display significantly more autistic features than age-and IQ-matched controls. They assert that a distinction must be made between the assigning of individuals to dichotomous, behaviorally defined diagnostic categories and a profile of behaviors associated with specific genetic factors.

**Social and Emotional Profile in Females with fraX.** Although there is less information available about females with fraX, evidence suggests that female heterozygotes demonstrate behavioral abnormalities that are similar in quality, but less severe than those seen in males with this condition (Hagerman 1991; Reiss and Freund 1990b). Even though the majority of females with fraX function intellectually within the average range they seem to be vulnerable to a spectrum of developmental and psychiatric disabilities. Descriptions of adult women with fraX commonly include symptoms of depression, hyperactivity, and social withdrawal (Reiss et al. 1988; Hagerman and Sobesky 1989). Several controlled investigations have found social disability, anxiety, depression, and stereotypic behavior to be important components of the female phenotype (Freund, Reiss, and Abrams 1993; Hagerman et al. 1992; Lachiewicz 1992; Reiss et al. 1988). Freund et al. (1992) reported on the frequency of impaired social interaction and communication in women who were cytogenetically positive for fraX compared to obligate carriers who were cytogenetically negative for fraX and controls. FraX-positive women were found to manifest symptoms associated with schizotypal features including poor modulation of affect, odd communication, and conceptual disorganization. In that study (Freund et al. 1992), the degree of fragility correlated positively with severity of schizotypal features, level of adaptive functioning, IQ, education, and socioeconomic status. Sobesky, Hull, and Hagerman (1992) also reported mood instability to be a concern of many women with fraX. Results from studies investigating parental inheritance of the fraX mutation show that women inheriting the fragile X chromosome from their mothers are more impaired educationally and psychiatrically than those with paternal fraX inheritance (Reiss et al. 1989; Hinton et al. 1992).Girls with fraX display more depression, shyness, social avoidance behavior, reduced eye contact, impulsivity, and distractibility when compared to their non-fraX female siblings (Hagerman et al. 1992; Freund, Reiss, and Abrams in press). Lachiewicz (1992) reported Child Behavior Checklist ratings by mothers of 38 girls with fraX (ages 4 to 11 years) indicating high percentages (26% to 46%) of the sample scoring two standard deviations above the mean on scales measuring depression, social withdrawal, and hyperactivity. Together, these reports suggest that the social and emotional disabilities observed in fraX-positive females may begin in childhood and may increase the risk for profound and enduring effects throughout life.

In summary, the spectrum of psychological effects observed in association with the fraX mutation provides a window into the study of genetic-brain-behavior associations. The fraX syndrome is the best established etiology for two constellations of social-emotional developmental disability. The more severe expression of the mutation occurs in males, producing a phenotype with many characteristics associated with the behaviorally defined syndrome of autism. In females, the fraX mutation is associated with less severe effects that resemble many aspects of nonverbal learning disability (particularly the social-emotional learning disability subtype). Taken together, studies of male and female children with fraX syndrome, suggest that the fragile X mutation leads to primary CNS dysfunction related to the processing or integration of nonverbal stimuli, the modulation of attention, motor behavior and affect, and executive dysfunction. The fact that fraX is a homogeneous etiology for this profile of disturbance allows for more productive investigation designed to delineate the interaction of these cognitive, affective, and behavioral deficits. For example, deficits in attention may interfere with perception and understanding of socially relevant information and may, in turn, be associated with deficits in the pragmatic use of language. Similarly, abnormally high levels of arousal, excessive social anxiety, or deficits in the modulation of affective states may preempt adequate processing of socially relevant information and response.

## Comparing Features of FraX, NLD, and ASD

Several reports (Voeller 1991; Denckla 1991; Rourke 1989) suggest theoretical models that may be applicable to the understanding of neurobehavioral dysfunction in both males and females with the fraX mutation. For example, the study of subjects with neuroradiologically documented cerebral lesions suggests that dysfunction of the right hemisphere may explain the co-occurrence of attention deficit, social and emotional disabilities, and arithmetic and visuospatial deficits. These reports suggest that autism and nonverbal learning disability are related points along a behaviorally defined spectrum and that this spectrum may be applicable to the fraX neurobehavioral phenotype (Pennington, Schreiner, and Sudhalter 1991; Voeller 1991). Within such a spectrum, females with fraX are viewed as representing the less affected (NLD) end of the spectrum, while males with fraX occupy the more severe (autistic) end (Voeller 1991). Accordingly, the core deficit linking the diagnoses of NLD and autism is impaired social competence or social-emotional learning disability (Voeller 1991). Distinctions are then based on severity and associated features such as attention deficits, visuospatial impairment, and so forth.

A classification nosology proposed by Pennington (1991) is useful for comparing the fraX neurobehavioral phenotype to NLD and ASD. Pennington (1991) has extended the nosology of learning disabilities beyond traditional boundaries to include autistic spectrum disorder and acquired memory disorders. He defines a learning disorder as dysfunction in one or more neuropsychological systems that affect academic performance. In addition to including social and emotional disability among the neuropsychological-based disorders of learning, this expanded nosology effectively shifts the focus of investigation away from being strictly achievement-based. Based upon neuropsychological theory and research, this type of nosology fosters a hypothesis-driven approach to learning disabilities research and classification.

The taxonomy assumes that symptoms of a disorder can be divided into four categories: primary (or core) symptoms, correlated symptoms, secondary symptoms, and artifactual symptoms. Neither the classes of symptoms nor the class of disorder refer to unique etiology. A primary symptom is a behaviorally observable characteristic that is most directly caused by the underlying neuropsychological deficit. Correlated symptoms share the same etiology as the primary symptoms, but result from involvement of different brain systems. Secondary symptoms arise as consequences of primary or correlated symptoms. Artifactual symptoms are those that only seem to be associated with the disorder, but are not causally related (Pennington 1991; Rapin 1987)[1].

From the preceding review of the fraX behavioral phenotype we can now make comparisons to the taxonomy of symptoms that define NVLD and ASD. Table I provides a global comparison of those symptoms that have been observed in fraX. Those marked by a plus (+) have been observed in research reports of either children or adults.

---

[1] Other taxonomic systems have been suggested for classifying symptoms of learning disabilities as primary, secondary or correlated. For example, see B. P. Rourke 1989.

Table I. Comparison of FraX Phenotype to Symptoms of NLD and ASD

*Right Hemisphere (Nonverbal) Learning Disorder\**

| | fraX Females | fraX Males |
|---|---|---|
| **Primary** | | |
| Math deficits | + | + |
| Handwriting/art | ? | ? |
| **Correlated** | | |
| Social cognition | + | + |
| Attention | + | + |
| Conceptual skills | + | + |
| **Secondary** | | |
| Opposition to written work | ? | ? |
| Spelling problems | ? | ? |
| Depression | + | ? |
| Social withdrawal | + | + |
| **Artifactual** | | |
| Dyslexia | + | ? |

*Autistic Spectrum Disorder \**

| | fraX Females | fraX Males |
|---|---|---|
| **Primary** | | |
| Social contact deficit | + | + |
| Social understanding deficit | + | + |
| **Correlated** | | |
| Mental retardation | + | + |
| Executive dysfunction | + | + |
| Other cognitive/language deficits | - | + |
| Self injurious behavior | + | + |
| Seizures | ? | + |
| **Secondary** | | |
| Pragmatic deficits | + | + |
| Echolalia | + | + |
| Stereotypes | + | + |
| Splinter skills | - | - |
| Symbolic play deficits | ? | ? |
| **Artifactual** | | |
| High SES | - | - |
| Physical agility | - | - |
| Attractiveness | ? | ? |

\*Adapted from *Diagnosing Learning Disorders: A Neuropsychological Approach*, B. F. Pennington, 1991. Used by permission of The Guilford Press.

Minus (–) indicates symptoms that have not been observed, and (?) indicates either equivocal findings or the absence of studies that have addressed the presence of the symptom.

Table I provides a comparison between the most prominent features of NLD and ASD. As suggested by this comparison, there are many symptoms of both NLD and ASD that are also found in the fraX neurobehavioral phenotype. It can also be seen that the areas in which symptoms are expressed are observed in both females and males with fraX. This finding reinforces the observation that males and females with fraX differ in severity of symptoms, not in the quality or type of symptoms. The observed symptoms also fall within domains of cognitive, behavioral, and social-emotional functioning and many are related to the processing of nonverbal information.

Therefore, the comparison of the fraX phenotype to a taxonomy of symptoms for NLD and ASD supports the hypothesis that the fraX mutation is a genetic/molecular etiology for nonverbal and social-emotional learning disability.

## Does the Fragile X Phenotype Help in Subtype Classification?

The question remains as to whether the behavioral phenotype associated with fraX syndrome provides construct validity for NLD and ASD, or does it simply add more complexity to previous attempts at categorization? There are many methodological and statistical issues that add complexity to this question. In addition, identifying valid subtypes of disabled learners would be made easier if there existed a mature science of normal neuropsychological development (Pennington, Schreiner, and Sudhalter 1991).

The initial goal of a nosology is to identify symptoms that reliably occur together, which may then lead to isolation of subtypes of individuals who are homogeneous by etiology, pathogenesis, or response to treatment. To achieve these goals a useful nosology must satisfy scientific requirements for internal and external validity (Pennington 1991). If a syndrome definition has internal validity, it will lead to: (1) correct numbers of patients classified; (2) homogeneity within the identified subtype; (3) reliable procedures for classification; (4) replicability across different procedures; and (5) replicability of the subtype or syndrome in other samples (Fletcher 1985). For a syndrome definition to have external validity it must be able to explain a syndrome in relation to external variables of interest (Pennington 1991). Criteria related to external validity include such issues as differential response to treatment, clinical significance, differential relation to measures that are independent of those used to define the syndrome, differential etiology, prognosis, and developmental course. The purpose of syndrome analysis and classification is similar to the objective of behavioral genetics, to uncover a causal chain linking etiology, brain mechanism, neuropsychology, and symptoms.

In this chapter, fraX syndrome, a disease caused by a specific genetic mutation, has been compared to the behaviorally defined syndromes of NLD and ASD. Although the neurobehavioral phenotype of fraX shares many features in common with NLD and ASD, it is important to highlight the etiologic differences between a disease state and a behavioral syndrome. Due to the current level of sophistication in diagnostic classification, it must be emphasized that behaviorally defined syndromes, such as NLD and ASD, are etiologically heterogeneous. This increases the likelihood of heterogeneity at the neurobiological level as well. Because of its homogeneity at the etiologic level, the fraX phenotype seems to provide construct validity for many of the features that make up the behaviorally defined syndromes of NLD and ASD. Therefore, study of the fraX syndrome provides an opportunity to elucidate specific neurobiologic pathways leading to the learning disabilities found in fraX syndrome and shared by heterogeneous groups of individuals with NLD and ASD.

Results derived from cognitive, neuropsychological, and behavioral assessment of individuals with the fraX mutation indicate that the fraX phenotype may involve both frontal and right hemisphere neural circuits. Right hemisphere areas are implicated by deficits in social perception and cognition, pragmatics, maintenance of attention, conceptual skills, and spatial awareness. Prefrontal areas are implicated by deficits in attention, organization, self-monitoring, social judgment, and perseverative behavior. Because the prefrontal area of the brain is an integrative neural center, deficits in prefrontal brain functioning may be expected to interfere with the regulation of motoric, affective, and cognitive behavior. It may be, as Freund and Reiss (submitted) suggest, that a nonverbal learning disorder and executive dysfunction are both useful in explaining a common underlying phenotype in males and females with fraX. It might, therefore, be hypothesized that the fraX neurobehavioral phenotype, which is etiologically homogeneous, provides evidence for the existence of genetic factors that affect the development of right hemisphere and prefrontal brain areas.

## SUMMARY

Although the fraX syndrome has been associated with a broad range of phenotypic features, effects on the central nervous system are unquestionably the most important from the standpoint of the affected individual's daily functioning. It has also been suggested that there is enough consistency in the quality of cognitive, neuropsychological, communication, and behavioral dysfunction in individuals with fraX syndrome to characterize a neuropsychiatric phenotype (Reiss and Freund 1992; Reiss and Freund 1990b).

The hypothesis that neurocognitive deficits underlie social cognition requires further controlled study to establish its validity, and to disentangle the competing hypothesis that social and emotional sequelae appear as secondary reactions to the experience of growing up with physical and learning disabilities. Most research into this topic recognizes the mediating role of the right hemisphere in social behavior, and that the right hemisphere plays an important part in academic, adaptive functioning. But frontal lobe dysfunction is also associated with impairments in social behavior and personality functioning (Eslinger et al. 1990). Network models of attention (Mesulam 1981; Heilman, Voeller, and Nadeau 1991) suggest that attention is not a unitary construct, but rather a faceted system mediated by a neural network involving frontal, parietal, and brain stem areas. This complexity makes the interpretation of deficits in specific cognitive domains difficult to disembed from processes of attentional and executive function (Denckla 1991).

Future studies integrating molecular analyses with behavioral, social, and neuropsychological variables should greatly increase specification of the clinical features of the fragile X syndrome for both males and females and lead to better understanding and prediction of normal and aberrant behavior. Much more research remains to be done that can better define and segment nonverbal abilities within a developmental framework and the extent to which nonverbal LD exist in the general population (Denckla 1991). Evidence supporting a nonverbal LD and an executive dysfunction hypothesis is sufficient to guide future hypothesis-driven research.

The material presented in this chapter has focused upon the neurobehavioral characteristics of fragile X syndrome. Over the past decade, observation has suggested similarities between the fraX neurobehavioral phenotype and two behaviorally defined syndromes, nonverbal learning disability (NLD) and autistic spectrum disorder (ASD). The data reviewed here suggest that fraX shares with these disorders a profile of social-emotional learning disability that is marked by deficits in attention, social cognition, and the psychiatric symptoms of depression, anxiety, and avoidance behavior.

Because the etiology of fraX is a specific X-linked mutation, its effects on brain development and function are potentially identifiable. The study of fraX using a behavioral genetics methodology offers a window through which to understand the complexity of causes and pathophysiological mechanisms of a subtype of learning disability associated with social and emotional impairment.

**REFERENCES**

Brainard, S. S., Schreiner, R. A., and Hagerman, R. J. 1991. Cognitive profiles of the carrier fragile X woman. *American Journal of Medical Genetics* 38:505–508.

Brown, W. T., Friedman, E., Jenkins, E. C., Brooks, J., Wisniewski, K., Raguthu, S., and French, J. H. 1982a. Association of fragile X with autism. *Lancet* 1:100.

Brown, W. T., Jenkins, E. C., Friedman, E., Brooks, J., Wisniewski, K., Raguthu, S., and French, J. H. 1982b. Autism is associated with the fragile X syndrome. *Journal of Autism and Developmental Disorders* 12:303–307.

Cohen, I. L., Vietze, P. M., Sudhalter, V., Jenkins, E. C., and Brown, W. T. 1989. Parent-childddyadic gaze patterns in fragile X males and in non-fragile X males with autistic disorder. *Journal of Child Psychology and Psychiatry* 30:845–56.

Cohen, I. L., Vietze, P. M., Sudhalter, V., Jenkins, E. C., and Brown W. T. 1991a. Effects of age and communication level on eye contact in fragile X males and non-fragile X autistic males. *American Journal of Medical Genetics* 38:498–502.

Cohen, I. L., Sudhalter, V., Pfadt, A., Jenkins, E. C., Brown, W. T., and Vietze, P. M. 1991b. Why are autism and the fragile X Syndrome associated? Conceptual and methodological issues. *American Journal of Human Genetics* 48:195–202.

Crowe, S., and Hay, D. 1990. Neuropsychological dimensions of the fragile X syndrome: Support for a non-dominant hemisphere dysfunction hypothesis. *Neuropsychologia* 28:9–16.

Denckla, M. B. 1983. The neuropsychology of social-emotional learning disabilities. *Archives of Neurology* 40:461–62.

Denckla, M. B. 1991. Academic and extracurricular aspects of nonverbal learning disabilities. *Psychiatric Annals* 21:717–24.

Dykens, E., Leckman, J., Paul, R., and Watson, M. 1988. Cognitive, behavioral and adaptive functioning in fragile X and non–fragile X retarded males. *Journal of Autism and Developmental Disorders* 18:41–52.

Dykens, E. M., Hodapp, R., Ort, S., Finucane, B., Shapiro, L., and Leckman, J. 1989. The trajectory of cognitive development in males with fragile X syndrome. *Journal of the American Academy of Child and Adolescent Psychiatry* 28:422–26.

Einfeld, S., and Hall, W. 1992. Invited editorial comment: Behavior phenotype of the fragile X syndrome. *American Journal of Medical Genetics* 43:56–60.

Einfeld, S., Molony, H., and Hall, W. 1989. Autism is not associated with the fragile X syndrome. *American Journal of Medical Genetics* 38:498–502.

Eslinger, P. J., Grattan, L. M., Damasio, A., and Damasio, H. 1990. Childhood frontal lobe lesion and psychosocial development: Patient D.T. *Journal of Clinical and Expermental Neuropsychology* 12:95–103.

Ferrier, L. J., Bashir, A. S., Meryash, D. L., Johnston, J., and Wolff, P. 1991. Conversational skills of individuals with fragile X syndrome: A comparison with autism and Down syndrome. *Developmental Medicine and Child Neurology* 33:776–88.

Fisch, G. S., Shapiro, L. R., Simensen, R., Schwartz, C. E., Fryns, J. P., Borghgraef, M., Curfs, L. M., Howard-Peebles, P. N., Arinami, T., and Mavrou, A. 1992. Longitudinal changes in IQ among fragile X males: Clinical evidence of more than one mutation? *American Journal of Medical Genetics* 43:28–34.

Fletcher, J. M. 1985. External validation of learning disability typologies. In *Neuropsychology of Learning Disabilities,* ed. B.P. Rourke. New York: Guilford Press.

Freund, L., and Baumgardner, T. 1992. The WISC-R profile and neuropsychological function in girls with fragile X. In 3rd International Fragile X Conference, Snowmass, CO.

Freund, L., and Reiss, A. L. 1991. Cognitive profiles associated with the fragile X syndrome in males and females. *American Journal of Medical Genetics* 38:542–47.

Freund, L. S., and Reiss, A. L. Submitted. A neurocognitive phenotype of young males and females with fragile X.

Freund, L., Reiss, A. L., and Abrams, M. 1993. Psychiatric disorders associated with fragile X in the young female. *Pediatrics* 91(2):321–29.

Freund, L. S., Reiss, A. L., Hagerman, R. J., and Vinogradov, S. 1992. Chromosome fragility and psychopathology in obligate female carriers of the fragile X chromosome. *Archives of General Psychiatry* 49:54–60.

Fu, Y–H., Kuhl, D. P., Pizzuti, A., Pieretti, M., Sutcliffe, J. S., Richards, S., Verkerk, A. J. M. H., Holden, J. J. A., Fenwick, R. G., Warren, S. T., and Oostra, B. A. 1991. Variation of the CGG repeat at the fragile X site results in genetic instability: Resolution of the sherman paradox. *Cell* 67:498–502.

Grigsby, J., Kemper, M. B., and Hagerman, R. J. 1992. Verbal learning and memory among heterozygous fragile X females. *American Journal of Medical Genetics* 43:111–15.

Hagerman, R. J. 1991. Physical and behavioral phenotype. In *Fragile X Syndrome: Diagnosis, Treatment and Research*, eds. R. Hagerman and A. Silverman. Baltimore: Johns Hopkins University Press.

Hagerman, R. J., and Smith, A. C. M. 1983. The heterozygous female. In *The Fragile X Syndrome: Diagnosis, Biochemistry, and Intervention*, eds. R. J. Hagerman and P. M. McBogg. Dillon, CO: Spectra Publishing.

Hagerman, R. J., and Sobesky, W. E. 1989. Psychopathology in fragile X syndrome. *American Journal of Orthopsychiatry* 59:142–52.

Hagerman, R. J., Jackson, C., Amiri, K., Cronister-Silverman, A., O'Connor, R., and Sobesky, W. 1992. Girls with fragile X syndrome: Physical and neurocognitive status and outcome. *Pediatrics* 89:395–400.

Heilman, K., Voeller, K. K. S., and Nadeau, S. E. 1991. A possible pathophysiologic substrate of attention deficit hyperactivity disorder. *Journal of Child Neurology* 6, Supplement.

Hinton, V. J., Dobkin, C. S., Halperin, J. M., Jenkins, E. C., Brown, W. T., Ding, X. H., Cohen, I. L., Rousseau, R., and Miezejeski, C. M. 1992. Mode of inheritance influences behavioral expression and molecular control of cognitive deficits in female carriers of the fragile X syndrome. *American Journal of Medical Genetics* 43:87–95.

Hodapp, R. M., Dykens, E. M., Ort, S. I., Zelinsky, D. G., and Leckman, J. F. 1991. Changing patterns of intellectual strengths and weaknesses in males with fragile X syndrome. *Journal of Autism and Developmental Disorders* 21:503–516.

Johnson, D. J., and Myklebust, H. R. 1971. *Learning Disabilities*. New York: Grune & Stratton.

Kemper, M. B., Hagerman, R. J., Ahmad, R. S., and Mariner, R. 1986. Cognitive profiles and the spectrum of clinical manifestations in heterozygous fragile X females. *American Journal of Medical Genetics* 23:139–56.

Lachiewicz, A. M. 1992. Abnormal behaviors of young girls with fragile X syndrome. *American Journal of Medical Genetics* 43:72–77.

Lachiewicz, A. M., Guillion, C. M., Spiridigliozzi, G. A., and Aylsworth, A. S. 1987. Declining IQs of young males with the fragile X syndrome. *American Journal of Mental Retardation* 92:272–78.

Lyon, M. F. 1991. The quest for the X-inactivation centre. *Trends in Genetics* 7:69–70.

Mazzocco, M. M. M., Hagerman, R. J., Cronister-Silverman, A., and Pennington, B. 1992. Specific frontal lobe deficits among women with the fragile X gene. *Journal of the American Academy of Child and Adolescent Psychiatry* 31:1141–1148.

Mesulam, M-M. 1981. A cortical network for directed attention and unilateral neglect. *Annals of Neurology* 10:309–325.

Miezejeski, C. M., Jenkins , E. C., Hill, A. L., Wisniewski, K., French, J. H., and Brown, W. T. 1986. A profile of cognitive deficit in females from fragile X families. *Neuropsychologia* 24:405–409.

Oberle, I., Rousseau, F., Heitz, D., Kretz, C., Devys, D., Hanauer, A., Boue, J., Bretheas, M. F., and Mandel, J. L. 1991. Instability of a 550-base pair DNA segment and abnormal methylation in fragile X syndrome. *Science* 252: 1097–1102.

Ozols, E., and Rourke, B. P. 1985. Dimensions of social sensitivity in two types of learning disabled children. In *The Neuropsychology of Learning Disabilities: Essentials of Subtype Analysis*, ed. B. P. Rourke. New York: Guilford Press.

Pennington, B. F. 1991. *Diagnosing Learning Disorders: A Neuropsychological Framework*. New York: Guilford Press.

Pennington, B. F., Schreiner, R. A., and Sudhalter, V. 1991. Towards a neuropsychology of fragile X syndrome. In *The Fragile X Syndrome:Diagnosis, Treatment, and Research*, eds. R. Hagerman and A. Silverman. Baltimore: Johns Hopkins University Press.

Rapin, I. 1987. Searching for the cause of autism: A neurologic perspective. In *Handbook of Autism and Pervasive Developmental Disorders*, eds. D. J. Cohen and A. M. Donnelan. New York: John Wiley & Sons.

Reiss, A. L., and Freund, L. 1990a. Fragile X syndrome, DSM-III-R and autism. *Journal of the American Academy of Child and Adolescent Psychiatry* 29:863–872.

Reiss, A. L., and Freund, L. 1990b. Neuropsychiatric aspects of fragile X syndrome. *Brain Dysfunction* 3:9–22.

Reiss, A. L., and Freund, L. 1992. The behavioral phenotype of fragile X syndrome: DSM-III-R autistic behavior in male children. *American Journal of Medical Genetics* 43:35–46.

Reiss, A.L., Freund, L., Vinogradov, S., Hagerman, R. J., and Cronister, A. 1989. Parental inheritance and psychological disability in fragile X females. *American Journal of Human Genetics* 45:697–705.

Reiss, A. L., Hagerman, R., Vingradov, S., Abrams, M., and King, R. 1988. Psychiatric disability in female carriers of the fragile X chromosome. *Archives of General Psychiatry* 45:25–30.

Rourke, B. P. 1989. *Nonverbal Learning Disabilities, the Syndrome and the Model*. New York, NY: Guilford Press.

Rousseau, F., Heitz, D., Biancalana, V., Blumenfeld, S., Kretz, C., Boue, J., Bretheas, M. F., and Mandel, J. L. 1991. Direct diagnosis by DNA analysis of the fragile X syndrome of mental retardation. *New England Journal of Medicine* 325:1673–1681.

Sherman, S. L. 1991. Epidemiology. In *The Fragile X Syndrome: Diagnosis, Treatment, and Research*, eds. R. Hagerman and A. Silverman. Baltimore: Johns Hopkins University Press.

Sobesky, W., Hull, C., and Hagerman, R. 1992. The emotional phenotype in mildly affected carriers. In 3rd International Fragile X Conference, Snowmass, CO.

Sudhalter, V. 1992. The language system of males with fragile X syndrome. In 3rd International Fragile X Conference, Snowmass, CO.

Sudhalter, V., Cohen, I. L., Silverman, W., and Wolf-Schein, E. G. 1990. Conversational analyses of males with fragile X, Down syndrome and autism. *American Journal of Mental Retardation* 94:431–41.

Sudhalter, V., Maranion, M., and Brooks, P. 1992. Expressive semantic deficit in the productive language of males with fragile X syndrome. *American Journal of Medical Genetics* 43:65–71.

Voeller, K. K. S. 1991. Social-emotional learning disabilites. *Psychiatric Annals* 21:735–41.

Weintraub, S., and Mesalum, M-M. 1983. Developmental learning disabilities of the right hemisphere: Emotional, interpersonal, and cognitive components. *Archives of Neurology* 40:463–68.

Wisniewski, K. E., French, J. H., Fernando, S., Brown, W. T., Jenkins, E. C., Friedman, E., Hill, A. L., and Miezejeski, C. M. 1985. Fragile X syndrome: Associated neurological abnormalities and developmental disabilities. *Annals of Neurology* 18:665–69.

Wolff, P. H., Gardner, J., Lappen, J., Paccia, J., and Meryash, D. 1988. Variable expression of the fragile X syndrome in heterozygous females of normal intelligence. *American Journal of Medical Genetics* 30:213–25.

# Chapter • 5

# Familial Dyslexia
## *Genetic, Behavioral, and Imaging Studies*

H. Lubs
K. Gross-Glenn
R. Duara, E. Feldman
B. Skottun
B. Jallad, A. Kushch
M. Rabin

Clustering of dyslexia in families has been known to both teachers and investigators since the early 1900s. Data consistent with an autosomal dominant mode of inheritance have been known since the study by Hallgren in 1950. Zahalkova, Vrzal, and Klobovkova (1972) and Omenn and Weber (1978) presented smaller but similar family studies. These reports, however, were not regarded as proof of autosomal dominant inheritance because the definitions of affected versus unaffected often were ill-defined and this mode of inheritance did not clearly explain the male preponderance found in most studies of dyslexia.

Several studies included all patients with normal intelligence, evidence of relatively pure reading disability, and absence of other etiologic factors into a genetic study of dyslexia. This resulted in the inclusion of a combination of families with generation-to-generation transmission (probable autosomal dominant inheritance) and affected siblings with normal parents (possible autosomal recessive inheritance or polygenic) (Finucci et al. 1976; Finucci and Childs 1981) and did not

Supported by NICHD Grant Number P1HD21885.

permit definition of a clear mode of inheritance, although the demonstration of the repeated occurrence of dyslexia in certain families was clear. The study by Smith, Kimberling, and Lubs (1983) provided additional data in three-generation families with dyslexia. Although more males were affected than females, the sex ratio was not significantly different from 1.0 when the (largely male) probands were omitted. Thus, this study provided further evidence of autosomal dominant inheritance. It could not, however, prove autosomal dominant inheritance because only three-generation families were selected for study and a precise segregation analysis could, therefore, not be done.

Studies of twins have provided increasingly strong evidence for the inheritance of dyslexia. The Colorado Reading Project now includes more than 200 twin pairs (DeFries et al. 1991). The concordance rate for 99 monozygous (MZ) twin pairs was 70%, compared to 48% in 112 dizygous (DZ) twin pairs. Several effective new techniques have been introduced to evaluate the relative contributions of genetics and environment including the use of expected differential regression towards the mean of reading performance data between DZ and MZ twins. Similarly, environmental influences were shown not to be an important source of variation (DeFries et al. 1991). The twin studies, however, have not clarified the mode or modes of inheritance in familial dyslexia.

Pennington et al. (1991) reviewed four studies relating to the inheritance of developmental dyslexia. In three of these projects (the Colorado family reading study, the study of Washington kindreds, and the study of Iowa kindreds) ascertainment was through probands with reading disabilities. The results of the segregation analysis in these studies are summarized in table I. The fourth study, which was a linkage study comparable to the present study (i.e., ascertainment was through large, three-generation families) is not included in the table because it was not appropriate to carry out segregation analysis. These results were consistent with a major locus transmission in two of the three samples, and with polygenic transmission in the third (Iowa) sample. There was not evidence of a recessive gene effect, but the hypothesis of a dominant gene effect could not be rejected. Thus, the results were best explained by either a major gene or dominant gene effect with sex-influenced transmission. Although the mode of diagnosis was similar in each of the studies, i.e., specific test criteria and exclusionary criteria were used, and the general approach to studying families was described, the details of the studies have not been published. In the Iowa sample, for example, a test based on a memory deficit subtype routine was used by the Iowa diagnostic clinic as the initial diagnostic criteria, but for the grandparents, self-reporting only was utilized. Other details of the testing and ascertainment are presented in the paper. Overall, these results represent the first analysis of

Table I.—Summary of Segregation Analyses and Genetics Data (adapted from Pennington et al. 1991)[*]

| | Colorado Family Reading Study (N=565) | Washington (N=131) | Iowa (N=660) |
|---|---|---|---|
| Number of families | 133.0 | 9.0 | 39.0 |
| Family type | Nuclear | Extended | Extended |
| Sex ratio, M:F | 1:7 | 1:5 | 1:3 |
| Affected first-degree relatives (%) | 47.0 | 71.0 | 30.0 |
| Compensation(%) | 22.0 | — | — |
| Null Hypothesis | | | |
| No transmission | Rejected[†] | Rejected[†] | Rejected[†] |
| No major gene | Rejected[†] | Rejected[†] | Consistent[‡] |
| No multifactorial/polygenic | Consistent[‡] | Consistent[‡] | Rejected[†] |
| No dominant gene effect | Rejected[†] | Rejected[†] | — |
| No recessive gene effect | Consistent[‡] | Consistent[‡] | — |
| No additive gene effect | Rejected[†] | Rejected[†] | — |

[*]These results were based on a population prevalence of 7.5%, a male: female ratio of 1.8:1, and appropriate ascertainment corrections.

[†]Null hypothesis rejected at $p < .001$.

[‡]Null hypothesis cannot be rejected at $p < .05$.

Reprinted with permission from B. F. Pennington. B. F. Pennington, et al. Evidence for major gene transmission of developmental dyslexia. *JAMA* 266(11), Table 1, p.1529 and Table 3, p. 1531.

relatively unbiased family data that support an autosomal dominant mode of transmission.

The existence of possible subtypes has been studied by many investigators. These reports have been reviewed by Newby and Lyon (Obrzut 1991) and by other authors in the same volume (Obrzut 1991). Several approaches to subtyping learning disabilities have been reported. Most frequently, subtyping is based on a specific battery of tests carried out in variably defined groups of children and matched controls. The most consistent subtyping pattern was based upon separation into phonologic and orthographic subtypes, but others, in related approaches, also have included developmental differences. Functional validity has, in part, often been reported. Few studies, however, have tested the biological validity of subtyping in extended families, under the hypothesis that the same gene would produce similar phenotypic (subtype) effects. Several studies (Wood et al. 1991; Hugdahl, Synnevag, and Satz 1990; DeFries et al. 1991), however, have approached the problem in nuclear or primary families and found a consistent pattern of phonologic problems between first-degree relatives with dyslexia. No evidence of a nonphonologic hereditary pattern has emerged. Additional data on extended families is critical for answering the question of the biologic validity of dyslexia subtypes and, indeed, whether more than one type exists.

Two broad goals have guided this study. The first goal has been to localize the gene or genes leading to dyslexia with a three-generation history of dyslexia. To achieve this, an independent assessment of the tentative linkage with chromosomal markers on the short arm of chromosome 15 was undertaken. The second broad goal has been to study these families as extensively as possible in order to characterize fully the effects of the dyslexia gene. These studies might detect a consistent abnormality that was more directly related to the mutant gene, and, therefore, would provide the basis for a more definitive test for dyslexia. Finally, these data could serve as a basis for possible subtyping in the event that several linkages or localizations were established.

The present study differs in concept from most other studies of dyslexia in several important ways. First, a highly selected group of families is the object of the study. These have been three-generation families selected largely for size, proximity to the study center, and interest in participating in the study. The study approaches the question of the mechanism of inheritance of at least one type of dyslexia through linkage-analysis. If there, indeed, is no form of dyslexia inherited in this fashion, significant linkage results are not likely to be found. The studies reported by Smith, Kimberling, and Lubs (1983) and by Pennington et al. (1991) utilized the same approach. Second, the study also differs from most studies in the way in which dyslexia is defined. Although dyslexia in these families is initially defined by conventional tests, as discussed above, there is an ultimate, planned, redefinition of dyslexia based on observations made by the combination of the gene localization results and the tests designed to screen for dyslexia—the neuropsychologic tests, and specially designed psychophysical tests of vision and speech perception, as well as PET and MRI studies. The final definition depends on the outcome of both the genetic studies and the total array of tests.

## THE PRESENT STUDY

### Genetics and Linkage Studies

Over the past five years, families with a three-generation history of dyslexia were identified through an initial structured telephone interview. Families with the largest number of available and interested family members were selected for participation. Generally, at least 10 potentially informative matings (for the linkage studies) were required. Family members with a history of dyslexia had to meet the study criteria for dyslexia. These were based on age-determined standard deviation discrepancies between IQ and reading and spelling performance on selected standardized tests in individuals with IQ scores above 90 with no known emotional, neurologic, and/or environmental reasons for reading impairment. A comprehensive psychoeducational battery to formalize the diagnosis of developmental dyslexia was administered to normal and dyslexic family members meeting these criteria. The battery currently assesses general intelligence and achievement in the areas of reading, spelling, and arithmetic. The Nonsense Passages test (Finucci et al. 1976; Gross-Glenn et al. 1990) was included because it has been shown to be sensitive to residual reading deficits among compensated dyslexics. The details of the tests and criteria have been published previously (Lubs et al. 1991) but require age-graded cutoffs in two of four areas ($\geq 1.0$ *SD* below IQ for grades 3–8 and $\geq 1.5$ *SD* below IQ > grade 8). The four areas were assessed by the following tests:

| | |
|---|---|
| Spelling | Wide-Range Achievement Test-Revised (WRAT-R): Spelling subtest (Jastak 1984) |
| Oral Reading | Gray-Oral Reading Test Revised (GORT-R) (Wiederholt and Bryant 1986) Woodcock-Johnson Psycho-Educational Battery Letter-Word Identification subtest (Woodcock and Johnson 1977) |
| Comprehension | Woodcock-Johnson Psycho-Educational Battery Passage Comprehension subtest (Woodcock and Johnson 1977) |
| Decoding | Woodcock-Johnson Psycho-Educational Battery Word-Attack Scale subtest (Woodcock and Johnson 1977) Nonsense Passages (Ages 16+) (Gross-Glenn et al. 1990; Finucci et al. 1976) |

A pedigree was obtained by contacting several family members, and an extensive questionnaire addressing educational, developmental, medical, and behavioral issues was administered to the largest possible number of dyslexic and non-dyslexic family members. In addition, blood was obtained for linkage studies and screening tests for vision and auditory acuity were carried out. A minimum of 3 hours of testing was required. A maximum of 20 hours of testing was required for those who participated in the full study, which included vision, speech perception, neuropsychological, and brain-imaging studies.

Seventeen families have been entered into the study. These pedigrees include more than 700 individuals of whom more than 200 have been studied. The pattern of inheritance is consistent with the original hypothesis of autosomal dominant inheritance (Lubs et al. in press). Penetrance was greater than 90%, a result consistent with other autosomal dominant disorders. The more informative pedigrees are shown in figure 1. Family members were classified by a combination of historical data and screening tests. Dyslexics were classified either as "affected" (by history and diagnostic criteria), as "compensated adults" (having a

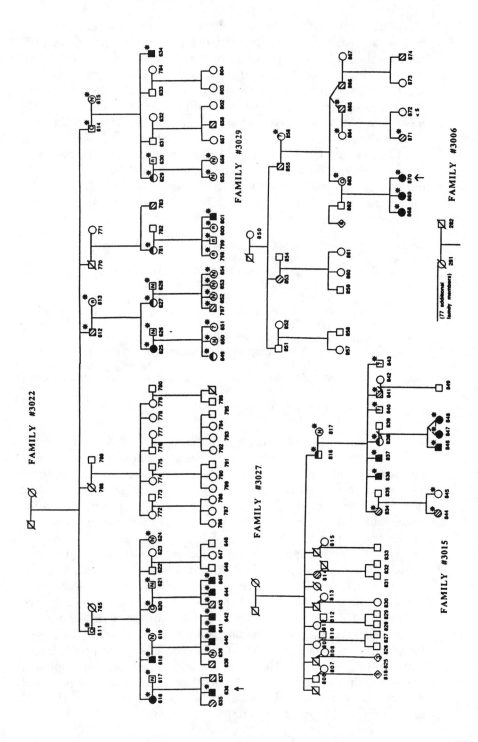

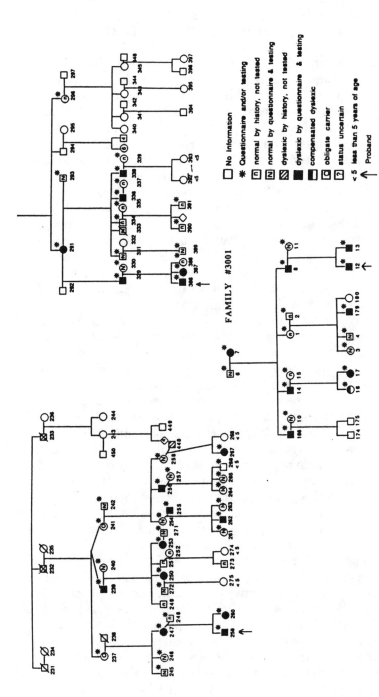

Figure 1. Selected Pedigrees. Family 3022 originally contributed most of the significant data indicating a linkage with chromosome 15. Restudy, which extended the pedigree by 30 individuals, has not confirmed this linkage. Families 3027 and 3029 represent 2 of the 5 families ascertained in the last 6 months and are still under study. Compensated adults are shown in 3027 (816, 817). Obligate carriers are shown in families #3015 (241, 237) and 3022 (611, 614).

clear, documented history of dyslexia during childhood but not testing now as affected), or as "obligate carriers" (negative by history and testing, but with an affected parent and child). Seventy-four family members were determined to have a gene leading to dyslexia. Of these, 61 were classified as currently affected. Seven individuals were considered to be compensated adults, with a clear history of dyslexia (usually including remediation) but who did not fall within the diagnostic criteria and had minimal or no problems in reading as adults. Six other individuals were classified as obligate carriers. They represented less than 10% of those classified as dyslexic. Four were female and two were male. Both males were over 60 years of age and denied reading or spelling problems. Both refused testing. It is possible both were affected, but for the genetic analysis, they were counted as obligate carriers. On a few occasions spouses who married into a family and had no history of dyslexia themselves or in their family were found to be outside the normal range in the screening battery, usually because of a poor performance on the Nonsense Passages. They were classified as normal spouses. No marriage between known dyslexics was encountered. Those with negative educational history for dyslexia and normal screening results were classified as not affected.

Although a formal segregation analysis to test the hypothesis of autosomal dominant inheritance cannot be done because of the biased mode of ascertainment, several points can be made about the mode of inheritance. In the larger pedigrees, three generations of dyslexics were also seen in branches that were not directly involved in ascertainment, such as 3022 and 3015. The sex ratio was not altered significantly from 1 (see below), and male-to-male transmission was frequently observed, which rules out X-linked dominant inheritance. No family with a pattern of inheritance suggestive of X-linked inheritance has been ascertained in our study or reported by others. Final proof of autosomal dominant inheritance awaits either the identification of a linkage (the purpose of the study) and cloning of the gene, or development of a specific diagnostic test that would make possible a less biased identification of families, but these data provide additional support for an autosomal dominant mode of inheritance in many families.

The finding that 7 of 74, or 9% of those having a gene leading to dyslexia had no evident effect from it; that is, the gene was nonpenetrant, is consistent with observations in many autosomal dominant disorders in which the nonpenetrance rate may be as high as 10%. In addition, if children were excluded (because the possibility that "normal" children might be obligate carriers cannot be ruled out), the frequency was still only 14% (7/51). Six of 51 dyslexics over the age of 21 (with a clear history of dyslexia) no longer tested as dyslexic, and were classified as compensated dyslexics. Thus, of the 51 adults determined to have the gene, 12 either never had significant dyslexia or were no longer dyslexic (24%). These results are strikingly like those found in the similar studies reviewed by Pennington et al. (1991). This high frequency of normally functioning adults (almost 1 in 4 in the present study) may have been a significant factor in obscuring possible autosomal dominant inheritance in earlier studies and illustrates the importance of extending the pedigree beyond parents and siblings in a child with possible dyslexia. The milder effect in females (Feldman et al. unpublished), as well as a frequent lack of awareness of dyslexia and less precise diagnostic tests several decades ago, also, are likely contributors to falsely negative family histories. The selection of very large, three-generation families for study allows the identification of obligate carriers and provides a more complete view of the genetics of this common disorder.

Other significant descriptive information has been derived from the pedigree and questionnaire data (Feldman et al. 1993). The more important findings are summarized here. The male/female ratio in dyslexics (including obligate carrier and compensated dyslexics) was 1.06 (38/36), which was not different from the usual ratio of 1.04. Among dyslexics, 13% (8/61) were left handed; 15% (11/74) were left handed if compensated dyslexics and obligate carriers were included. These values did not differ significantly from 14% in normal family members (4/28), from 10% in normal spouses (3/29), or from 12% (7/57) in the combined set of normals. An unusually high frequency of non–right handedness was not observed in any family. These data were derived from a direct question relating to handedness. The Edinburgh Inventory (Oldfield 1971), which was available on a smaller sample, yielded comparable results. No clinically significant differences between dyslexics and normals in these families were found in their prenatal and perinatal history. The overall frequency of neurologic complaints among dyslexics (19%) was the same as in unaffected family members. Similarly, the reported frequency of individuals with seizures was no different in the two groups. Familial dyslexics were not more likely than unaffected family members to have oculomotor or visual problems, right-left confusion, or head injuries. There were no reports of Tourette syndrome in any of the eleven families.

The degree of dyslexia among affected individuals was evaluated by a *Severity Index* (Feldman et al. unpublished). This was designed to create a quantitative description of the extent of the reading deficits among our subjects. It was derived using the individual's score on selected tests from the diagnostic screening battery. The reading/spelling tests included the Gray Oral Reading Test-Revised (Wiederholt and Bryant 1986), the Nonsense Passages test (Finucci et al. 1976; Gross-Glenn et al. 1990) (average of time and errors), and the spelling subtests of the Wide Range Achievement Test-Revised (WRAT-R) (Jastak 1984). The index was calculated by subtracting the score on each of these three tests from the subject's IQ score and then averaging the three deviation scores so that all three tests were equally weighted. The results of this analysis showed a significantly greater severity in the adult males compared to the adult females (Feldman et al. unpublished). The mean severity score in 18 males was 27.2 compared to 19.3 in 19 females ($p \leq .001$) and the distribution of scores clearly showed this difference (Feldman et al. unpublished). This observation, in part, may explain the high male/female ratio found in many studies, because males would be more likely to be recognized in the school systems as dyslexic if they were more severely affected. Other factors, such as associated attention deficit disorder in males and difference in behavior of the two sexes in school could contribute to this (presumed) bias in the recognition or identification of children as dyslexic. The suggestion of Shaywitz et al. (1991) that there is a reporting bias against diagnosing females as dyslexic may also be explained by the greater severity of the disorder in males. A better test (psychometric, psychophysical, or genetic) may resolve the issue in the future.

Data from the questionnaire have also been utilized to compare the long-term educational, occupational, and social effectiveness in the adult dyslexic and nondyslexic family members (Feldman et al. 1993). No difference in income, years of education, or marital status between the dyslexic and nondyslexic individuals were found. Dyslexic family members were not more likely than controls to have drug or alcohol problems. A particularly high frequency of attention deficit disorders with hyperactivity (ADHD, DSM III) and minor psychiatric symptoms (depression and phobias) were noted. Both were particularly frequent in Family 3017.

These observations are important both from the standpoint of counseling families about the risk of future children being affected as well as the obvious importance of the knowledge to families that essentially normal reading ability may be reached by some children, particularly female children. Whether the improved reading ability that occurs in some adults is due to remediation, the development of more effective strategies for reading, or simply reflects the variation in severity that accompanies most autosomal dominant disorders is not currently clear, but the phenomenon seems to be real. Problems with spelling, difficulty with nonsense passages and tests for nonwords (Finucci et al. 1976; Gross-Glenn et al. 1990; Wood et al. 1991) still remain for the majority of adult dyslexics.

## Studies of Immune Function

The frequency of allergy (51% compared to 54%), autoimmune disorders (26% compared to 21%), and premature graying (13% compared to 14%) was no different among those with and without a gene of dyslexia and other family members. There was no obvious clustering of autoimmune disorders in any family, including Family 3017.

Similarly, the battery of tests designed to detect immune dysfunction did not reveal more positive studies than expected in the first four years of the study and were discontinued. Tests designed to assay T-lymphocyte subsets were carried out in 41 dyslexic and 29 normal family members. No clinical abnormalities were observed, and the frequency of an elevated T4/T8 lymphocyte ratio was similar in dyslexic and nondyslexic individuals: 8/41 dyslexics (20%) and 4/74 (15%) nondyslexics (Lubs et al. 1991).

The first study by Pennington et al. (1987) showed an increase in autoimmune disorders in dyslexics (7/70) compared to unaffected family members (1/66). Only medically documented autoimmune disorders were included. When one family in which there were three reports of autoimmune disease was omitted, however, the frequency of the association fell from 10% to 7.8% and the difference between dyslexic and normal individuals was no longer significant. As discussed by these authors, it is possible that there is a genetic subtype of dyslexia in which there is an association with autoimmune disease, but this was clearly not observed in the present study. In a second similar study of the families of twins in the Colorado Reading Project (DeFries et al. 1991) neither an increased frequency of allergy nor an increased frequency of autoimmune disorder was found. No cosegregation of these disorders and dyslexia, and no correlation with dyslexia was found. Thus, the overall results of the studies by Pennington et al. (1987) and DeFries et al. (1991) and the present study clearly do not support an etiological relationship or consistent association between autoimmunity and dyslexia as originally proposed by Geschwind and Behan (1982).

## Linkage Studies

Linkage and gene localization studies currently play a critical role in the study of the genetics of dyslexia. These studies have been described in prior publications (Lubs et al. 1991). In essence, these are based upon a comparison of the likelihood of a putative gene for dyslexia and any marker gene being coinherited through several branches of a number of families with the chance occurrence of the same event. This is expressed as a LOD score (logarithm of the odds of linkage). A LOD score of 3, the usual level for accepting the findings as significant, indicates $10^3$ (or 1000 to 1) odds of linkage. This must, however, be confirmed by a second study, because, although unlikely, the results could be due to chance. One of the advantages of this approach is that LOD scores (as logarithms) can be directly summed over many families. LOD scores, however, are determined at many intervals along a chromosome, because several instances of recombination between paired homologous chromosomes occur at each meiosis. The frequency of such recombination is related to the proximity of any two loci and is described by the recombination frequency (θ). Genes that are close have a recombination frequency of 0.01, and genes that are far apart, or on different chromosomes, show a pattern of random transmission, with θ=0.50. A recombination frequency of 0.01 is approximately equivalent to 1 centimorgan (cM) and, in physical terms, represents about 1,000,000 base pairs. The gene localization screening program now in progress (see below) is designed to screen at roughly 20 cM intervals.

In an earlier study, Smith, Kimberling, and Lubs (1983) reported a LOD score of 3.3 with normal variants of the short arm of chromosome 15 and dyslexia at a recombination frequency (θ) of 0.20. Most of the statistical significance was contributed by one family (6432 in the original report, which is family 3022 in the present report). This family had also been restudied (DeFries et al. 1991) and the LOD scores with chromosomal polymorphisms, as well as a multipoint linkage with DNA polymorphisms (in 22 families), remained high but not significant. The overall linkage analysis in all families, however, did not support linkage (DeFries et al. 1991). The first goal of the present study was to confirm or negate the possible linkage to chromosome 15. Eight independently ascertained families, studied with DNA polymorphisms localized to the proximal long arm of 15 (15cen-15q13), gave no evidence of linkage. We, therefore, decided to restudy the original family that provided most of the prior evidence of linkage to chromosome 15 using four DNA restriction fragment markers (D15S13, D15S11, D15S24, and D15S10) and a highly informative repetitive (dC-dA)n repeat marker localized to the proximal 15q (figure 2). As shown in table II, no evidence of linkage was found.

There was essentially complete agreement between the two studies on the classification of family members as abnormal or dyslexic. One boy, however, who had preliminarily been classified as normal, was found to be dyslexic when restudied by us at an older age. When the original chromosome 15 variant data was recalculated with this single reclassification, the LOD score was not indicative of linkage (i.e., 1.8). Thus, from our study of DNA markers as well as the more recent report by DeFries et al. (1991), it must be concluded that there is no significant evidence of linkage between dyslexia and chromosome 15. Moreover, no precedent exists for localizing unique coding sequences to the short arms of chromosome 15 and the other associated chromosomes, and an individual without any one or two of these

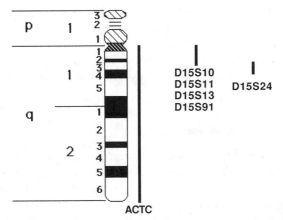

Figure 2. Map of chromosome 15 markers. Cytogenetic localization of the polymorphic DNA markers is indicated by the vertical bars. Reprinted with permission from H. Lubs and M. Rabin. Lubs, H., Rabin, M. et al. Genetic bases of developmental dyslexia: Molecular studies. In *Neuropsychological Foundations of Learning Disabilities*, edited by J. E. Obrzut and G. W. Hynd. 1991. San Diego: Academic Press.

short arms (as in a Robertsonian translocation, which deletes 2 short arms) is perfectly normal and does not have dyslexia.

More than 40 other markers, largely blood groups and protein polymorphisms, have also been studied in these families (Lubs et al. 1991). In most instances no suggestive LOD scores have been detected. Only 10% of the genome, however, has been excluded (with a likelihood of 100:1, i.e., a negative LOD score ≤ 2.0). Screening of the entire genome is now much more feasible than when the study began and

Table II. LOD Scores for Family 3022 with Polymorphic Chromosome 15 DNA Markers

| Marker | \(Recombination Fraction—Θ\) | | | | | | | | |
|--------|------|-------|-------|-------|-------|-------|-------|-------|-------|
|  | 0.0 | 0.05 | 0.10 | 0.15 | 0.20 | 0.25 | 0.30 | 0.35 | 0.40 |
| ACTC | $-\infty$ | −3.55 | −2.43 | −1.70 | −1.20 | −0.83 | −0.56 | −0.36 | −0.20 |
| D15S10 | 0.04 | 0.03 | 0.03 | 0.02 | 0.01 | 0.01 | 0.01 | 0.00 | 0.00 |
| D15S11 | −2.57 | −1.53 | −0.98 | −0.66 | −0.44 | −0.29 | −0.17 | −0.09 | −0.04 |
| D15S13 | −1.80 | −0.09 | 0.09 | 0.14 | 0.15 | 0.13 | 0.11 | 0.08 | 0.05 |
| D15S24 | −3.57 | −1.20 | −0.72 | −0.48 | −0.34 | −0.24 | −0.18 | −0.13 | −0.08 |
| D15S91 | $-\infty$ | −0.98 | −0.70 | −0.53 | −0.41 | −0.32 | −0.24 | −0.17 | −0.10 |

Adapted from Lubs, H., Rabin, M., et al. Genetic bases of developmental dyslexia: Molecular studies. In *Neuropsychological Foundations of Learning Disabilities*, edited by J. E. Obrzut and G. W. Hynd. 1991. San Diego: Academic Press. Used with permission.

we are beginning more intensive screening, with repeat markers at approximately 20 cm. Among these 40 markers, a suggestive LOD score of 1.9 ($\theta$=.20) has been found in eight families with dyslexia and the Rh locus. A DNA repeat polymorphism, closely linked to Rh, has also yielded similar LOD scores and we are currently pursuing this possible linkage.

### Behavioral and Psychophysical Studies

*Neuropsychological Studies.* The objective of the neuropsychological studies has been to provide a behavioral phenotype of the familial dyslexic subject through a description of cognitive and neuropsychological functioning. Five major areas of functioning were assessed including language, executive functions, nonverbal attention and memory, verbal attention and memory, and visuospatial/constructive abilities. The battery was administered to as many members as possible of families meeting criteria for inclusion in this study. In our adult sample, 30 subjects were dyslexic and 32 were unaffected. Our pediatric sample was not large enough for statistical analyses; therefore, only adult data analyses are reported.

In these families, dyslexic adults were found to exhibit deficits on select language abilities, namely receptive vocabulary and syntactic comprehension, and within visuospatial/constructive functions, dyslexic subjects obtained lower scores on simple and complex graphomotor tasks (Lubs et al. 1991). Verbal and nonverbal memory performance was comparable for dyslexic and unaffected subjects. Dyslexics were slower on tasks requiring rapid naming, were less efficient on tasks requiring rapid set shifting when naming alternating sequences of letters and numbers, and numbers, letters, and colors, and had more difficulty retaining a string of three consonants following a counting interference period (Levin et al. 1991; Lubs et al. 1991). These findings suggest a specific pattern of neuropsychological dysfunction among familial dyslexics (Feldman unpublished data), and are similar to the results reported by Wood et al. (1991b).

*Psychophysical Studies of Vision.* As part of the overall goal of studying these families as extensively as possible, we characterized visual function in some detail. We did so by comparing the visual contrast sensitivity of dyslexic (*N*=18) and normal (*N*=22) readers at two spatial frequencies: 0.6 and 12 cycles/degree under a series of different conditions. Those with clinically significant problems with vision were not included in these studies.

First we assessed the effect of stimulus onset and offset transients. We did this by comparing sensitivity: (1) under a ramped stimulus condition in which the contrast was gradually increased over time; and, (2) under a nonramped condition in which contrast was turned on and off abruptly.

We found that for both groups of subjects the inclusion of stimulus onset and offset transients resulted in an increase in contrast sensitivity relative to the ramped baseline condition. This increase was more pronounced for the low-frequency condition (i.e., 0.6 c/deg) and, more importantly, was equal for dyslexic and normal readers. This shows that dyslexic readers do not have a deficit in their ability to detect stimulus transients.

We went on to determine contrast sensitivity as a function of stimulus duration (this test was only carried out with nonramped stimuli). Five different durations were tested: 17, 34, 102, 306, and 1088 milliseconds. In the case of the low spatial frequency stimuli (i.e., 0.6 c/deg), there was no difference between dyslexic and normal readers, over the full range of durations tested. On the other hand, when using the high-frequency grating (i.e., 12.0 c/deg), we found that the dyslexic individuals have markedly inferior contrast sensitivity at the shortest stimulus durations (i.e., 17, 34, and 102 msec). This deficit seems to reflect a more sluggish temporal summation on the part of the dyslexic observers.

In our last test, we determined the effect of forward masking. This experiment was identical to the preceding experiment except that the test stimulus was preceded by a masking stimulus (a high-contrast grating presented briefly, 102 msec). The presence of the masking stimulus reduced the sensitivity to brief stimuli for both groups. This reduction was more pronounced for low-frequency (i.e., 0.6 c/deg) stimuli. After controlling for any difference in contrast sensitivity in the unmasked condition, we found no difference in susceptibility to masking between the dyslexic and the control group.

These results are of particular significance in light of the proposed transient system deficit theory of dyslexia (Martin and Lovegrove 1984, 1987, 1988; Slaghuis and Lovegrove 1984; Lovegrove, Martin, and Slaghuis 1986; Lovegrove et al. 1986; Lovegrove, Garzia, and Nicholson 1990; Williams, Molinet, and LeCluyse 1989; Lovegrove 1991). The transient system is commonly thought to be particularly sensitive to low spatial frequencies and high temporal frequencies, to mediate the detection of stimulus transients, and to be specifically susceptible to masking by brief stimuli. Although we did find deficits associated with brief stimuli (equivalent to high temporal frequencies), we did not find deficits in the detection of low spatial frequency gratings. Neither did we find deficits in the ability of dyslexic readers to detect stimulus transients, nor did we find any reductions in the susceptibility to masking. Therefore, the transient system deficit theory is largely inconsistent with the results we obtained. However, our data have emphasized temporal factors (i.e., brief stimulus presentations or high temporal frequencies) in the study of sensory and perceptual functions in dyslexic readers. It is of considerable interest that comparable findings in rapid processing of auditory stimuli have been observed in this same set of families (Steffins et al. 1992). Greater periods of silence, for example, were required for dyslexic individuals to distinguish /sta/–/sa/, than for unaffected family members.

## Brain Imaging Studies

The neurobiological basis of behavior was initially thought to be represented by the size of certain brain regions, thus launching the "science" of phrenology. Although most of the tenets of this "science" have been rejected, the morphology of some brain regions have been found to be correlated to aspects of behavior. For example, the left planum temporale (PT), located in Wernicke's area, is larger than the right PT in 65% of adult brains (Geschwind and Levitsky 1968), suggesting, perhaps, that the function of the language dominant left hemisphere is related to the larger left planum. It has been shown in several studies (reviewed by Hynd and Semrud-Clikeman 1990) that in normal individuals, the posterior part of the brain is wider on the left than on the right. These studies all suggest, but do not prove, the relationship of left hemisphere dominance for language to left-dominant posterior hemispherical asymmetry. The size of certain brain regions may be predictive of aspects of functional ability. Moreover, because the dimensions of brain structures are stable variables (assuming high reliability of measurement), as opposed to brain metabolism or blood flow, the size of a brain region can be incorporated very effectively in genetic studies where the inheritance of particular behavior may be associated with the size, shape, or asymmetry of a particular brain structure. Data on the relationship of the size and asymmetry of target brain structures and the inheritance of a dyslexic trait in the present families are, therefore, currently being obtained.

Studies done on brains of dyslexics who have come to autopsy have yielded valuable data. Galaburda, Rosen, and Sherman (1988) and Galaburda (1991) have reported that in all six male and three female dyslexics who came to autopsy, the PT, a structure located on the inferior bank of the Sylvan fissure, posterior to Heschl's gyrus, failed to show the usual left-greater-than-right asymmetry, but was symmetric instead. Furthermore, it was found in the sample that this symmetry was not caused by a smaller left PT, but by a larger-than-normal right PT. This finding has led Galaburda (1991) to hypothesize that a large right PT is associated with dyslexia. Extrapolating from findings in rat brains (of a negative correlation between the degree of asymmetry for a given architectonic area and the total number of neurons in that architectonic area), Galaburda (1991) proposed that a pathological event in dyslexia may be an excess of neurons in the right planum and a larger-than-normal right PT, representing a failure of the usual regressive events in neurogenesis. Galaburda (1991) has also shown that, in rats, an abnormally large complement of neurons in a particular architectonic area is associated with a larger number of callosal fibers connecting the right and left sides of the structure.

With the development of magnetic resonance imaging (MRI) and the improvements in its technology from 2-D to 3-D imaging, and the recent ability to obtain slices as thin as 1 mm, many brain morphologic studies have become possible in living humans. Studies done between 1978 and 1989, using CT scans on reading-impaired individuals, have been reviewed by Hynd and Semrud-Clikeman (1990). Most of these studies suggested reversed or reduced asymmetry of posterior brain structures in dyslexic as compared to normal subjects. Hier et al. (1978) showed that those dyslexic individuals with reversed parieto-occipital asymmetry (R>L) had worse verbal IQ scores than those with the normal asymmetry (L>R). They considered reversed asymmetry to be a risk factor for dyslexia.

In a recently published study (Duara et al. 1991), we showed that the segments of a horizontal brain slice at the level of the Foramen of Monroe showed right-greater-than-left asymmetry in the anterior half of the brain and left-greater-than-right symmetry of the posterior 10% of the brain in normal and dyslexic individuals. Furthermore, a mid-posterior brain segment, corresponding roughly to the angular gyrus, was significantly more asymmetrical toward the left in normal readers as compared to dyslexic subjects who tended to have either symmetry, or right-greater-than-left asymmetry, in this region. This result is consistent with those of previous CT scan studies, but is more specific as to the brain regions involved. We also showed that the splenium of the corpus callosum was larger in dyslexic than normal readers, and larger in female than male dyslexics. The larger splenium of the corpus callosum in dyslexic individuals is consistent with Galaburda's hypothesis of a failure of the usual pruning of excess neurons and their axons during development. It is clear from these results that gender effects may mask disease effects and should always be accounted for.

As a follow up to this study, we measured the area of the superior temporal plane (STP), a region that includes the planum temporale and Heschl's gyrus, using serial coronal MRI slices of 5 mm thickness, in a group of normal and dyslexic subjects (Kushch et al. 1991). There is a highly significant difference in the asymmetry of the STP between normals who had L>R asymmetry, and dyslexics, who had symmetrical or R>L STPs. To the extent that the STP can be equated with the planum temporale, our findings so far are somewhat inconsistent with those of Galaburda (of a larger R planum in dyslexics). Rather, the data suggest a normal sized R planum but a smaller L planum in dyslexics. Our results are consistent with those of Larson et al. (1990) and Leonard et al. (1993), both of whom found that the L planum was smaller than normal in dyslexics and the R planum was of normal size. We were also able to show a correlation between the degree of asymmetry between R and L STP and the size of the splenium of the corpus callosum. We found a significant correlation (r=0.53, p=.002) between the L/R asymmetry of the STP and the score on a test of passage comprehension (Woodcock and Johnson 1977). This correlation was significant even after correcting for multiple comparisons and also after removing the most prominent outliers in the data. Although this correlation was significant for dyslexic readers alone and for dyslexic and normal readers together, it was not significant for normal readers alone. Thus, it seems unlikely that superior temporal plane asymmetry in the R>L direction, by itself, is associated with poor verbal performance, but in subjects already prone to dyslexia, asymmetry in this direction may worsen the severity of the dyslexia, or act as a risk factor for dyslexia. This finding represents the first demonstration of a possible direct relationship between the relative size of a brain structure and performance on a behavioral test. Confirmation with a large group of subjects and with direct measurement of the planum temporale is necessary.

## SUMMARY AND CONCLUSION

A wide variety of studies suggests that most families with dyslexia have a significantly more global problem than anticipated. This seems to include rapidly presented visual and auditory information, and, at least in certain families, an increased frequency of phobias, depression, and attention deficit disorder with hyperactivity. From the neuropsychologic studies, a pattern also emerges of high-functioning familial dyslexic subjects who exhibit specific and selective deficits in their ability to process and integrate information rapidly and efficiently, including rapid set shifting. These findings are also accompanied by significant differences in brain anatomy and function. Immunologic differences between dyslexic and unaffected family members have not been detected. Although the differences described above occur with high frequency in familial dyslexics, they do not ordinarily interfere with successful completion of education or the capacity to function well in contemporary society.

The genetic information in 11 large families was consistent with autosomal dominant inheritance with 90% penetrance. The severity of dyslexia was greater in adult males. It is also of interest that almost a quarter of adults determined to have a gene resulting in dyslexia were either compensated adults who tested normally, or obligate carriers who transmitted the gene but did not have a history of testing consistent with dyslexia. This may have obscured the pattern of dominant inheritance in the past and indicates the importance of obtaining extensive documented family histories in children found to have isolated problems in reading and spelling. Linkage studies have not confirmed the prior tentative linkage with chromosome 15 and screening of the entire genome is in progress at 20 cm intervals.

## REFERENCES

DeFries, J. C., Olson, R. K., Pennington, B. F., and Smith, S. D. 1991. Colorado reading project: An update. In *The Reading Brain: The Biological Basis of Dyslexia*, eds. D. D. Duane and D. B. Gray. Parkton, MD: York Press.

Duara, R., Kushch, A., Gross-Glenn, K., Jallad, B., Pascal, S., Loewenstein, D. A., Sheldon, R., Rabin, M., Levin, B., and Lubs, H. 1991. Neuroanatomical differences between dyslexic and normal readers on MR scans. *Archives of Neurology* 48:410–16.

Feldman, E., Jallad, B., Kushch, A., Gross-Glenn, K., Duara, R., Rabin, M., and Lubs, H. A. Unpublished. Gender differences in the severity of adult familial dyslexia.

Feldman, E., Levin, B. E., Lubs, H., Rabin, M., Lubs, M.-L., Jallad, B., and Kushch, A. 1993. Adult familial dyslexia: A retrospective developmental and psychosocial profile. *Journal of Neuropsychiatry and Clinical Neurosciences:* 195–99.

Finucci J. M., and Childs, B. 1981. Are there really more dyslexic boys than girls? In *Sex Differences in Dyslexia*, eds. A. Ansara, N. Geschwind, A. Galaburda, M. Albert, and N. Gartrell. Towson, MD: The Orton Dyslexia Society.

Finucci, J. M., Guthrie, J. T., Childs, A. L., Abbey, H., and Childs, B. 1976. The genetics of specific reading disability. *Annals of Human Genetics* 40:1–23.

Galaburda, A. M. 1991. Anatomy of dyslexia. Argument against phrenology. In *The Reading Brain: The Biological Basis of Dyslexia*, eds. D. D. Duane and D. B. Gray. Parkton, MD: York Press.

Galaburda, A. M., Rosen, G. D., and Sherman, G. F. 1988. Symmetric and asymmetric neocortical architectonic areas differ in callosal connectivity. *International Journal of Developmental Neuroscience* 7:8.

Geschwind, N., and Behan, P. O. 1982. Left handedness: Association with immune disease migrain and developmental learning disorder. *Proceedings of the National Academy of Science* 79:5097–5100.

Geschwind, N., and Levitsky, W. 1968. Human brain: Left-right asymmetries in the temporal speech region. *Science* 161:186–87.

Gross-Glenn, K., Jallad, B., Novoa, L., Helgren-Lempesis, V., and Lubs, H. A. 1990. Nonsense passage reading as a diagnostic aid in the study of adult familial dyslexia. *Reading and Writing: An Interdisciplinary Journal* 2:161–73.

Hallgren, B. 1950. Specific dyslexia (congenital word-blindness): A clinical and genetic study. *Acta Psychiatrica Neurologica Scandinavia* 65 (suppl):1–287.

Hier, D. B., LeMay, M., Rosenberger, P. B., and Perlo, V. P. 1978. Developmental dyslexia: Evidence for a sub-group with reversal of cerebral asymmetry. *Archives of Neurology* 35:90–92.

Hugdahl, K., Synnevag, B., and Satz, P. 1990. Immune and autoimmune diseases in dyslexic children. *Neuropsychologia* 28:673–79.

Hynd, G. W., and Semrud-Clikeman, M. 1990. Dyslexia and brain morphology. *Psychological Bulletin* 106:447–82.

Jastak, S. 1984. *Wide Range Achievement Test-Revised*. Wilmington, DE: Jastak Associates, Inc.

Kushch, A., Duara, R., Gross-Glenn, K., Jallad, B., Levin, B., Rabin, M., and Lubs, H. 1991. Superior temporal plane measurements on MRI in normal and dyslexic readers. *Neurology* 40:19–86.

Larson, J. P., Hoien, T., Lundberg, I., and Odengaard, H. 1990. MRI evaluation of the symmetry of the planum temporale in adolescents with dyslexia. *Brain and Language* 39:289–301.

Leonard, C. M., Voeller, K. K. S., Lombardino, L. J., Morris, M. K., Hynd, G. W., Alexander, A. W., Andersen, H. G., Garofalakis, M., Honeyman J. C., Mao, J., Agee, O. F., and Staab, E. V. 1993. Anomalous cerebral structure in dyslexia revealed with MR imaging. *Archives of Neurology* 50:461–69.

Levin, B. E., Jallad, B., Gross-Glenn, K., Kushch, A., and Lubs, H. 1991. Possible frontal lobe dysfunction in adult dyslexia. *Journal of Clinical and Experimental Neuropsychology* 13:111.

Lovegrove, W. 1991. Spatial frequency processing in dyslexic and normal readers. In *Vision and Visual Dyslexia*, ed. J. F. Stein. Boca Raton, FL: CRC Press, Inc.

Lovegrove, W., Martin, F., and Slaghuis, W. 1986. A theoretical and experimental case for a visual deficit in specific reading disability. *Cognitive Neuropsychology* 3:225–67.

Lovegrove, W., Slaghuis, W., Bowling, A., Nelson, P., and Geeves, E. 1986. Spatial frequency processing and the prediction of reading ability: A preliminary investigation. *Perception and Psychophysics* 40:440–44.

Lovegrove, W. J., Garzia, R. P., and Nicholson, S. B. 1990. Experimental evidence for a transient system deficit in specific reading disability. *American Optometric Association Journal* 61:137–46.

Lubs, H., Duara, R., Levin, B., Jallad, B., Lubs, M.-L., Rabin, M., Kushch, A., and Gross-Glenn, K. 1991. Dyslexia subtypes: Genetics, behavior, and brain imaging. In *The Reading Brain: The Biological Basis of Dyslexia*, eds. D. D. Duane and D. Gray. Parkton, MD: York Press.

Lubs, H. A., Rabin, M., Feldman, E., Jallad, B. J., Kushch, A., Gross-Glenn, K., Duara, R., and Elston, R. C. In press. Familial dyslexia: Genetic and medical findings in eleven 3-generation families. *Annals of Dyslexia*.

Martin, F., and Lovegrove, W. 1984. The effects of field size and luminance on contrast sensitivity differences between specifically reading disabled and normal children. *Neuropsychologia* 22:73–77.

Martin, F., and Lovegrove, W. 1987. Flicker contrast sensitivity in normal and specifically disabled readers. *Perception* 16:215–21.

Martin, F., and Lovegrove, W. 1988. Uniform-field flicker masking in control and specifically-disabled readers. *Perception* 17:203–14.

Obrzut, J. E., and Hynd, G. W. (eds.) 1991. *Neuropsychological Foundations of Learning Disabilities*. New York: Academic Press, Inc.

Oldfield, R. C. 1971. The assessment of handedness: The Edinburgh Inventory. *Neuropsychologia* 9:97–113.

Omenn, G. S., and Weber, B. A. 1978. Dyslexia: Search for phenotypic and genetic heterogeneity. *American Journal of Medical Genetics* 1:333.

Pennington, B. F., Gilger, J. W., Paul, D., Smith, S. A., Smith, S. D., and DeFries, J. C. 1991. Evidence for major gene transmission of developmental dyslexia. *Journal of the American Medical Association* 266(11);1527–1534.

Pennington, B. F., Smith, S. D., Kimberling, W. J., Green, P. A., and Haith, M. M. 1987. Left-handedness and immune disorders in familial dyslexics. *Archives of Neurology* 44:634–39.

Shaywitz, B., Shaywitz, S., Liberman, I., Fletcher, J., Shankweiler, D., Duncan, J., Katz, L., Liberman, A., Francis, D., Dreyer, L., Crain, S., Brady, S., Fowler, A., Kier, L., Rosenfield, N., Gore, J., and Makuch, R. 1991. Neurolinguistic and biologic mechanisms in dyslexia. In *The Reading Brain: The Biological Basis of Dyslexia*, eds. D. D. Duane and D. Gray. Parkton, MD: York Press.

Slaghuis, J. W. L., and Lovegrove, W. 1984. Flicker masking of spatial-frequency-dependent visible persistence and specific reading disability. *Perception* 13:527–34.

Smith, S. D., Kimberling, W. J., and Lubs, H. A. 1983. Specific reading disability: Identification of an inherited form through linkage analysis. *Science* 219:1345–1347

Steffins, M. L., Eilers, R. E., Gross-Glenn, K., and Jallad, B. 1992. Speech perception in adult subjects with familial dyslexia. *Journal of Speech and Hearing Research* 35:192–200.

Wiederholt, J. L., and Bryant, B. R. 1986. *Gray Oral Reading Test-Revised*. Austin, TX: PRO-ED.

Williams, M. C., Molinet, K., and LeCluyse, K. 1989. Visual masking as a measure of temporal processing in normal and disabled readers. *Clinical Vision Sciences* 4:137–44.

Wood, F., Felton, R., Flowers, L., and Naylor, C. 1991. Neurobehavioral definition of dyslexia. In *The Reading Brain: The Biological Basis of Dyslexia*, eds. D. D. Duane and D. B. Gray. Parkton, MD: York Press.

Woodcock, R. W., and Johnson, M. B. 1977. *Woodcock-Johnson Psycho-Educational Battery*. Allen, TX: DLM Teaching Resources.

Zahalkova, M., Vrzal, V., and Klobovkova, E. 1972. Genetic investigations in dyslexia. *Journal of Medical Genetics* 9:48.

# Chapter • 6

## Interrelationships Between Reading Disability and Attention Deficit-Hyperactivity Disorder

*Bennett A. Shaywitz,*
*Jack M. Fletcher, and*
*Sally E. Shaywitz*

Attention deficit-hyperactivity disorder (ADHD)[*] and learning disabilities (LD) represent the most common neurobehavioral disorders of childhood, affecting children from early childhood through school and into adult life. Estimates suggest that ADHD affects as many as 10% to 20% of the school-age population (Shaywitz and Shaywitz 1988; Szatmari, Boyle, and Offord 1989), and that the prevalence of learning disabilities ranges from 5% to 10% (Interagency Committee on Learning Disabilities 1987).

Supported by Grant # PO1 HD21888 and 1P50 HD25802 from NICHD.

[*]We use the term *attention deficit-hyperactivity disorder* (ADHD) (American Psychiatric Association 1987, 1991) to encompass what DSM-III referred to as attention deficit disorder (ADD). ADHD is used synonymously with hyperactivity. We use the term *learning disability* in a generic sense to include all types of learning disability. *Dyslexia* represents a particular type of learning disability in which reading is primarily affected. Although dyslexia is the most frequently observed learning disability, other learning disabilities may reflect arithmetic (dyscalculia), handwriting (dysgraphia), or spelling disabilities.

## DEFINITION

In this chapter we review evidence that supports the belief that although attention deficit-hyperactivity disorder (ADHD) and learning disabilities frequently co-occur in the same child, each (ADHD and LD) is a separate problem. Diagnosis of ADHD is established on the basis of a history of symptoms representing the cardinal constructs of ADHD—inattention, impulsivity, and sometimes hyperactivity (American Psychiatric Association 1980, 1987, 1991). In contrast, the diagnosis of learning disability is established on the basis of performance on tests of ability and achievement. Historically, LD has been conceptualized as the inability to learn in children with otherwise normal or above normal intelligence. Guidelines (provided as an attempt at the operationalization of Public Law 94-142 [P.L. 94-142]) of "a severe discrepancy between achievement and intellectual ability" (U.S.O.E. 1977) offer the most generally accepted criteria throughout the English-speaking world (Cone and Wilson 1981; Frankenberger and Fronzaglio 1991; Pennington 1991; Reynolds 1984; Rutter 1970; Thorndike 1963).

## HISTORICAL PERSPECTIVE

Historically, the antecedents of the current controversies surrounding the relationship between ADHD and LD can be traced to the late nineteenth–early twentieth century. By the beginning of the twentieth century, descriptions of attentional difficulties experienced by children, which are similar to those known today as ADHD, began to appear in the medical literature, linking the behaviors to disorders causing brain damage. In a remarkably prescient report, Still (1902) described children with significant inattention affecting their school performance which he attributed to "morbid defects in moral control" (p. 1008). Although his descriptions are remarkable for their similarity to current diagnostic criteria, Still's concepts of etiology remained poorly defined. In that same era, however, other physicians linked the description of similar behaviors to traumatic brain injury (Meyer 1904; Goldstein 1936), sequelae of von Economo encephalitis (Hohman 1922), or a variety of other childhood CNS infections (Bender 1942). Strauss and associates wrote a series of reports in which they formulated the concept of the "brain-injured (damaged) child" (Werner and Strauss 1941; Strauss and Lehtinen 1947).

By the 1950s, investigators had become disillusioned by these notions and the concept of the hyperkinetic behavior disorder was promulgated in the pediatric literature. Laufer and Denhoff (1957) argued that underlying the hyperkinetic syndrome was some sort of dysfunction of the diencephalon. These theories influenced many physicians and educators and persisted into the 1960s. However, by the early 1960s, many investigators and clinicians were becoming increasingly uncomfortable with the assumption that structural brain damage could be inferred on the basis of behavioral symptomatology alone. Thus, by 1962, both the Oxford International Study Group on Child Neurology (Bax and MacKeith 1963) as well as an NIH Task Force (Clements 1966) had recommended that the term *minimal brain damage* be discarded and replaced by *minimal brain dysfunctions* (MBD). Building on the work of Strauss and of Kennard (1960), who believed that, for example, the "equivocal" Babinski sign was a manifestation of brain injury, Clements and Peters (1962) introduced the belief that the demonstration of abnormalities on neurologic examination, however minor, were important indicators of the syndrome. In their view, minimal brain dysfunctions could be inferred from the presence of a cluster of symptoms including specific learning deficits, hyperkinesis, impulsivity, and short attention span and confirmed by findings on examination of "equivocal" neurological signs and borderline-abnormal or abnormal EEG.

In the 1960s, MBD was viewed as a real advance in incorporating the diverse manifestations of the syndrome, while not emphasizing a particular interpretation thought to reflect the nature of the brain insult. With time, it became increasingly apparent that the concept of MBD was seriously flawed, and, in an operational sense, unworkable. Thus, the amalgamation of both the learning disability and the behavioral disorder within the diagnosis of MBD served only to compound the already existing confusion. An even more serious criticism of MBD was the absence of any rigorous diagnostic criteria. This deficiency was a reflection of the lack of progress in the general classification (or nosology) of behavioral disorders. Strategies for the elaboration of scientifically valid classification schemata emerged in the 1970s, as exemplified by the work of Feighner, Robins, and Guze (1972) on diagnostic criteria for affective disorder and schizophrenia. Specific inclusion and exclusion criteria were developed that could be used within the framework of both research studies and clinical practice. Their approach spread rapidly within the psychiatric community and resulted in the elaboration of research diagnostic criteria (RDC) and were codified in DSM-III (American Psychiatric Association 1980) and more recently in DSM-III-R (American Psychiatric Association 1987). The evolution of our concepts of ADHD from its conception as a global entity reflecting brain damage to increasingly more specific diagnostic entities with inclusion and exclusion criteria is shown in figure 1.

The term *learning disabilities* was first used by Samuel A. Kirk (1962) in the first edition of his textbook *Educating Exceptional Children* and gained immediate acceptance by educators and parent groups fol-

## HISTORICAL TRENDS

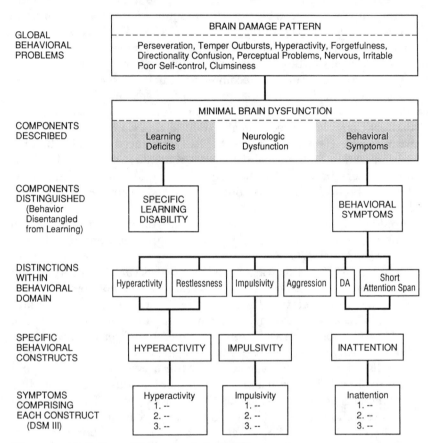

Figure 1. Evolution of the concept of ADHD.

lowing his presentation at the 1963 Conference on Exploration into the Problems of the Perceptually Handicapped Child (Berk 1984). The evolution of the term is discussed more fully by Berk (1984) and by Myers and Hammill (1982).

### PREVALENCE OF ADHD AND LD

Evidence from a number of investigative groups suggests considerable overlap between attention disorder and learning disabilities. The prevalence of learning disabilities in the ADHD population is substantial (Keogh 1971; Wender 1971). Results of studies to date support this belief, with estimates of learning disabilities in a hyperactive population ranging between 9% (Halperin et al. 1984) and 80% (McGee and Share

1988) to 92% (Silver 1981). Estimates of hyperactivity in a learning-disabled population range from 26% to 41% (Holborow and Berry 1986) to 50% (Lambert and Sandoval 1980), to 80% (Safer and Allen 1976). In a sample survey of Connecticut school children, 11% of children with attention disorder were classified as learning disabled in either reading or arithmetic, whereas 33% of children with learning disabilities satisfy criteria for ADHD (Shaywitz 1986). Studies examining the academic achievement of hyperactive compared to control children support the notion that significantly more children with ADHD experience academic achievement problems. They are more likely to perform below expectations in reading and arithmetic and, compared to controls, are behind both in their academic subjects and in more subjects (Cantwell 1978). Holborow and Berry (1986) found seven times as many children rated as hyperactive were described as experiencing "very much" difficulty in all academic areas compared to their nonhyperactive classmates.

## PATHOGENESIS OF READING DISABILITY

The proposed pathogenic mechanisms for ADHD and RD are quite distinct, involving very different brain regions and mechanisms. The overwhelming evidence relates reading and dyslexia to language and not, for example, to deficits in visuospatial function. Central to such a view is the conceptualization that reading is not an entirely new system, but rather one that is based on language. One hypothesis suggests that the language apparatus forms a distinct biological system, or module (Fodor 1983), which is served by specific brain mechanisms and structures that have been adapted to serve the reading task (Liberman, Shankweiler, and Liberman 1989; Liberman and Mattingly 1989). Much has been learned about the nature of the reading process and the component skills necessary for the acquisition of reading, particularly the importance of phonological processes (Brady and Shankweiler 1991; Goswami and Bryant 1990; Perfetti 1991; Gough, Ehri, and Treiman 1992; Vellutino 1991). Evidence from a number of investigative groups has now converged to indicate that poor readers have difficulty understanding that words are composed of units in the form of phonemes, syllables, and morphemes (see Brady and Shankweiler 1991; Goswami and Bryant 1990; Liberman, Shankweiler, and Liberman 1989; Vellutino 1991 for reviews). Evidence from a number of lines of investigation supports the belief that the neural processes related to language (and, as indicated above, for reading as well) seem to be mediated by brain structures in the perisylvian association cortex usually in the left hemisphere (Caplan 1992; Ojemann et al. 1989).

Neurobiologic correlates of attention deficit hyperactivity disorder are less well established, however, they are clearly considerably different from those mechanisms subserving the reading process. Posner and associates (Posner 1988; Posner and Petersen 1990) suggest that attention systems in the brain are anatomically separate from the data-processing systems. In his view, these attention systems encompass a network of anatomic areas with particular areas responsible for different functions, such as orienting, detection, and alerting. Anatomically, these systems involve posterior parietal areas, the superior colliculus, thalamus, and anterior cingulate regions. Frontal areas are involved as well. Other conceptualizations of attentional mechanisms are reviewed by Cooley and Morris (1990), LaBerge (1990), Colby (1991), Benson (1991), and Heilman, Voeller, and Nadeau (1991). Positron emission tomography (PET) provides a unique opportunity to examine metabolic factors in vivo in a variety of disorders. Zametkin et al. (1990) examined cerebral glucose metabolism in young adults with histories of ADHD as children. Their findings suggested global reductions in glucose metabolism in ADHD, with largest reductions in premotor and superior prefrontal cortex, areas similar to what Posner (1988; Posner and Petersen 1990) proposes as anterior attentional brain regions.

## COGNITIVE PROFILES IN RD COMPARED TO ADHD

We illustrate the relationship between ADHD and RD by findings from a recent study. Children (*n*=312) in this study (age range 7.5 to 9.5 years) were participants in an ongoing study of the classification of learning, attention, and behavioral disorders (Shaywitz et al. 1991; Shaywitz, Shaywitz, and Fletcher 1992). The children were recruited through a variety of sources, including schools, parent groups, and media announcements. None had severe emotional problems, uncorrected vision problems, hearing loss, acquired neurological disorders, or absence of English as a primary language. No restrictions were placed according to gender, race, or socioeconomic status.

The learning-disabled children were identified using two definitions of learning disability. One definition (discrepancy) identified a child as learning disabled on the basis of a regression-based discrepancy between reading (and/or arithmetic) achievement and IQ. The other definition (low achievement) identified learning-disabled children on the basis of a score below the 25th percentile on a measure of academic achievement. Also included was a group of children with no learning or attention problem or other handicap.

As discussed earlier, we focus the discussion on dyslexia, the most common type of learning disability. For reading disability, the measures were the decoding (real words and pseudowords) and reading cluster scores subtests on the Woodcock-Johnson Psychoeducational Test Battery (Woodcock and Johnson 1977), and Full Scale IQ on the Wechsler Intelligence Test for Children-Revised (WISC-R; Wechsler 1974). ADHD was defined on the basis of parent report using either the Yale Children's Inventory (DSM-III criteria) or a DSM-III-R symptom checklist (DSM-III-R criteria).

Each child received an assessment of academic ability, cognitive skills, and behavioral adjustment. Comparisons were made on variables representing measures of language and cognitive ability with hypothesized relationships to reading ability and disability. Measures of phonological awareness were expected to be strongly related to reading disability and measures of visual-spatial, nonverbal memory, and attentional skills to be weakly related. In contrast, we would expect phonological measures to be only weakly related to ADHD.

Two multivariate methods of data analysis were used, a multivariate approach to repeated measures (ANOVA) and multiple regression. In brief, groups were formed by combining reading disability (based on either discrepancy or low achievement) with definitions of ADHD. A second analytic approach was based on multiple regression. This approach evaluated whether the presence of ADHD accounts for variability in measures of reading achievement beyond that explained by the set of cognitive measures described above. Regression analysis employed hierarchical methods and models based on four independent variables representing measures of reading achievement (word decoding, oral reading, listening comprehension, and silent reading). Linguistically based measures, visual motor tasks, and a composite measure of attention served as dependent measures.

Four subject groups are considered here: RD only, ADHD only, RD + ADHD, and a nonimpaired contrast group. The cognitive profiles for reading-disabled children with and without ADHD are quite similar, with severe deficits in linguistic measures noted in both groups. Regression analyses indicate that a large proportion of the variance of reading is explained, not surprisingly, by linguistic measures. The inclusion of attention variables to the equation resulted in only a small additional proportion of variance explained, an increment that varied depending on the reading measure used as the independent variable. For example, when word reading was used, a very small additional increment was noted (figure 2). However, when silent reading comprehension was the reading measure, a much larger proportion of variance was explained by attention (figure 3).

## ADHD AND RD: THE NATURE OF THE ASSOCIATION

Our findings add support to the conceptualization proposed at the beginning of this review; this is, that ADHD and LD, more specifically

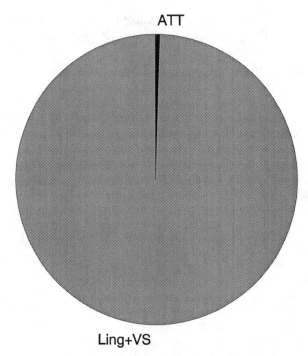

Figure 2.   Additional proportion of variance of reading (measured by word reading) explained by attentional measures.

RD, are separate disorders that frequently co-occur. Furthermore, our results are consonant with increasing evidence from a number of lines of investigation that reading disability is characterized by linguistic deficits, primarily in phonological processing; in contrast, such linguistic deficits are not characteristic of ADHD unless the attention disorder is associated with reading disability. Thus, utilizing factor analytic studies, Lahey et al. (1978; 1988) found separate LD and hyperactivity factors. Felton et al. (1987) examined children with ADHD alone compared to children with reading disability. Reading-disabled children exhibited difficulty with tasks involving confrontation naming and rapid automatized naming; children with ADHD had most trouble with word-list learning and recall. August and Garfinkel (1990) reported that ADHD and RD contribute separate sources of cognitive morbidity. Thus, children with both ADHD and RD exhibited deficits in lexical decoding and rapid word naming, in contrast to children with ADHD without RD. Ackerman, Dykman, and Gardner (1990) found that children with ADHD and dyslexia performed poorly on a test of phonologic sensitivity. Such findings support a language-based deficit for reading disability in these ADHD children with a co-occurring reading disability.

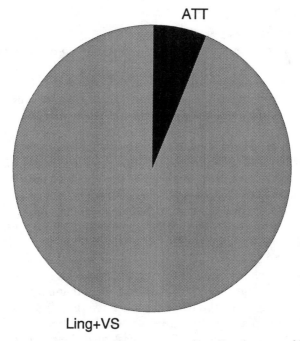

Figure 3.   Additional proportion of variance of reading (measured by silent reading comprehension) explained by attentional measures.

In contrast, other studies (McGee et al. 1989) found very few measures on which the ADHD and LD groups differed, results contrary to the notion that the two are discrete subgroups. In the McGee et al. study, criteria for selection of the reading disabled group were far different from those used in most studies, indexing as reading disabled all children whose reading performance was below the median of reading in the ADHD group. Most investigators employ an ability-achievement discrepancy or reading achievement below the 25th percentile. McGee et al.'s use of less impaired readers may have biased the findings of their study, producing results inconsistent with those of other investigators.

A recent report may reconcile these conflicting data. Thus, in a large cross-sectional study, Rowe and Rowe (1992) have demonstrated a reciprocal relationship between inattention and reading achievement. Their data indicate that problems with behavior may lead to reading difficulties and, conversely, that reading difficulties may result in behavior problems.

**IMPLICATIONS**

We suggest that the appreciation that learning disabilities and attention disorder are separate disorders that may co-occur in the same individual has important theoretical and clinical implications. From a theoretical perspective we should not be surprised that the proposed pathogenic mechanisms for each (ADHD and RD) are quite different, involving very different brain regions and mechanisms (see *Pathogenesis* section).

At a more clinical level, this conceptualization provides a rationale that drives both evaluation and intervention. Thus, in evaluating the child with school problems we need to consider both ADHD and LD (RD) as diagnostic possibilities, and as a consequence, we need reliable and valid measures for each. Our findings suggest that attentional mechanisms do, indeed, play a role in the reading process, particularly during the silent reading task, a procedure where the child is provided text and then told to read and answer the questions. Most school-based evaluations (e.g., tests in most academic subjects) involve just such a procedure, and it is this kind of task that may be quite difficult for the child with ADHD as well as a reading disability. We suggest that, when dealing with children who have both a reading disability and a co-occurring ADHD, professionals be aware of the influence of inattention on tests that use silent reading comprehension as a measure of reading ability. Other reading tasks, such as word reading, are less likely to be influenced by attentional factors and may provide an assessment of the child's reading that is less biased by any co-occurring inattention.

Any rational intervention should be tailored to the results of the diagnostic evaluation. For example, if we find that the child has primarily a reading disability, interventions focused on language, particularly phonological processing, should be incorporated into the treatment plan. Similarly, if the child's problems relate to ADHD, specific behavioral, environmental, and pharmacologic interventions used successfully in ADHD are most reasonable. For those children who are found to satisfy criteria for ADHD and RD, a rational treatment plan must incorporate interventions directed at both. Awareness that RD and ADHD represent two separate disorders provides for a more focused assessment for the possibility of each of these disorders and should result in more meaningful, appropriately targeted and, one hopes, more effective interventions.

**SUMMARY**

In this chapter we examined the interrelationships between ADHD and LD and proposed a conceptualization that although ADHD and learning disabilities frequently co-occur in the same child, each (ADHD and LD) is a separate problem. Beginning with the definition of each disorder, we reviewed the historical antecedents of ADHD and LD, examined the epidemiologic evidence relating ADHD and LD, and briefly reviewed current views of pathogenesis of RD, the most common of the learning disabilities. Using an example from one of our own studies as well as data from other investigations, we indicate that reading disability is characterized by linguistic deficits, primarily in phonological processing. In contrast, such linguistic deficits are not characteristic of ADHD, unless the attention disorder is associated with reading disability.

These findings support the conceptualization that reading disability and attention disorder represent separate diagnostic entities that frequently co-occur in the same individual. Such a conceptualization provides a rationale that drives both evaluation and intervention. In evaluating the child with school problems we need to consider both ADHD and LD as possibilities, and interventions must then be tailored to the particular diagnosis.

**REFERENCES**

Ackerman, P. T., Dykman, R. A., and Gardner, M. Y. 1990 ADD students with and without dyslexia differ in sensitivity to rhyme and alliteration. *Journal of Learning Disabilities* 23:279–83.

American Psychiatric Association. 1980. *Diagnostic and Statistical Manual of Mental Disorders*, third edition (DSM-III). Washington, DC: American Psychiatric Association.

American Psychiatric Association. 1987. *Diagnostic and Statistical Manual of Mental Disorders*, third edition, revised (DSM-III-R). Washington, DC: American Psychiatric Association.

American Psychiatric Association. 1991. *DSM-IV Options Book: Work in Progress*. Washington, DC: American Psychiatric Association. Task Force on DSM-IV.

August, G. J., and Garfinkel, B. D. 1990. Comorbidity of ADHD and reading disability among clinic-referred children. *Journal of Abnormal Child Psychology* 18:29–45.

Bax, U., and MacKeith, R. C. 1963. "Minimal brain damage"—A concept dysfunction. In *Minimal Cerebral Dysfunction*, ed. R. C. MacKeith and M. Bax. London: SIMP with Wm. Heinemann.

Bender, L. 1942. Post encephalitic behavior disorders in childhood. In *Encephalitis: A Clinical Study*, ed. J. B. Neal. New York: Grune & Stratton.

Benson, F. D. 1991. The role of frontal dysfunction in attention deficit hyperactivity disorder. *Journal of Child Neurology* 6:S9–S12.

Berk, R. A. 1984. Evaluation of current screening procedures. In *Screening and Diagnosis of Children with Learning Disabilities*. Springfield, IL: Charles C Thomas.

Brady, S. A., and Shankweiler, D. P., eds. 1991. *Phonological Processes in*

*Literacy: A Tribute to Isabelle Y. Liberman.* Hillsdale, NJ: Lawrence Erlbaum Associates.

Cantwell, D. P. 1978. Hyperactivity and antisocial behavior. *American Academy of Child Psychiatry* 17:252-62.

Caplan, D. 1992. *Structure, Processing and Disorders.* Cambridge, MA: MIT Press.

Clements, S. D. 1966. Minimal brain dysfunction in children.NINDB Mono-graph #3. U.S. Department of Health, Education and Welfare. Washington DC.

Clements, S. D., and Peters, J. E. 1962. Minimal brain dysfunctions in the school-aged child. *Archives of General Psychiatry* 6:185–87.

Colby, C. L. 1991. The neuroanatomy and neurophysiology of attention. *Journal of Child Neurology* 6:S90–S131.

Cone, T. E., and Wilson, L. R. 1981. Quantifying a severe discrepancy: A critical analysis. *Learning Disability Quarterly* 4:359–71.

Cooley, E. L., and Morris, R. D. 1990. Attention in children: A neuropsychologically based model for assessment. *Developmental Neuropsychology* 6:239–74.

Feighner, J. P., Robins, E., and Guze, S. B. 1972. Diagnostic criteria for use in psychiatric research. *Archives of General Psychiatry* 18:746–56.

Felton, R. H., Wood, F. B., Brown, I. S., Campbell, S. K., and Harter, M. R. 1987. Separate verbal memory and naming deficits in attention deficit disorder and reading disability. *Brain and Language* 31:171–84.

Fodor, J. A. 1983. *The Modularity of Mind.* Cambridge: MIT Press.

Frankenberger, W., and Fronzaglio, K. 1991. A review of states' criteria and procedures for identifying children with learning disabilities. *Journal of Learning Disabilities* 24:449–512.

Goldstein, K. 1936. Modification of behavior consequent to cerebral lesion. *Psychiatric Quarterly* 10:539–610.

Goswami, U., and Bryant, P. 1990. *Phonological Skills and Learning to Read.* U.K.: Lawrence Erlbaum.

Gough, P. B., Ehri, L. C., and Treiman, R., eds. 1992. *Reading Acquisition.* Hillsdale, NJ: Lawrence Erlbaum Associates.

Halperin, J. M., Gittelman, R., Klein, D. F., and Ruddel, R. G. 1984. Reading disabled hyperactive children: A distinct subgroup of attention deficit disorder with hyperactivity? *Journal of Abnormal Child Psychology* 12:1–14.

Heilman, K. M., Voeller, K. K. S., and Nadeau, S. E. 1991. A possible pathophysiologic substrate of attention deficit hyperactivity disorder. *Journal of Child Neurology* 6:S76–1.

Hohman, L. B. 1922. Post encephalitic behavior disorders in children. *Johns Hopkins Hospital Bulletin* 380:372–75.

Holborow, P., and Berry, P. 1986. A multinational, cross-cultural perspective on hyperactivity. *American Journal of Orthopsychiatry* 56:320–22.

Interagency Committee on Learning Disabilities. 1987. *Learning Disabilities: A Report to the U.S. Congress.* Washington, DC: U.S. Government Printing Office.

Kennard, M. A. 1960. Value of equivocal signs in neurologic diagnosis. *Neurology* 10:753–64.

Keogh, B. K. 1971. Hyperactivity and learning disorders: Review and speculation. *Exceptional Children* 38:101–9.

Kirk, S. A. 1962. *Educating Exceptional Children.* Boston: Houghton Mifflin.

LaBerge, D. 1990. Thalamic and cortical mechanisms of attention suggested by recent positron emission tomographic experiments. *Journal of Cognitive Neuroscience* 2:358–72.

Lahey, B., Pelham, W. E., Schaughency, E. A., Atkins, M. S., Murphy, H. A.,

Hynd, G., Russo, M., Hartdagen, S., and Lorys-Vernon, A. 1988. Dimensions and types of attention deficit disorder. *Journal of the American Academy of Child and Adolescent Psychiatry* 27:330–35.

Lahey, B. B., Stempniak, M., Robinson, E. J., and Tyroler, M. J. 1978. Hyperactivity and learning disabilities as independent dimensions of child behavior problems. *Journal of Abnormal Psychology* 87:333–40.

Lambert, N. M., and Sandoval, J. 1980. The prevalence of learning disabilities in a sample of children considered hyperactive. *Journal of Abnormal Child Psychology* 8:33–50.

Laufer, M., and Denhoff, E. 1957. Hyperkinetic behavior syndrome in children. *Journal of Pediatrics* 50:463–74.

Liberman, A. M., and Mattingly, I. G. 1989. A specialization for speech perception. *Science* 243:489–94.

Liberman, I. Y., Shankweiler, D., and Liberman, A. M. 1989. The alphabetic principle and learning to read. In *Phonology and Reading Disability, Solving the Reading Puzzle. International Academy for Research in Learning Disabilities Monograph Series*, Number 6, ed. D. Shankweiler and I. Y. Liberman. Ann Arbor: University of Michigan Press.

McGee, R., and Share, D. L. 1988. Attention deficit disorder-hyperactivity and academic failure: Which comes first and what should be treated? *Journal of the American Academy of Child and Adolescent Psychiatry* 27:318–25.

McGee, R., Williams, S., Moffitt, T., and Anderson, J. 1989. A comparison of 13-year-old boys with attention deficit and/or reading disorder on neuropsychological measures. *Journal of Abnormal Child Psychology* 17:37–53.

Meyer, A. 1904. The anatomical facts and clinical varieties of traumatic insanity. *American Journal of Insanity* 60:373–441.

Myers, P. I. and Hammill, D. D. 1982. *Learning Disabilities*. Austin, TX: PRO-ED.

Ojemann, G., Ojemann, J., Lettich, E., and Berger, M. 1989. Cortical language localization in left, dominant hemisphere. *Journal of Neurosurgery* 71:316–26.

Pennington, B. F. 1991. *Diagnosing Learning Disorders: A Neuropsychological Framework*. New York: Guilford Press.

Perfetti, C. A. 1991. Representations and awareness in the acquisition of reading competence. In *Learning to Read: Basic Research and Its Implications*, ed. L. Rieben and C. A. Perfetti. Hillsdale, NJ: Lawrence Erlbaum Associates.

Posner, M. 1988. Structures and functions of selective attention. In *Clinical Neuropsychology and Brain Function: Research, Measurement, and Practice*, ed. T. Boll and B. K. Bryant. Washington, DC: American Psychological Association.

Posner, M., and Petersen, S. E. 1990. The attention system of the human brain. *Annual Review of Neuroscience* 13:25–42.

Public Law 94-142. 1975. Education for All Handicapped Children Act, S.6, 94th Congress [Sec. 613(a) (4)] 1st Session, June 1975, Report No. 94-168.

Reynolds, C. R. 1984. Critical measurement issues in learning disabilities. *The Journal of Special Education* 18:451–76.

Rowe, K. J., and Rowe, K. S. 1992. The relationship between inattentiveness in the classroom and reading achievement (Part A): Methodological issues. *Journal of the American Academy of Child and Adolescent Psychiatry* 31:349–56.

Rutter, M. 1970. Psychological development—Predictions from infancy. *Journal of Child Psychology and Psychiatry* 11:49–62.

Safer, D. J., and Allen, R. D. 1976. *Hyperactive Children: Diagnosis and Management*. Baltimore: University Park Press.

Shaywitz, B. A., Shaywitz, S. E., and Fletcher, J. M. 1992. The Yale Center for the Study of Learning and Attention Disorders. *Learning Disabilities* 3:1–12.

Shaywitz, B. A., Shaywitz, S. E., Liberman, I. Y., Fletcher, J. M., Shankweiler, D. P., Duncan, J. S., Katz, L., Liberman, A. M., Francis, D. J., Dreyer, L. G., Crain, S., Brady, S., Fowler, A., Kier, L. E., Rosenfield, N. S., Gore, J. C., and Makuch, R. W. 1991. Neurolinguistic and biologic mechanisms in dyslexia. In *The Reading Brain: The Biological Basis of Dyslexia*, ed. D. D. Duane and D. B. Gray. Parkton, MD: York Press.

Shaywitz, S. E. 1986. Early recognition of vulnerability-EREV. Technical report to Connecticut State Department of Education.

Shaywitz, S. E., and Shaywitz, B. A. 1988. Attention deficit disorder: Current perspectives. In *Learning Disabilities: Proceedings of the National Conference*, eds. J. F. Kavanagh and T. J. Truss. Parkton, MD: York Press.

Silver, L. 1981. The relationship between learning disabilities, hyperactivity, distractibility, and behavioral problems. *Journal of the American Academy of Child Psychiatry* 20:385–97.

Still, G. F. 1902. The Coulstonian lectures on some abnormal physical conditions in children. *The Lancet* 1:1008–1012, 1077–1082, 1163–1168.

Strauss, A. A., and Lehtinen, L. E. 1947. *Psychopathology and Education in the Brain-Injured Child*. New York: Grune & Stratton.

Szatmari, P., Boyle, M., and Offord, D. R. 1989. ADDH and conduct disorder: Degree of diagnostic overlap and differences among correlates. *Journal of the American Academy of Child and Adolescent Psychiatry* 28:865–72.

Thorndike, R. L. 1963. *The Concepts of Over- and Under-Achievement*. New York: Bureau of Publications, Teachers College, Columbia University.

United States Office of Education. 1977. Assistance to states for education for handicapped children: Procedures for evaluating specific learning disabilities. 42:62082: Federal Register 1977.

Vellutino, F. R. 1991. Introduction to three studies on reading acquisition: Convergent findings on theoretical foundations of code-oriented versus whole-language approaches to reading instruction. *Journal of Educational Psychology* 83:437–43.

Wechsler, D. 1974. *Wechsler Intelligence Scale for Children–Revised*. New York: The Psychological Corporation.

Wender, P. H. 1971. *Minimal Brain Dysfunction in Children*. New York: John Wiley & Sons.

Werner, H., and Strauss, A. A. 1941. Pathology of the figure-background relation in the child. *Journal of Abnormal Social Psychology* 36:236–48.

Woodcock, R. W., and Johnson, M. B. 1977. *Woodcock-Johnson Psychoeducational Battery*. Hingham, MA: Teaching Resources Corporation.

Zametkin, A. J., Nordahl, T. E., Gross, M., King, A. C., Semple, W. E., Rumsey, J., Hamburger, S., and Cohen, R. M. 1990. Cerebral glucose metabolism in adults with hyperactivity of childhood onset. *New England Journal of Medicine* 323:1361–1366.

# Chapter • 7

# Early Detection
# of Learning Disability

*Bruce K. Shapiro*

Specific Learning Disability (SLD), and its associated dysfunctions, is the most common disorder of higher cortical function in childhood. It is the most common chronic neurologic disorder seen by primary care providers and the most common disorder seen by child psychiatrists, pediatric neurologists, and psychologists (Tibbles 1976; Wender 1971). Almost 2 million (43.6%) children enrolled in federally supported special education programs receive services for learning disability (U.S. Department of Education 1990). Learning disability is diagnosed in approximately 5% of all school children, but this *underestimates* the actual prevalence of these disorders because it does not account for those children who remain unidentified, who receive services under a different category, or those who drop out of school. The importance of SLD is attested to by the funding provided to its detection, diagnosis, and remediation by local, state, and federal governments; efforts by communities and private industry to address the lasting difficulties encountered by some with SLD; and federal research programs.

Learning disabilities have been recognized for approximately one hundred years, but the definition and classification of SLD is still evolving. The most commonly used definition of SLD is that of the federal government.

Specific Learning Disability means a disorder in one or more of the basic psychological processes involved in understanding or using language, written or spoken, which may manifest itself in an imperfect ability to listen, think, speak, read, write, spell, or to do mathematical calculations. The term includes such conditions as perceptual handicaps, brain injury, minimal brain dysfunction, dyslexia, and developmental aphasia. The term does not include children who have learning problems which are primarily the result of visual, hearing, or motor handicaps, of mental retardation, of emotional disturbance, or of environmental, cultural or economic disadvantage (Office of Education 1977, p. 65083).

This definition has three fundamental characteristics. The first characteristic delineates the boundaries of learning disabilities—(1) academic abilities as distinguished from more general retardation, (2) processes that give rise to deficient language, and (3) a central nervous system mechanism (basic psychologic processes). The second characteristic seeks to incorporate the many manifestations of SLD, which previously were viewed as independent entities, into a single construct. The last characteristic is the most misunderstood. The exclusion clauses were not meant to imply that SLD could not occur with other handicapping conditions, poverty, or social or cultural disadvantage, but were added for fiscal reasons: Congress already had programs that addressed these problems. Later efforts to clarify some aspects of the earlier definition emphasized the heterogeneity of SLD, recognized that it extended beyond childhood, and acknowledged co-morbidity among disorders (Hammill et al. 1987).

There are several immediate applications for the early identification of SLD: early intervention for learning problems, fuller understanding of the natural history of SLD, development of meaningful classification, determination of therapeutic efficacy, prevention of secondary emotional disorders, and evaluation of other interventions. Of these applications perhaps the most compelling justification for early identification is the provision of early intervention. Effective techniques of early identification serve to make early intervention more specific. Most attempts at early intervention are directed toward improving long-term academic performance, while some focus on prevention of secondary emotional and self-esteem problems. No attempt is made to distinguish children who require a nonacademic therapy during the preschool period from those whose therapy should be delayed until a specific readiness can be reached or from those who would benefit from nonspecific intervention. Similarly, criteria to distinguish children for whom therapy is unnecessary or ineffective are lacking.

## EARLY DETECTION BY EARLY DIAGNOSIS

Specific learning disability is not a unitary construct. SLD is a group of disorders of function arising from abnormal neural systems. The manifestations of SLD are protean and change across the age span. Therefore, early detection may be achieved in several different ways.

Most current attempts at early detection focus on early diagnosis of the disorder.

The heterogeneity of SLD is reflected in the number of different types of SLD that exist. SLD may exist in oral expression, listening comprehension, written expression, basic reading skills, reading comprehension, mathematics calculation, and/or mathematics reasoning; however, these disorders are not random. Most studies have found four syndromes of SLD: language-based disorder, visual-perceptual-motor diffuse dysfunction, and transitional syndromes.

Language-based disorders are characterized by disordered oral language, articulation errors, difficulty in decoding, relative sparing of arithmetic, written language problems secondary to oral language dysfunction, and attention deficit hyperactivity-like behaviors. By contrast the visual-perceptual-motor syndromes are characterized by normal language development, good basic reading, poor arithmetic skills (usually calculation), written language difficulties related to motor problems, and poor social comprehension. Children with diffuse dysfunction generally show depression of IQ and a variable pattern of disabilities, while transitional syndromes show isolated deficiencies (such as spelling).

Not all these disorders are apparent at the start of academic instruction. Most present when there is mismatch between the academic demands and the child's capacity. Table I lists the age-related presentations of SLD. When viewed from the context of "developmental failure," it is easy to understand why most attempts at early identification by diagnosis have focused on reading and why some types of SLD are not subject to "early" identification.

The use of a discrepancy-based model for the early diagnosis of reading disability has proved to be unsuccessful. In a study of 222 children who were followed prospectively from birth until age $7^1/2$ years, Shapiro and co-investigators (1990a), applying five commonly used formulas to define reading disability to the population, attempt-

Table I. Presentations of SLD

| | |
|---|---|
| Kindergarten | Motor problems (especially fine motor)<br>Sequencing difficulty<br>Language dysfunction (including articulation)<br>Hyperactivity/aggressiveness |
| Early primary | Decoding<br>Behavior |
| Late Primary | Underachievement<br>Writing<br>Reading comprehension<br>Behavior |
| Middle School | Behavior |

ed to assess how well the formulas discriminated the 22 children who received extra help in reading from the larger population. While the ability to classify normals correctly ranged from 74% to 99%, the ability to detect children receiving reading help ranged from 0 to 45%. This led the authors to conclude that, while a young child may obviously require additional educational assistance, he or she may not meet criteria for a severe discrepancy.

## PRESCHOOL DETECTION OF SLD

If one requires academic exposure to diagnose SLD, then the appropriate time for SLD detection is in the early school years. Other methods for the early identification of SLD that do not require academic underachievement include: detection of neurodevelopmental dysfunction, recognition of associated conditions, and historical risk factors. Such methods may be applicable to preschool children or infants.

Many preliteracy assessments of preschool children assess "readiness." This is an ill-defined concept that presumes the prerequisite skills for academic success are known, can be measured, and are predictive for the individual child. Kindergarten populations have been tested with such instruments as the Metropolitan Readiness Test, Denver Developmental Screening Test, Pediatric Examination of Educational Readiness, Florida Screening, and Wide Range Achievement Test, and, although some of these tests show modest predictability, the prediction of academic outcomes for individual children is not justified (Tramontana, Hooper, and Selzer 1988; Cadman et al. 1987; Blackman et al. 1992; Satz et al. 1978).

Perhaps the major reasons the broad-ranging tests of educational readiness may not succeed in identifying children with SLD can be deduced from the perspectives of application and measurement. The purpose of tests of educational readiness is to identify those children who lack readiness and therefore are likely to do poorly in early education. These tests do not distinguish children with specific deficits from those who have more general delays. Furthermore, the tests are composites, and relative strength in one area may result in underidentification of children with SLD. Finally, children with specific deficits, in contrast to global delays, may not have consistent rates of development or may compensate for their developmental deviations. Therefore a cross-sectional sampling may not adequately describe a longitudinal picture.

Little is known about the earlier development of items chosen for tests of educational readiness, and therefore we cannot tell if we are dealing with a continuous function, appropriate for measurement on an interval scale and prognostication, or a threshold function, which would require measurement in a categorical fashion and preclude prognostication for the individual when used in a cross-sectional fashion. An example of this is in the visual-motor area where the Bender Gestalt, Test of Visual Motor Integration, and Rey-Osterreith Complex Figure all have similar curves with the number of errors halving between 5 and 7½ years (figure 1). It is also possible that poor school performance and the measured deviation result from a common cause and the observed relationship is due to covariation. Finally, the relationship between measures of educational readiness and academic achievement is not always direct, as in the case of the preschool neurological examination.

Given the breadth of SLD it is impossible for "one size to fit all," so some have focused on specific areas of development, rather than trying to approach the problem of prediction broadly. Bashir and Scavuzzo (1992) posit at least three essential functions of language in school: (1) representation and analysis of knowledge and information; (2) facilitation of social relations and cultural membership; and (3) development of personal identity and the capacity for self-regulation of behavior. Language disorders have been noted to persist in approximately two-thirds of children (Aram, Ekelman, and Nation 1984; Garvey and Gordon 1973; Hall and Tomblin 1978; Strominger and Bashir 1977).

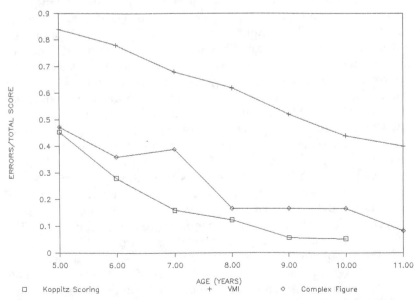

Figure 1. Curves depicting proportion of errors by age on three visual motor tests—Bender Gestalt (using Koppite scoring), Beerly Test of Visual Motor Integration (VMI), and Rey-Osterreith Complex Figure. Note similar curves for all three measures.

Approximately half of children with language disorders have persistent academic problems (Aram and Hall 1989). Resolution of problems by 5½ years was associated with a favorable prognosis for reading attainment (Bishop and Adams 1990). However, it is not clear whether a deficit in a specific language ability (e.g., phonological processing) or a general linguistic deficiency is more directly responsible for reading failure.

Studies of language development in early preschool and infancy would support a more general deficit. Delay in acquisition of phrases at age three was associated with poorer performance on a variety of academic, intellectual, and social measures throughout school and into early adulthood (Klackenberg 1980). In the Dunedin longitudinal study (Silva, Williams, and McGee 1987), between 58% and 67% of children with either comprehension or expressive delays at age 3 had a low IQ or a low reading score at ages 7, 9, and 11 (in contrast to 19% to 22% of the remainder of the sample). In the same study, between 71% and 86% of children with general language delay had a low IQ and/or reading difficulties across the three ages studied. While phonological production deficits were noted in 30-month olds who were later found to be dyslexic, syntactic differences more closely corresponded to the childrens' eventual outcomes (Scarborough 1990).

Relationships have also been noted between infant language development and later academic outcomes. Lyle (1970) noted an association between early language delay (as early as 6 to 24 months), articulatory difficulties (age 2½ to 4 years) and reading difficulty in the primary grades. In a study of normal development, Capute and co-workers (Shapiro et al. 1989) prospectively followed a cohort of infants from birth until age 7½ years and recorded early language and motor milestone attainment at each well-child visit through 2 years and performed a psychoeducational evaluation at discharge. Statistical modeling that captured the rate and sequence of development was employed instead of focusing on individual milestone attainment, and indices and gradients were developed to describe gross motor, receptive language, and expressive language development. Using data collected by age 2 years it was possible to predict correctly 78% of children who experienced reading delay at age 7½ while correctly classifying 74% of normals (Shapiro et al. 1990b).

Preschool children who exhibit motor dysfunction have been found to have later SLD (Gilberg 1992). These deficits are milder than those in cerebral palsy and may be more subtle in their presentations. Deficits in fine motor function may manifest themselves in difficulty with coloring, cutting, or writing. Mild abnormalities in tone or coordination frequently are manifested as clumsiness. Children who have experienced delayed motor development also are at risk for school dysfunction. In a report from the Collaborative Perinatal Project, 118 (of 229) who "lost" their diagnosis of cerebral palsy by seven years had higher frequencies of mental retardation, nonfebrile seizures, articulation defects, abnormal eye movements, and increased rates of immaturity and hyperactivity when compared to children who were never diagnosed as having cerebral palsy (Nelson and Ellenberg 1982). The Dunedin Multidisciplinary Child Development Study found that more than half of the children who walked after 18 months were later found to have low IQs or reading difficulties at age seven years (Silva, McGee, and Williams 1982). However, when looking at reading diffi- culties alone, the differences were not statistically different. The inabil- ity of late walking to predict academic achievement has been con- firmed by others (Shapiro et al. 1989).

Although preschool neurologic examination does not predict SLD well, the neonatal neurologic examination, alone and in conjunc- tion with later evaluations in the first year of life, has been associated with SLD. Prechtl (1965) serially evaluated children with agreement for all three examinations noted in 50% and concordance between the neonatal and later examinations in 75%. Rubin and Balow (1980) fol- lowed 1613 children who were examined at birth, 4 months, and 12 months. Children were grouped by the number of normal examina- tions during the first year. Significant intergroup differences were noted, with those in suspect groups exhibiting poorer performance (independent of social class and birth weight) on measures of intelli- gence, motor skills, language, and school achievement.

## ASSOCIATED DEFICITS

SLD is the functional manifestation of abnormal neurologic functions and consequently coexists with other disorders. As noted above, per- haps the most clear-cut relationships are those seen in children with disordered language (e.g., developmental language disorders, devel- opment dysphasias, central communication disorders). Associated dysfunctions are seen in areas that are less directly related to cogni- tive/academic function as in the case of motor function (e.g., develop- mental coordination disorder, minimal nervous system dysfunction, choreiform syndrome, clumsy child syndrome) or behavioral distur- bance (e.g., attention deficit hyperactivity disorder [ADHD], opposi- tional defiant disorder, conduct disorder, dysthymia, and depression).

The use of associated deficits to identify SLD would be warrant- ed if the following criteria could be met: (1) a close relationship with the associated disorder and SLD; (2) the associated disorder can be operationally defined in a fashion that would facilitate large-scale application; and (3) the age of presentation of the associated disorder is substantially younger than that of SLD. The second criterion would exclude the use of most motor deficits as proxy for SLD. The third criterion would rule out most of the behavioral disturbances with the exception of ADHD.

Hyperactivity is frequently associated with SLD. The prevalence of hyperactivity in children with SLD approximates 50% (Shaywitz and Shaywitz 1988). ADHD is a difficult diagnosis to establish in preschool children. This is in part due to the inability to discern pathologic inattentiveness and hyperactivity from that which is normally seen in preschoolers. Diagnosis is further complicated by the transient nature of inattentiveness and hyperactivity seen in preschoolers. Therefore, it has been suggested that the DSM-III-R criteria for diagnosis be altered to require that problems be present for 12 months rather than 6 (Barkley 1990).

Approximately half of hyperactive 3-year olds maintain their hyperactivity and approximately one third are reading disabled at age 15 (McGee et al. 1991). However, simply screening preschoolers for ADHD is not sufficient. Some authors have reported almost a one-to-one correspondence between ADHD and SLD, whereas others have suggested that SLD does not occur any more frequently in ADHD than in the general population (cf Shaywitz and Shaywitz 1988). On the other hand, milder ADHD may be underidentified because preschoolers lack exposure to the stress of formal school instruction. If these assertions are shown to be true for the general population, then preschool screening using ADHD alone may be precluded by too high a rate of misclassification—both under- and over-identification. Whether using factors that have been associated with persistence of hyperactive behavior and less favorable outcomes, such as language disorder or aggressive behavior (Campbell and Ewing 1990; Palfrey et al. 1985), improved predictive validity is a subject for future investigation.

## HISTORICAL RISK

Historical factors may be used to indicate that a child is at greater or lesser risk of having a condition. Risk is a statistical concept and not a diagnosis. Most children do not have the condition that they are "at risk" of having. Ascertainment of risk allows for increased surveillance and may aid early identification. However, the costs of tracking and monitoring large populations of at-risk children may diminish the effective funding of services for children with established diagnoses.

Factors obtained from birth certificates such as race and level of maternal education may be used to predict school failure. While statistically significantly related to the outcome, many other factors seem to influence whether children succeed in school, as evidenced by the substantial residual variance (Ramey et al. 1978). Other factors related to prenatal, natal, or postnatal factors have been associated with SLD, but when controlled studies have not confirmed such associations. In a recent study of eight-year olds with extremely low birthweight (501–1000 grams) the prevalence of SLD was 26%, while that of controls matched for age, sex, and social class was 19% (Saigal et al. 1990).

## LOW ORDER PROCESSING

Basic perceptual processing can be distinguished from higher order processing by the choice of stimuli (clicks, flashes, or discrete word stimuli) and measures (frequency, amplitude, temporal, integration, or recall). It is presumed that basic perceptual processing is more reflective of primary brain functions and may be independent of experience and cognition. If such processing were found to be a necessary condition for SLD, then it may be possible to detect the neural dysfunction before academic experience.

Children with language impairment have been found to be impaired in their ability to respond correctly to nonverbal sensory information that enters the nervous system quickly and the amount of time required for sensory information processing is substantially greater than in normal children (cf Tallal 1988). Six variables, when used in combination, were found to discriminate correctly between language-impaired and normally developing children 98% of the time (Tallal, Stark, and Mellits 1985). These variables were related to producing or perceiving basic sensory information presented over a short period of time and included tactile, speech, nonverbal cross-modal integration, and through verbal and nonverbal visual information. Similar temporal deficits have been noted in language impaired children for nonverbal motor planning (Johnston et al. 1981). Children with reading impairment who also showed language deficits also demonstrated perceptual temporal impairment (Tallal 1980a, b).

Presently measures of basic processing must be viewed as "potentially useful" in the early identification of SLD. For potential to be translated into reality it is necessary to: (1) develop tools that can be easily applied to large numbers of preschool children; (2) determine the classification characteristics of these measures; (3) delineate subgroups who will not be identified by these approaches; and (4) establish whether the degree of deficit is related to the degree of academic underachievement (predictive validity). Obtaining the results will require multisite, longitudinal study.

## PHYSIOLOGIC MEASURES

Physiologic measures include such techniques as electrophysiologic assessments, regional cerebral blood flows, and positron emission tomography (PET). Each of these techniques yields information about brain function in a more direct fashion than more traditional psycho-education approaches. Despite the excitement engendered by these techniques, they should be subjected to the same scrutiny as other assessment instruments. Studies that address standardization, reliability, validity (predictive and concurrent), and classification issues are critical before widespread application of these measures.

Physiologic measures have additional limitations. Some of the measures (e.g., positron emission tomography or regional cerebral blood flow), are quite good at localizing the site of the altered brain function (spatial resolution); however, they require repetitive performance of tasks and, therefore, they lack the ability to be measured in "real" time (temporal resolution) that the electrophysiologic measures possess. Specialized equipment, radiation, and need for cooperation may prove limiting for application of these techniques to preschool populations.

## ELECTROPHYSIOLOGIC MEASURES

Electroencephalography (EEG) has not been found useful to distinguish children with dyslexia. The type of EEG pattern and the presence of epileptiform activity have not been helpful in classifying dyslexics. Despite the lack of discriminatory ability, EEG abnormalities have been associated with inadequate visual perception, abnormal stereopsis, oculomotor disorders, visual disorders, decreased photic responses, short attention, abnormal ideation, delayed speech and motor development, and deafness, among other disorders of higher cognitive function (cf Hughes 1985).

While standard application of EEG technology is limited for detecting SLD, other investigators have attempted to assess brain function by evaluating brain responses to a stimulus. Studies of visual evoked responses have reported inconsistent findings that can be attributed, at least in part, to differences in methodology and populations. Auditory evoked potentials (AEPs) are following the lead of visual evoked responses. However, AEPs are enjoying considerable clinical attention as a means of defining central auditory processing disorders. Event-related potentials (ERPs) refer to the very late responses that depend upon the informational content of the stimulus or the psychological state of the patient. Although preliminary, reports have suggested different modes of processing task-relevant information with dyslexics likely to be less efficient and less effective than with normals (Lovrich and Stamm 1983). Evoked responses are subject to modification based on the attention of the subject. Thus, their ability to provide early identification may be limited, especially in preschool children with ADHD.

Perhaps the most excitement in the diagnosis of higher cortical function disorders by electrophysiologic methods has resulted from computer-assisted analysis of EEG results. Neurometrics seeks to gather data sensitive to sensory, perceptual, and cognitive functions and to extract and quantify critical features that extend more traditional psychological and clinical classifications (John et al. 1988). Normative data are available for children as young as 6 years and are derived from 60 seconds of artifact-free EEG. The results are said to be reliable, objective, and independent of race, sex, culture, or socioeconomic status (Prichep et al. 1983). However, the ability of the method to discern "pure" dyslexia has been challenged (Yingling et al. 1986).

Brain electrical activity mapping (BEAM) is another computer-assisted method of EEG analysis that uses EEG and evoked potential data recorded from multiple electrodes to develop a computer-derived topographic map. Duffy and co-workers (1980a) developed rules to distinguish boys with dyslexia from normals. They then applied the rules to a larger group of children with 80% to 90% accuracy (Duffy et al. 1980b). Unfortunately, a longitudinal study that included BEAM analysis at 6 years did not replicate the earlier studies of 9 to 10.7 year olds (Badian et al. 1990).

## Blood Flow Studies

Regional blood flow studies use xenon 133 inhalation techniques to assess function in localized areas of brain while a subject performs various tasks. Minimal differences were noted for dyslexic and normal groups, but asymmetric findings were seen when one hemisphere was compared to the other on a semantic classification task, and decreased anteroposterior differences were seen on another task (Rumsey et al. 1987). Flowers and co-workers (1991), in a study of adults, found that childhood reading ability was inversely correlated with focal activation in the left temporoparietal lobe, although this was not related to adult reading capacity. The differences between studies were attributed to patient selection and sample size characteristics. Positron emission tomography studies have found significant differences between dyslexics who also had a first degree relative with reading disability and normals in normalized regional metabolic values in prefrontal cortex and in the lingual (inferior) region of the occipital lobe (Gross-Glenn et al. 1991).

## ANATOMIC APPROACHES

Anatomic approaches to SLD began as a result of neuropathologic studies of dyslexia. Later studies employed computerized axial tomography to assess hemispheric symmetries, while subsequent studies have used magnetic resonance imaging techniques to target specific areas (morphometric analysis) as well as assess hemispheric differences. In one study (Hynd et al. 1990) only 10% of dyslexic subjects showed left greater than right pattern of plana asymmetry, while 70% of normal and ADHD children evidenced this finding. While these differences seem large, if applied to a population of 100 children and a 5% prevalence of dyslexia is assumed, 29 would be misclassified by missing 11% of dyslexics and over calling 30% of normals: 57 normals would be misclassified for each dyslexic correctly identified. MRI blood flow studies may prove of use in defining structure-function relationships in children because radioisotopes and intra-arterial punctures used for regional blood flow studies are not required for this method (Filipek and Kennedy 1991). Imaging studies have the advantage of being applied to in vivo populations but are limited in discerning the finer abnormalities of structure that were noted in the neuropathologic studies (Galaburda et al. 1985).

## GENETIC APPROACHES

SLD has been noted to run in families and a genetic etiology has been posited. While it is likely that a single gene does not explain the full spectrum of SLD, attempts at gene identification are hampered by heterogeneity of the population. It is likely that heterogeneity exists even among families that evidence autosomal dominant transmission (Pennington et al. 1991). Methods to obtain homogeneous populations have included twin studies, family studies, pedigree studies, segregation analysis, neurophysiologic studies, neuropsychologic assessments, and genetic linkage analysis (Childs and Finucci 1983). The detection of specific genes for SLD would permit diagnosis that is independent of age and behavioral or laboratory test performance. Unfortunately, linkage studies have not yielded a clearly confirmed linkage (Lubs et al. 1991).

## CODA

Attempts at the early identification of SLD are justified because they are felt to facilitate early intervention. However, efforts at early identification must proceed with caution. Identification of children in the presymptomatic state may alter the parent-child relationship and lead to stigmatization by others or the child. Misclassification may result in delayed provision of services for the child with SLD who was missed by early identification attempts or parental anxiety or lowered expectations in those who were incorrectly deemed "SLD." Finally, early identification without a coexisting policy that provides therapy is pointless.

Current methods of identification are based on test performance, hypothetical mechanisms of dysfunction, and associated dysfunctions. Although group associations are found, the evidence that these techniques can be applied to individual children is lacking. It is unlikely that all children with SLD can be identified using these methods.

Newer techniques to detect neural dysfunction must be regarded as still being developed. They must demonstrate the validity and reliability characteristics that are required of other measures. They must be applicable to large populations of preschool children and, possibly, infants. Finally, the neural dysfunction that is detected must be predictive of later functional outcomes for individual children.

Early identification seeks to make possible improvement in the quality of life of those with SLD by direct intervention; but the outcome of this disorder is not known. Given the prevalence of SLD, a significant public health problem would exist if only a small percentage of people with SLD experience an unfavorable outcome. Similarly, small positive effects on outcome would be expected to result in large gains. Such effects may result from nonspecific factors associated with early identification and monitoring, and this should be studied as well as the efficacy of the identification process.

Early intervention should be on the same scientific base as early identification. Current studies of the natural history of SLD are inconclusive and factors that favorably influence outcome or prognosticate poor outcomes are yet to be delineated. All outcomes have been reported: some children do well and some adapt. Adverse outcomes have been reported in academic and cognitive development, mental health problems, and social functioning (cf reviews by Bruck 1987; Horn, O'Donnell, and Vitulano 1983; Schonhaut and Satz 1983; Spreen 1988). Thus, consideration of interventions should not be limited to remedial reading or mathematics, but should address the continuum of disordered higher cortical and neurobehavioral dysfunctions.

## REFERENCES

Aram, D. M., and Hall, N. E. 1989. Longitudinal follow-up of children with preschool communication disorders: Treatment implications. *School Psychology Review* 18:407–501.

Aram, D. M., Ekelman, B. L., and Nation, J. E. 1984. Preschoolers with language disorders: 10 years later. *Journal of Speech and Hearing Research* 27:232–44.

Badian, N. A. , McAnulty, G. B., Duffy, F. H., and Als, H. 1990. Prediction of dyslexia in kindergarten boys. *Annals of Dyslexia* 40:152–69.

Barkley, R. 1990. *Attention Deficit Hyperactivity Disorder: A Handbook for Diagnosis and Treatment.* New York: Guilford Press.

Bashir, A. S., and Scavuzzo, A. 1992. Children with language disorders: Natural history and academic success. *Journal of Learning Disabilities* 25: 53–65.

Bishop, D. V. M., and Adams, C. 1990. Prospective study of the relationship between specific language impairment, phonological disorders and reading retardation. *Journal of Child Psychology and Psychiatry* 31:1027–1050.

Blackman, J. A., Bretthauer, J., Gressard, R. P., and Nelson, R. P. 1992. Predictive validity of a preschool neurodevelopmental instrument. *Journal of Developmental and Behavioral Pediatrics* 13:112–17.

Bruck, M. 1987. The adult outcomes of children with learning disabilities. *Annals of Dyslexia* 37:252–63.

Cadman, D., Chambers, L. W., Walter, S. D., Ferguson, R., Johnston, N., and McNamee, Jr. 1987. Evaluation of public health preschool child development screening: The process and outcomes of a community program. *American Journal of Public Health* 77:45–51.

Campbell, S. B., and Ewing, L. J. 1990. Follow-up of hard-to-manage preschoolers: Adjustment at age 9 and prediction of continuing symptoms. *Journal of Child Psychology and Psychiatry* 31:871–89.

Childs, B., and Finucci, J. M. Genetics, epidemiology, and specific reading disability. In *Developmental Neuropsychiatry*, ed. M. Rutter. New York: Guilford Press.

Duffy, F. H., Denckla, M. B., Bartels, P. H., and Sandini, G. 1980a. Dyslexia: Regional differences in brain electrical activity by topographic mapping. *Annals of Neurology* 7:412–20.

Duffy, F. H., Denckla, M. B., Bartels, P. H., Sandini, G., and Kiessling, L. S. 1980b. Dyslexia: Automated diagnosis by computerized classification of brain electrical activity. *Annals of Neurology* 7:421–28.

Filipek, P. A., and Kennedy, D. N. 1991. Magnetic resonance imaging: Its role in the developmental disorders. In *The Reading Brain: The Biological Basis of Dyslexia*, eds. D. D. Duane and D. B. Gray. Parkton, MD: York Press.

Flowers, D. L., Wood, F. B., and Naylor, C. E. 1991. Regional cerebral blood flow correlates of language processes in reading disability. *Archives of Neurology* 48:637–43.

Galaburda, A. M., Sherman, G. F., Rosen, G. D., Aboitz, F., and Geschwind, N. 1985. Developmental dyslexia: Four consecutive cases with cortical anomalies. *Annals of Neurology* 18:222–33.

Garvey, M., and Gordon, N. 1973. A follow-up study of children with disorders of speech. *British Journal of Disorders of Communication* 8:17–28.

Gilberg, C. 1992. Deficits in attention, motor control and perception and other syndromes attributed to minimal brain dysfunction. In *Diseases of the Nervous System in Childhood*, ed. J. Aicardi. London: MacKeith Press.

Gross-Glenn, K., Duara, R., Barker, W. W., Lowenstein, D., Chang, J. Y., Yoshii, F., Apicella, A. M., Pascal, S., Boothe, T., Sevush, S., Jallad, B. J., Novoa, L., and Lubs, H. A. 1991. Positron emission tomographic studies during serial word-reading by normal and dyslexic adults. *Journal of Clinical and Experimental Neuropsychology* 13:531–44.

Hall, P., and Tomblin, B. 1978. A follow-up study of children with articulation and language disorders. *Journal of Speech and Hearing Disorders* 43:227–41.

Hammill, D. D., Leigh, J., McNutt, G., and Larsen, S. 1987. A new definition of learning disabilities. *Journal of Learning Disabilities* 21:109.

Horn, W. F., O'Donnell, J. P., and Vitulano, L. A. 1983. Long-term follow-up studies of learning-disabled persons. *Journal of Learning Disabilities* 16: 542–55.

Hughes, J. R. 1985. Evaluation of electrophysiological studies of dyslexia. In *Biobehavioral Measures of Dyslexia*, eds. D. Gray and J. Kavanagh. Parkton, MD: York Press.

Hynd, G. W., Semrud-Clikeman, M., Lorys, A. R., Novey, E. S., and Eliopulos, D. 1990. Brain morphology in developmental dyslexia and attention deficit disorder/hyperactivity. *Archives of Neurology* 47:919–26.

John, E. R., Prichep, L. S., Fridman, J., and Easton, P. 1988. Neurometrics: Computer-assisted differential diagnosis of brain dysfunctions. *Science* 239:162–69.

Johnston, R. B., Stark, R. E., Mellits, E. D., and Tallal, P. 1981. Neurological status of language impaired and normal children. *Annals of Neurology* 10: 159–63.

Klackenberg, G. 1980. What happens to children with retarded speech at 3? *Acta Paediatrica Scandinavica* 69:681–85.

Lovrich, D., and Stamm, J. S. 1983. Event related potential and behavior correlates of attention in reading retardation. *Journal Clinical Neuropsychology* 5:13–37.

Lubs., H., Duara, R., Levin, B., Jallad, B., Lubs, M. L., Rabin, M., Kushch, A., and Gross-Glenn, K. 1991. Dyslexia subtypes: Genetics, behavior, and brain imaging. In *The Reading Brain: The Biological Basis of Dyslexia*, eds. D. D. Duane and D. B. Gray. Parkton, MD: York Press.

Lyle, J. G. 1970. Certain antenatal, perinatal, and developmental variables and reading retardation in middle class boys. *Child Development* 41:481–91.

McGee, R., Partridge, F., Williams, S., and Silva, P. A. 1991. A twelve-year follow-up of preschool hyperactive children. *Journal of the American Academy of Child and Adolescent Psychiatry*. 30:224–32.

Nelson, K. B., and Ellenberg, J. H. 1982. Children who "outgrew" cerebral palsy. *Pediatrics* 69:529–36.

Office of Education. 1977. Assistance to states for education of handicapped children: Procedures for evaluating specific learning disability. *Federal Register* 42:65083.

Palfrey, J. S., Levine, M. D., Walker, D. K., and Sullivan, M. 1985. The emergence of attention deficits in early childhood: A prospective study. *Journal of Developmental and Behavioral Pediatrics* 6:339–48.

Pennington, B. F., Gilger, J. W., Pauls, D., Smith, S. A., Smith, S. D., and DeFries, J. C. 1991. Evidence for major gene transmission of developmental dyslexia. *Journal of the American Medical Association* 266:1527–34.

Prechtl, H. 1965. Prognostic value of neurological signs in the newborn. *Proceedings of the Royal Society of Medicine* 53:3–4.

Prichep, L., John, E. R., Ahn, H., and Kaye, H. 1983. Neurometrics: Quantitative evaluation of brain dysfunction in children. In *Developmental Neuropsychiatry*, ed. M. Rutter. New York: Guilford Press.

Ramey, C., Stedman, D., Borders-Patterson, A., and Mengel, W. 1978. Predicting school failure from information available at birth. *American Journal of Mental Deficiency* 82:525–34.

Rubin, R., and Balow, B. 1980. Infant neurological abnormalities as indicators of cognitive impairment. *Developmental Medicine and Child Neurology* 22:336–43.

Rumsey, J. M., Berman, K. F., Denckla, M. B., Hamburger, S. D., Kruesi, M. J., and Weinberger, D. R. 1987. Regional cerebral blood flow in severe developmental dyslexia. *Archives of Neurology* 44:1144–49.

Saigal, S., Szatmari, P., Rosenbaum, P., King, S., and Campbell, D. 1990. Learning disabilities (LATE) and school problems in a regional cohort of extremely low birthweight (ELBW) children: A comparison with matched controls. *Pediatric Research* 27:254A.

Satz, P., Taylor, H. G., Friel, J., and Fletcher, J. 1978. Some developmental and predictive precursors of reading disabilities. In *Dyslexia*, eds. A. L. Benton and D. Pearl. New York: Oxford University Press.

Scarborough, H. S. 1990. Very early language deficits in dyslexic children. *Child Development* 61:1728–43.

Schonhaut, S., and Satz, P. 1983. Prognosis for children with learning disabilities: A review of follow-up studies. In *Developmental Neuropsychiatry*, ed. M. Rutter. New York: Guilford Press.

Shapiro, B. K., Palmer, F. B., Antell, S., Bilker, S., Ross, A., and Capute, A. J. 1989. Neurodevelopmental precursors of learning disability. In *Proceedings from the 1988 Tri-regional Conference on Completed MCH Research*. Washington, DC: NCEMCH.

Shapiro, B. K., Palmer, F. B., Antell, S. E., Bilker, S., Ross, A., and Capute, A. J. 1990a. Detection of young children in need of reading help: Evaluation of specific reading disability formulas. *Clinical Pediatrics* 29:206–213.

Shapiro, B. K., Palmer, F. B., Antell, S., Bilker, S., Ross, A., and Capute, A. J. 1990b. Precursors of reading delay: Neurodevelopmental milestones. *Pediatrics* 85:416–20.

Shaywitz, S. E., and Shaywitz, B. A. 1988. Hyperactivity/attention deficits. In *Learning Disabilities: Proceedings of the National Conference*, eds. J. F. Kavanagh and T. J. Truss. Parkton, MD: York Press.

Silva, P. A., McGee, R., and Williams, S. 1982. The predictive significance of slow walking and slow talking: A report from the Dunedin Multidisciplinary Child Development Study. *British Journal of Disorders of Communication* 17:133–39.

Silva, P. A., Williams, S., and McGee, R. 1987. A longitudinal study of children with developmental language delay at age three: Later intelligence, reading and behaviour problems. *Developmental Medicine and Child Neurology* 29:630–40.

Spreen, O. 1988. Prognosis of learning disability. *Journal of Consulting and Clinical Psychiatry* 56:836–42.

Strominger, A. Z., and Bashir, A. S. 1977. A nine year follow-up of language disordered children. Paper presented at the meeting of the American Speech and Hearing Association, Chicago, November.

Tallal, P. 1980a. Auditory temporal perception, phonics and reading disabilities in children. *Brain and Language* 9:182–98.

Tallal, P. 1980b. Language and reading: Some perceptual prerequisites. *Bulletin of The Orton Society* 30:170–78.

Tallal, P. 1988. Developmental language disorders. In *Learning Disabilities: Proceedings of the National Conference*, eds. J. F. Kavanagh and T. J. Truss. Parkton, MD: York Press.

Tallal, P., Stark, R. E., and Mellits, D. 1985. Identification of language-impaired children on the basis of rapid perception and production skills. *Brain and Language* 25:314–22.

Tibbles, J. A. R. 1976. The functions and the training of a pediatric neurologist. *Developmental Medicine and Child Neurology* 18:167–72.

Tramontana, M., Hooper, S. R., and Selzer, S. C. 1988. Research on the preschool prediction of later academic achievement: A review. *Developmental Review* 8:89–146.

Wender, P. 1971. *Minimal Brain Dysfunction in Children*. New York: John Wiley & Sons.

U.S. Department of Education. 1990. *Digest of Educational Statistics*. Washington, DC: National Center for Educational Statistics (NCES-91-660).

Yingling, C. D., Gallin, D., Fein, G., Peltzman, D., and Davenport, L. 1986. Neurometrics does not detect 'pure' dyslexia. *Electroencephalography and Clinical Neurophysiology* 63:426–30.

# Chapter • 8

# The Role of Language in Learning Disabilities

*Elisabeth H. Wiig*

### PERSPECTIVES OF LANGUAGE-LEARNING DISABILITIES

The nature and characteristics of language disorders in learning disabilities (LLD) have received extensive attention in the last decades. Language disorders are highly prevalent (70% to 80%) among children and adolescents with diagnosed learning disabilities. The chronicity and changing nature of the disorders as a function of age, academic, professional or vocational, and social demands have received attention. The broad scope of language deficits and their implications across the life span have also been recognized.

### Assessment Perspectives

Speech-language pathologists and special educators have gained acumen in using norm-referenced tests to identify language-learning disabilities, determine the nature and degree of the deficits, identify areas of strengths and weaknesses, and determine eligibility and needs for services (Wiig and Secord 1991). The field has also extended traditional assessments to include criterion-referenced, portfolio, ecological, and ethnographic evaluation to gain a broader view of the dynamics of the disorders (Damico 1992; Wiig 1990; Wiig and Secord in press).

Language disorder syndromes associated with learning disabilities persist into adolescence and adulthood (Bashir and Scavuzzo 1992; Wiig 1989). Students with language-learning disabilities do not catch up. It concurs that the language and communication deficits persist and emerge in new forms with changes in academic and social demands. The students affected often reach a plateau or stagnate in development at pre-adolescent levels when appropriate intervention is not provided (Wiig and Freedman 1992). Language-learning disabilities occur in varying degrees of severity and in different patterns (receptive-expressive, primarily receptive, primarily expressive). Single-factor norm-referenced measures may suggest that LLD represents the lower end of a normal distribution of language ability, but this may be an artifact. Qualitative differences from normal developmental trajectories emerge on closer examination. They emerge when evaluations are broad in scope, multifactored, account for measurement error by relying on confidence intervals rather than single scores, and are sensitive to linguistic or metalinguistic transitions from skill to strategy use in all areas of communication.

### Intervention Perspectives

Speech-language pathologists and special educators have embraced new perspectives and paradigms for providing language intervention across the educational life span. The predominant perspectives for language intervention are now collaborative, contextual-pragmatic, curriculum-related, and strategy-based (Secord 1989; Secord and Wiig 1991; Wiig 1989). In contrast, former intervention perspectives were generally clinical, linguistic skill-based, and developmentally based (Wiig and Semel 1984).

Professionals increasingly take a holistic perspective on the nature and implications of language disorders in learning disabilities and apply this perspective to intervention (Wiig and McCracken 1992; Wiig and Freedman 1993). The holistic perspective suggests that there is inter-relatedness among language, cognition, and affect and that all processes develop within a social context (Bruner 1973; Luria 1980; Vygotsky 1962).

### WORD AND CONCEPT KNOWLEDGE

Vocabulary and word knowledge provide an excellent thermometer for cognitive and linguistic growth and development throughout the school years. Research indicates that vocabulary (word knowledge) is the best single predictor of reading achievement and of life-time learning potential (McKeown and Curtis 1987). A glimpse at the developmental trajectory can explain why this may be so.

### Development and Deficits

During the early years, a child's world knowledge translates into word knowledge (Crais 1990). A child develops spontaneous concepts from reflections about everyday experiences, events, and life (Rieber and Carton 1987). During the school years, scientific concepts are developed. They are defined logically and originate in the structured, specialized activities of education and classroom instruction. During the middle and late school years, we observe that a student's word knowledge translates into world knowledge.

Studies of receptive vocabulary (knowledge of references for content words) in children with learning disabilities suggest that they acquire spontaneous concepts adequately. We find deficits in word knowledge when we explore beyond the limits of referential word knowledge (receptive vocabulary) (Wiig and Freedman 1993; Wiig and Secord 1992). On probing word knowledge informally in a group of adolescents with LD, Vygotsky (1962) found they had developed "pseudoconcepts" for many words. For example, several students with LD argued that there was no such thing as a year 0 "because zero means nothing." As a result, they were unable to deal with historical time, differences in historical-religious time references and calendars, or the concept that time lines are arbitrary.

Formal research with the recent *Test of Word Knowledge* (Wiig and Secord 1992), which goes beyond receptive vocabulary, indicates that deficits in word and concept knowledge emerge as tasks require higher level, abstract word and concept knowledge. Deficits generally occur in the knowledge of meaning relationships among words (word definitions, word opposites, synonyms) and of metalinguistic aspects of meaning (multiple contexts and meanings, figurative usage, conjunctions, and transition words). The nature of the deficits suggest that students with language-learning disabilities approach the task of acquiring new words and concepts from a holistic rather than an analytic perspective (McKeown and Curtis 1987).

### Intervention

The types of deficits in word and concept knowledge observed among students with language-learning disabilities negatively influence listening, speaking, reading, and writing. These students tend to be concrete in speaking, writing, and thinking and often show a plateau at Grades 4 and 5 in literacy and reading comprehension. Fortunately, word and concept knowledge can be developed collaboratively in the classroom setting across the curriculum. We have observed significant gains on a broad norm-referenced language test in all aspects of language functioning (listening, speaking, reading, writing, vocabulary, grammar) after classroom-based, curriculum-integrated, thematic-holistic intervention (Wiig, Freedman, and Secord 1992). The intervention focused on developing word and concept knowledge in an analytic approach. It included comparing and contrasting semantic features in words, developing semantic word webs and thematic-conceptual webs, building semantic networks, and providing a contextual framework for learning (Wiig and Freedman 1992).

Intervention that integrates meaning and structure in a thematic-holistic approach can result in significant gains in syntactic, as well as semantic, aspects of language and communication in pre-adolescent and adolescent students with LLD (Wiig and Freeman in press; Wiig, Freedman, and Secord 1992). In this approach, thematic units were designed collaboratively by a special education teacher, an LD specialist, and a speech-language pathologist. The units responded to curriculum requirements, focused on key concepts and vocabulary, integrated listening, speaking, reading, and writing, and developed relevant study and social skills. For example, when the regular curriculum focused on media and communication, the thematic-holistic units designed for junior-high students with learning disabilities developed knowledge of preconcepts and advanced concepts in activities that focused on, among others: (1) the human senses and communication; (2) modes and modalities; (3) tools and equipment; (4) codes, symbols, and languages; (5) communication functions, intentions, and conventions; and (6) media, audiences, purposes, and effects.

## LINGUISTIC RULE KNOWLEDGE

Words are the central elements in the social system of communication. However, linguistic rules (morphology and syntax) add structure and predictability to our messages and to communication in context. Deficits in acquiring and using basic rules for word inflection (e.g., noun plural, past tense) and derivation (e.g., noun, adverb) can be observed predictably in students with LLD in the preschool and early elementary school years (Semel, Wiig, and Secord 1987; Wiig and Semel 1984; Wiig, Secord, and Semel 1992).

In the middle and late school years, deficits in acquiring and using rules for complex sentences (e.g., subordination of clauses, relative clauses) tend to stand out (Semel, Wiig, and Secord 1987; Wiig and Secord 1992). The structural linguistic deficits associated with LLD have been related to central auditory processing, auditory and working memory, and rule-learning deficits, for example. On one norm-referenced language test the best discriminators of LLD versus non-LLD were: (1) oral directions and knowledge of word formation rules (morphology) for ages 5 to 7 and (2) sentence formulation and sentence recall for ages 8 to 12 (Semel, Wiig, and Secord 1987). Higher level syntactic rule learning (transformational grammar) depends heavily on inductive reasoning abilities. The problems in the acquisition and use of complex sentences can, therefore, be related to higher level difficulties, as well as to auditory processing and memory deficits. Among them are difficulties in recognizing and abstracting patterns in complex linguistic stimuli, and integrating the structural rules within a pragmatic system for how language is used in context.

Limitations in using the structural rules for English become evident when a structured, multidimensional assessment profile[1] is developed in portfolio evaluation (Wiig, Sherbenou, and Hresko in progress). When we assign and evaluate the performance on multidimensional, language-based tasks, such as writing a "Once upon a time..." story, giving an oral report, or writing an essay, deficits in linguistic skills (morphology and syntax) generally stand out. The performance levels for *use of skills or mechanics* tend to be unacceptable. With pre-adolescents and adolescents with LLD, intervention that integrates meaning and structure in a thematic-holistic approach can, as indicated earlier, result in significant gains in syntactic, as well as semantic, aspects of language and communication (Wiig and Freedman 1993).

## COMMUNICATION STRATEGIES AND PRAGMATICS

### Communication as Game

Mature communication can be likened to game playing. Speakers or writers must adhere to principles and maxims for the quantity and quality of communication. They must respond to the controlling variables for when, what, and how to communicate. Among these variables are the participants, settings, media, topics, and objectives. They must take the affective and conceptual perspective of a listener or reader and follow accepted underlying schema for discourse, narrative, or written communication. They must also use stored linguistic knowledge to formulate messages with appropriate social register (politeness and style), attenuation (softening and indirectness), or amplification (emphasis and directness). Communication, whether by speaking or writing, involves risky decision making (Gilhooly 1988),

---

[1]Portfolio assessment is commonly associated with the whole language approach to teaching. It uses a global, holistic approach to evaluate students' work samples. The assessment approach can be focused to identify which performance dimensions are adequate and which are deficient. In focused-holistic portfolio assessment, the educational specialist elicits integrated work samples such as spoken or written stories, essays, projects, or interviews. The samples are then analyzed in a focused approach to determine the levels of performance for critical dimensions of the integrated, multidimensional task (e.g., level of conceptualization or creativity, use of information or knowledge, organization or structure, and rules, skills, or conventions). The educational outcome is to identify performance dimensions in need of enrichment or direct teaching.

because there is always a degree of uncertainty about the outcome or effectiveness of any approach. Mature communication requires multi-attribute and stage decisions because they occur within a multidimensional, verbal, and nonverbal system.

## Developmental Patterns

The normal trajectory in communication strategy and pragmatic development is a path that parallels that of cognition. Between 5 and 7 years of age, children communicate from a self-oriented, concrete, and skill-based linguistic-use perspective. They use straightforward language forms to express themselves and make things happen. For example, they might say, "Open the door!" and "You always forget your bag."

Between ages eight and ten there is a gradual transition to strategic communication. Communications become other-oriented, recognize listener needs and expectations, respond to expectations for politeness and social register, and become increasingly abstract in content and reference. For example, they might say, "Could you please open the door?" and "Remember to take your bag." Between ages 11 and 13, communication and metalinguistic strategies are in place. For example, they might say, "Would you mind helping me with the door?" and "Aren't you supposed to bring your bag?" Preadolescents have integrated maxims for the quantity and quality of communication, linguistic and pragmatic rules, and social-cultural conventions. They can also take into account both the conceptual (shared knowledge) and affective (emotional needs) perspectives of listeners or readers.

Students with LLD often progress to the transitional stages typical for ages seven to eight. They frequently fail to complete the transition to mature, strategic communication in listening, speaking, reading, and writing. Several factors may contribute to the failure to move toward maturity; among these it may be that the prerequisite linguistic rules and word and concept knowledge are inadequate. Students with LLD frequently have problems recognizing patterns in both the verbal and nonverbal aspects of communication. They tend to focus on only one aspect or dimension of communication, either verbal or nonverbal. The patterns they abstract are often incomplete and therefore they cannot form efficient hypotheses, test them, nor develop and generalize strategies. Students with LLD often have trouble alternating between looking at the parts and looking at the whole of communication. In other words, they tend to have a limited and rigid focus and, therefore, they do not take risks when communicating. As listeners and readers, they have problems with, among other things, discerning characterization and relationships expressed in discourse. As speakers and writers they have problems expressing subtle meanings, characteristics, or relationships. The deficits can be identified by norm-referenced testing, portfolio or descriptive assessment, and/or observation (Damico 1992; Wiig and Secord 1989, 1992; Wiig, Sherbenou, and Hresko in progress).

### Nonverbal Communication

Unfortunately, some students with LLD also have visual perception and integration problems (Rourke 1989; Semrud-Clikeman and Hynd 1990). For them the visual-spatial patterns that convey nonverbal communication cues, especially those that are based in movement, may not be recognized consistently. As a result, they may not identify and abstract nonverbal communication that expresses for example higher-level, complex emotions, intentions, and reactions such as avoidance, empathy, frustration, or indecisiveness. They may fail to develop strategies for interpreting others and expressing themselves nonverbally and may not generalize from one communication context to another.

### Types of Intervention

Intervention to develop verbal and nonverbal communication strategies should occur in natural contexts, and be relevant to the students' communication needs. Goals and procedures should be curriculum- , vocation- , or life-related, and should emphasize communication strategy acquisition. Training for communication strategy acquisition should follow a trajectory in which simple rules and strategies are taught first. The basic strategies can then be reworked, transformed, and integrated into more efficient and complex strategies (Swanson 1989). In this process, the learner can be supported in transforming and refining communication strategies by reducing complex, multidimensional information to rules with fairly constant relationships. The acquired rules can then be readily available and become highly automated with practice. The learner can also be supported in chunking several strategies into single, abstract units or schema for communication in context and in deleting parts of strategies that are not generic or generally necessary.

Schema development for communication is especially important in strategy training. This is because the internalized schema for communication in context can provide reference knowledge that can be used for in-depth analysis of oral and written communication in general. Literacy training in the upper grades often requires that students investigate particular aspects of texts or situations, such as in plays, novels, or films, that are part of the curriculum. For example, they may be asked to describe the personalities of major characters on the basis of their verbal expressions and interactions only.

Social drama is among several approaches that can be used for intervention when students with LD show social interaction and communication deficits (Wiig and McCracken 1992). Skits used in the process portray common conflicts in the daily lives of pre-adolescents and adolescents with learning disabilities. After viewing or performing a skit, the students with LD participate actively in cognitive processing. This process emphasizes sharing of emotions and reactions, experiencing what actually occurred, interpreting the conflict and dynamics of the interactions, generalizing observations and new strategies for coping and compensation, and applying the strategies in communication and social interaction. Processing is supported by guided questioning and scaffolding.

## ORGANIZATIONAL ABILITIES

Organization of spoken and written language and task and time management are often areas of great difficulty for children and adolescents with learning disabilities. At first glance, it would seem that the two abilities should not be related. The relationship becomes clearer when we consider that organized behavior in any domain is guided by recognition and adherence to plans, goals and objectives, and perspectives. Let's look at some plans that underlie extended communication.

### Script Knowledge

Narratives and spoken or written communications (descriptive, expository, or argumentative) follow underlying plans (schema). In the most simple form, a story plan dictates that there must be a clear beginning (identifies characters and settings), middle (introduces conflicts and efforts at resolution), and ending (provides resolution and closure). As stories, descriptions, and arguments become more complex, the intricacies of the underlying plans for speaking or writing also increase in complexity.

Discourse and conversation are also conducted within an organized structure or plan. In goal-oriented communication with strangers it is especially easy to recognize a plan. The interaction is expected to begin with an attention getter (preparatory) and an acknowledgment (enabler). Preconditions are then stated (negotiation of terms), the objective is carried out (action), postconditions are fulfilled (contract), and there is a well-defined, often ritualistic closure.

We organize the world around us in similar ways. Events and experiences are structured into plans (scripts) (Schank 1982). From these scripts we can abstract higher level schema that serve as templates for actions and reactions. There are three generic types of scripts: (1) the situational script (e.g., visiting a fast-food restaurant); (2) the cause-effect script (e.g., baking a pie); and (3) the personal script (e.g., selecting a political candidate and voting). There are also combined scripts. Script knowledge and internalization are important aids for understanding, remembering, predicting, making inferences, and communicating.

As we approach language-learning disabilities from a pragmatic, holistic, curriculum-related perspective, it becomes evident that students with LLD often possess inadequate script knowledge. They often lack knowledge of important classroom scripts for aspects such as how the teacher gives directions, for completing workbook assignments, and for test taking. As a result, they must depend on short-term and working memory to function in the classroom and these memory abilities are often inadequate. Several factors may contribute to the difficulties; among them are lower processing rates and holistic (rather than analytical) cognitive styles.

Limitations in organizational abilities among students with language-learning disabilities become apparent when a structured, multi-dimensional assessment profile is developed for portfolio evaluation (Wiig, Sherbenou, and Hresko in progress). When we assign and evaluate the performances on multidimensional tasks and projects such as writing a story, making a collage, or developing methods and reminders for converting American measures for spatial dimensions (length, width, depth), volume, and speed into metric equivalents in an applied math or physics problem, the organizational inadequacies generally stand out. The performance levels on the dimension *use of organization or composition* may be marginal or unacceptable in the presence of superior performance on the dimension *level of conceptualization or creativity*.

One objective for language intervention is to make underlying plans, scripts, and schema explicit and clear to students with LLD. These students must become able to recognize the underlying organization and abstract it into internalized symbolic scripts. They must be supported to use these scripts for learning and performing in school, on the job, and in life.

## Task Management

Problems in task management and organization may be related to, among other things, visual-spatial deficits and/or difficulties in time perception or conceptualization. The negative effects of language disorders should not be overlooked. Students with learning disabilities who have visual-spatial and time perception deficits, without concomitant language disorders, can often compensate by verbal mediation. They can refer to internalized scripts for action sequences and tasks and make inferences and predictions on the basis of script knowledge.

Because inner language and verbal mediation are deficient in language disorders, compensation is often difficult for students with LLD. Language provides a powerful, sequential code for internalizing, reconstructing, and determining order in action sequences and, therefore, for organizing and managing tasks. Language, including words and concepts, is also a valuable code for guiding categorization, a productive approach to organization and task management. Intervention to develop understanding of the functional components and underlying sequences in concrete tasks can generate script knowledge. This can occur when tasks are demonstrated, broken down into smaller units, and talked about (self-talk).

## REASONING AND PROBLEM SOLVING

We have mentioned several times that the recognition of patterns in linguistic and in nonverbal communication stimuli and contexts is a prerequisite for, among other things, linguistic rule learning and script and schema development. Recognizing and abstracting patterns, drawing inferences, and arriving at conclusions based on observations, facts, examples, and/or models is an inherent feature of inductive reasoning. Unfortunately, inductive reasoning seems to be deficient in many students with learning disabilities. Stone and Forman (1988) reported three deficit patterns on a formal operational reasoning task (the bending rods task[2]) among adolescents with diagnosed learning disabilities. Close to one third (29%) exhibited specific developmental delays in hypothesis testing and in using isolation-of-variables strategies. About another third (26%) showed poor awareness of implicit task demands and arrived at highly general conclusions about solving the problem. Only a small group (7%) exhibited a general conceptual deficit that influenced all aspects of problem solving negatively. Among adolescents with LLD these researchers observed hypothesis testing deficits in about one third of the sample (30%). Poor awareness of task demands and/or general conceptual deficits were less common. Each occurred in about ten percent of the sample.

Wansart (1990) used the Tower of Hanoi[3] task to assess problem

---

[2]The bending rods task is a Piagetian problem designed to probe formal operational reasoning. It evaluates the attainment of conservation of weight and requires estimates and predictions.

[3]The Tower of Hanoi problem is a task in which the problem solver is presented with an array of three pegs. The first peg holds five disks of increasing size toward the bottom. The objective is to move the disks so that the tower is duplicated on the third peg in the array.

solving strategies among 10- to 12-year-old students. Academic achievers used a final representational strategy that allowed transfer of a solution. Students with learning disabilities, on the other hand, tended to be bound to situationally specific aspects of the task and transfer was limited. The same approach, a final procedural strategy, is commonly used by 7- to 8-year-olds with normal development and achievement (Blanchet 1981).

There is other evidence that students with learning disabilities may have problems discerning relevant from irrelevant information when solving a problem (Swanson 1989). Students with LD tend to make ad hoc best guesses that may be opportunistic and do not guarantee a solution (heuristics). Academic achievers, in contrast, tend to use procedural routines (algorithms) that result in a solution when one is feasible.

These observations have important implications for communication and metalinguistic strategy acquisition by students with LLD. Strategy acquisition from naturalistic communication contexts will be limited by both perceptual and conceptual inadequacies. The plateaus observed in linguistic rule learning and communication (metalinguistic) strategy acquisition among students with LLD may reflect limitations in moving beyond experiential (physical demonstration) and deductive (building from prior knowledge) learning and reasoning. Use of inductive (pattern abstraction), abductive (probabilistic resolution), and analogous (combining deduction and induction) reasoning approaches are required to move from concrete operations to formal operations for communication (Wiig 1992).

There are several implications for language intervention. Among them are that intervention formats to develop pattern recognition and strategy use should control the progression of reasoning approaches. With pre-adolescents and adolescents with LLD it may be necessary to begin by demanding experiential reasoning and then progress to demanding deductive, inductive, analogous, and, finally, abductive reasoning. Teaching strategies, such as guided questioning and scaffolding, support this movement, as does constant explication of underlying patterns (structure, script, schema) in verbal and nonverbal communication stimuli and contexts (Wiig 1989, 1992).

## CREATIVITY

Creativity is an important variable for a student's educational and professional options through life. Creativity can take many forms. It is characterized by divergence in conceptualization and/or imaging. Many students with learning disabilities show creativity in some area. Some show ability to create divergent images and incorporate creativity in artistic expression or crafts. Others may show evidence of conceptual and verbal creativity. In childhood they may tell "tall" or scary stories, play act, or stage games that require verbal cunning. They may speak and write creatively in adolescence and in adulthood. From a linguistic perspective, they show a high degree of metalinguistic ability or, in other words, ability to use language as a tool and medium for expressing creativity. The presence of a language disorder often spells an end to verbally based expressions of creativity for students with LLD. Many students with LLD may, nonetheless, show creativity in imagery, artistic, or scientific expression.

The level of creativity in an individual student can best be evaluated by using portfolio assessments. As mentioned above, creativity is often the dimension that stands out when portfolio samples of multidimensional tasks and projects are evaluated in a focused holistic approach (Wiig, Sherbenou, and Hresko in progress). We find that even when performance levels on the dimensions *skills or mechanics, use of information or prior knowledge,* and *use of organization or composition* are marginal, the level of creativity may be rated as excellent.

When natural, often nonverbal, creative talents and strengths are fostered, the expressions can be used as a point of departure for fostering divergent verbal expression and metalinguistic maturity. Students with LLD who are creative in imagery and visual thinking often show significant improvements in the attainment of metalinguistic abilities such as use of figurative language. The improvements follow when the student with LLD is taught recognition of underlying linguistic or structural patterns, develops script and schema knowledge, and superimposes strategies on this recognition (Wiig 1989, 1992).

## AFFECT AND MENTAL HEALTH

The last decade has seen growing awareness of the mental health problems of persons with learning disabilities. The field has long acknowledged that the frustrations, anxieties, and tensions associated with learning disabilities may result in secondary emotional problems. Some of the origins of the frustrations, anxieties, and tensions have been depicted vividly in the PBS program *F.A.T. City* (Lavoie 1990). The reactions may be reflected in withdrawal, defensiveness, insensitivity, or aggression. There is often a discernible relationship between the behavioral manifestations and the underlying language and communication problems (Bashir, Wiig, and Abrams 1987). As an example, adolescents with LLD and social-verbal communication (pragmatics) deficits are often described as direct, rude, stubborn, defensive, or aggressive. Many of the secondary emotional reactions and behaviors change as linguistic and metalinguistic competence are developed.

Recently there has been growing evidence that some persons with learning disabilities may be predisposed for mood disorders in the forms of depression or, less frequently, manic-depression (bipolar disorder). Right hemisphere dysfunction, cortical or subcortical, has been implicated, and nonverbal learning disabilities, attention deficit disorder (ADD) with hyperactivity, and pathological depression have been linked (Breslau 1990; Hudson and Pope 1990; Rourke 1989; Semrud-Clikeman and Hynd 1990). This relationship is stressed in other chapters in this volume.

Medical intervention results in significant improvements of mood disorders in the majority of cases. The presence of language-learning disabilities can, however, impair the effectiveness of associated counseling or psychotherapy. We have recorded and transcribed several interactions with children and adolescents with LLD during psychotherapy. In each case, the presence of LLD interfered with the process. Some typical patterns emerged. Some clients with LLD did not interpret accurately or consistently the complex sentences and/or abstract concepts used by therapists or remember previous references to the same situation. As a result, the same conflicts or issues were discussed over and over without obvious understanding or resolution.

When therapists relied on the client's ability to abstract patterns in behaviors (inductive reasoning), perceive similarities among situations or reactions (analogous reasoning), think divergently and probabilistically (abductive reasoning), or generalize, the efforts generally failed. When therapists used figurative language (idioms or metaphors) to convey images or stress universal features, the clients with LLD were generally unable to interpret them or respond appropriately. As an illustration, one therapist working with a 13-year-old boy with LLD tried to use a previous conflict situation in the classroom as an analogy to resolve a current conflict. The student exhibited two problems in dealing with the previous experiences. First, he had misperceived essential elements of the prior conflict. Second, he had forgotten linking events and no longer retained the chronology of the events in the conflict. The therapist also used indirect requests and references and time relationships that the student did not understand or could not deal with. The following interactions serve as illustrations.

T: "Wasn't someone else involved?"
S: "Sure."
T: "Didn't you tell me about that before?"
S: "No."
T: "How about last week?"
S: "Last week was vacation."

(Vacation had actually been three weeks earlier.)

The therapist then used a common figurative expression to hint, sum up, or elicit descriptions and resolutions. It fell on deaf ears.

T:  "Have you heard of being a square peg in a round hole?"
S:  "I don't do crafts."

Several measures may be used to increase the effectiveness of counseling or therapy. Among them are the use of calendars, family photos, videos, or other illustrations of similar instances for cuing, memory support, and perceiving analogies. The counselor or therapist can also learn to adapt the language used to conform to the client's level of language competence. Among other possible language adaptations, the therapist can use direct rather than indirect requests and references, avoid or elaborate on temporal references, and limit the use of abstract, multiple meaning, and figurative expressions. If these measures fail, a speech-language pathologist may serve as a consultant on how to modify the language of therapy, collaborate as a team member, or serve as a mediator in the counseling process.

## CONCLUSION

We have stressed that the language disorders associated with learning disabilities persist but change, across a child's educational life span and continue into adulthood. As a child with language-learning disabilities matures, the interactions between language and cognition become more apparent. Language-learning disabilities are often described in relation to the observed deficits in the acquisition of content (semantics), form (morphology and syntax), and use (pragmatics). We have broadened this perspective to consider related and/or concomitant strengths or deficits in organization and task management, reasoning and problem solving, creativity, and affect and mental health. Throughout, the perspectives taken for intervention have been collaborative, contextual, thematic, holistic, and strategy based.

## REFERENCES

Bashir, A. S., and Scavuzzo, A. 1992. Children with learning disabilities: Natural history and academic success. *Journal of Learning Disabilities* 25:53–65.

Bashir, A. S., Wiig, E. H., and Abrams, J. C. 1987. Language disorders in childhood and adolescence: Implications for learning and socialization. *Pediatric Annals* 16:145–58.

Blanchet, A. 1981. Étude génétique des significations et des modèles utilisés par l'enfant lors de résolution de problèmes. Doctoral dissertation, University of Geneva, Switzerland.

Breslau, N. 1990. Does brain dysfunction increase children's vulnerability to environmental stress? *Archives of General Psychiatry* 47:15–20.

Bruner, J. S. 1973. *Beyond the Information Given: Studies in the Psychology of Knowing*. New York: W. W. Norton.

Crais, E. R. 1990. World knowledge to word knowledge. *Topics in Language Disorders* 10:45–62.

Damico, J. 1992. Descriptive/nonstandardized assessment in the schools. *Best Practices in School Speech-Language Pathology*, Vol. 2. San Antonio, TX: Psychological Corporation.

Gilhooly, K. J. 1988. *Thinking: Directed, Undirected and Creative*. New York: Academic Press.

Hudson, J. I., and Pope, H. G. 1990. Affective spectrum disorder. *American Journal of Psychiatry*. 1464:552–64.

Lavoie, R. D. 1990. *How difficult can this be? The F.A.T. City Learning Disability Workshop*. Alexandria, Va: PBS Video.

Luria, A. R. 1980. *Higher Cortical Functions in Man*. New York: Basic Books.

McKeown, M. G., and Curtis, M. E. 1987. *The Nature of Vocabulary Acquisition*. Hillsdale, NJ: Lawrence Erlbaum Associates.

Rieber, R. W., and Carton, A. S. 1987. *The Collected Works of S. Vygotsky*, Vol. 1. New York: Plenum.

Rourke, B. P. 1989. *Nonverbal Learning Disabilities*. New York: Guilford.

Schank, R. C. 1982. *Reading and Understanding: Teaching from the Perspective of Artificial Intelligence*. Hillsdale, NJ: Lawrence Erlbaum Associates.

Secord, W. A. 1989. Collaborative programs in the schools: Concepts, models, and procedures. *Best Practices in School Speech-Language Pathology*, Vol. 1. San Antonio, TX: Psychological Corporation.

Secord, W. A., and Wiig, E. H. 1991. *Developing a Collaborative Language Intervention Program*. Buffalo, NY: EDUCOM Associates.

Semel, E. M., Wiig, E. H., and Secord, W. A. 1987. *Clinical Evaluation of Language Fundamentals–Revised*. San Antonio, TX: Psychological Corporation.

Semrud-Clikeman, M., and Hynd, G. W. 1990. Right hemispheric dysfunction in nonverbal learning disabilities. *Psychological Bulletin* 107:196–209.

Stone, C. A., and Forman, E. A. 1988. Differential patterns of approach to a complex problem-solving task among learning disabled adolescents. *The Journal of Special Education* 22:167–85.

Swanson, H. L. 1989. Strategy instruction: Overview of principles and procedures for effective use. *Learning Disabilities Quarterly* 12:3–15.

Vygotsky, L. S. 1962. *Thought and Language*. Cambridge, MA: M.I.T.

Wansart, W. L. 1990. Learning to solve a problem: A microanalysis of the solution strategies of children with learning disabilities. *Journal of Learning Disabilities* 23:164–70.

Wiig, E. H. 1989. *Steps to Language Competence: Developing Metalinguistic Strategies*. San Antonio, TX: Psychological Corporation.

Wiig, E. H. 1990. *Wiig Criterion Referenced Inventory of Language*. San Antonio, TX: Psychological Corporation.

Wiig, E. H. 1992. Strategy training for people with language-learning disabilities. In *Strategy Assessment and Training for Students with Learning Disabilities: From Theory to Practice*, ed. L. Meltzer. Austin, TX: Pro-Ed.

Wiig, E. H., and Freedman, E. 1993. *The WORD Book: Developing Words by Concepts*. Columbus, OH: SRA/DLM.

Wiig, E. H., and McCracken, J. 1992. *Daily Dilemmas: Coping, Compensation, and Communication Strategies through Social Drama*. Buffalo, NY: EDUCOM Associates.

Wiig, E. H., and Secord, W. A. 1991. *Measurement and Assessment: A Marriage Worth Saving*. Buffalo, NY: EDUCOM Associates.

Wiig, E. H., and Secord, W. A. 1992. *Test of Word Knowledge*. San Antonio, TX: Psychological Corporation.

Wiig, E. H., and Secord, W. A. In press. *Classroom Language Assessments*. Buffalo, NY: EDUCOM Associates.

Wiig, E. H., and Semel, E. M. 1984. *Language Assessment and Intervention for the Learning Disabled*, 2nd ed. Columbus, OH: Merrill Publishing.

Wiig, E. H., Freedman, E., and Secord, W. A. 1992. Developing words and concepts in the classroom: A holistic-thematic approach. *Intervention in School and Clinic* 27:278–85.

Wiig, E. H., Secord, W. A., and Semel, E. H. 1992. *Clinical Evaluation of Language Fundamentals—Preschool*. San Antonio, TX: Psychological Corporation.

Wiig, E. H., Sherbenou, R., and Hresko, W. In progress. Portfolio for students with special needs: Structured, multidimensional assessment profiles. Dallas, TX: The Winston School.

# Chapter • 9

# Social Deficits in Children with Learning Disabilities

*Wendy L. Stone*
*Annette M. La Greca*

In the past 15 years, there has been a surge of interest in the social correlates of learning disabilities (LD). Considerable research has focused on the social acceptance of children with LD, on the quality of their social interactions, and on how they perceive and interpret social cues. Impetus for this investigation comes from research suggesting that peer acceptance in childhood is an important predictor of later social and emotional adjustment. Empirical studies have revealed that children with poor peer relationships are at risk for later difficulties, including dropping out of school, criminal behavior, and mental health problems (Parker and Asher 1987).

Moreover, peer friendships serve a number of important and unique functions considered critical for social-emotional development. Friendships provide the senses of belonging, acceptance, and affection, and represent an important source of companionship and intimacy (Furman 1982; Furman and Robbins 1985). Friends also play a major role in the process of socialization. Through friendships, children learn interpersonal skills such as problem solving, aggression control, and self-disclosure. Friends also help to shape children's values and beliefs, and form their self-identities (Furman 1982; Hartup 1983).

## SOCIAL COMPETENCE

Social competence has been defined and operationalized in numerous ways by different investigators. In this chapter, we adopt Vaughn and

Hogan's (1990) conceptualization of social competence as a multidimensional construct that includes the following components: positive relations with others; adequate social-cognitive skills; effective social behaviors; and absence of maladaptive behaviors. These social competence components also have been discussed by other investigators (e.g., Dodge et al. 1986; Gresham and Reschly 1988).

Many strategies for assessing social competence are available, and can range from conducting structured interviews with children, to collecting behavioral ratings during role plays, to obtaining subjective judgments from peers. Naturally, the type of assessment used will vary according to the aspect of social competence under study. Table I lists some common methods for assessing the different components of social competence.

An important dimension on which assessment techniques differ is social validity, which refers to the relevance of the measure to important social outcomes (e.g., peer acceptance, future emotional adjustment) (Gresham 1983). Peer sociometric assessment, which involves eliciting children's judgments about their peers, is generally considered to be one of the most valid means of assessing social competence. Children often possess an understanding of peer group norms and standards for behavior that adults simply do not. Moreover, peer judgments have been found to predict social adjustment difficulties in adulthood (e.g., Cowen et al. 1973; Roff, Sells, and Golden 1972). Interested readers are referred to review articles by Gresham and Elliott (1989), Landau and Milich (1990), and McConnell and Odom (1986) for further discussion of specific assessment techniques.

Multiple factors contribute to the development and demonstration of social competence. These factors can be external or internal, and direct or indirect in their mode of influence (see table II). Environmental variables constitute the most distal influences on the development of social competence. At this level the concern is primarily with the availability of socially competent models and opportuni-

Table I.   Common Methods for Assessing Social Competence

| Dimension of Social Competence | Type of Assessment |
|---|---|
| Quality of peer relationships | • Subjective judgments from teachers, parents, and peers (e.g., teacher rankings, peer sociometrics) |
| Social-cognitive skills | • Children's self-reports<br>• Tasks of social perception, information processing, and problem solving |
| Behavioral repertoire | • Naturalistic observations<br>• Role plays<br>• Behavioral checklists/rating scales |

Table II.   Factors Contributing to Children's Social Competence

| Environmental | Situational | Personal |
|---|---|---|
| Availability of social models | Interaction setting | Cognitive/language abilities |
| Opportunities for peer interaction | Interaction partner(s) | Motivation to interact |
| Parental and other family influences | Type of activity | Social perception and understanding |
| | Previous history of interactions | Repertoire of appropriate social behaviors |
| | | Ability to self-monitor and self-regulate |

ties for social interaction. In addition, a number of direct and indirect parental influences on the development of peer acceptance and social competence have been described. These influences include parental involvement, warmth, physical playfulness, moderate levels of directiveness, and affective expressiveness (MacDonald and Parke 1984; Parke et al. 1989; Putallaz and Heflin 1990).

Situational factors also affect the development and expression of social competence. At this level, we are referring primarily to the context in which the interaction is occurring, such as the setting and the interaction partner. For example, a child's social competence may vary as a function of the specific child with whom he or she is interacting, the number of children involved in the situation, or his or her familiarity with the given setting or activity.

Finally, personal characteristics are also important determinants of a child's ability to interact in a socially competent manner. In addition to a child's social-behavioral repertoire, factors such as cognitive ability and language skills, accurate perception and understanding of social situations, motivation to interact, and ability to self-monitor are likely to influence his or her social behavior.

## SOCIAL COMPETENCE IN NONHANDICAPPED CHILDREN

Study of social competence in the developmental literature has overwhelmingly emphasized the use of peer sociometric assessment techniques. Over the past several years, these assessments have been refined to provide more fine-grained distinctions between sociometric status categories. Positive and negative peer nominations can be used to derive five categories of social status: popular, average, rejected, neglected, and controversial (Coie, Dodge, and Coppotelli 1982). This refinement has enabled us to differentiate two types of low-status children: those actively rejected by their peers; and those neglected or ignored. This distinction has important implications for children with LD.

Meaningful distinctions between different status groups have been made with respect to their associated social behavior, the stability of their status, and their risk for future adjustment difficulties. For example, popular children evidence the highest rates of prosocial behavior. They tend to be cooperative, friendly, helpful, and considerate. These children typically comply with group rules, and are able to handle verbal aggression without retaliating (Coie, Dodge, and Coppotelli 1982; Coie, Dodge, and Kupersmidt 1990; Dodge 1983). Table III lists some correlates of peer acceptance described in the literature.

In addition to behavioral characteristics, peer popularity is also related to a number of nonbehavioral factors, including: physical appearance, athletic ability, academic skills and achievement, and language and communication skills (Hartup 1983; La Greca 1987). The vast majority of children with LD are low achievers, and some may also have language or communication deficits. As a consequence, these children are likely to be at a disadvantage in terms of their peer acceptance. Popular peer status is also associated with specific parental behaviors, such as parents' sociability, use of an inductive discipline strategies such as reasoning, provision of verbal stimulation, emotional expressiveness, as well as the nature of their play with the child (MacDonald and Parke 1984; Putallaz 1987).

Children rejected by their peers are characterized as verbally and physically aggressive, disruptive, and attention seeking. Moreover,

Table III.   Correlates of Peer Acceptance

| Behavioral Characteristics | Personal Attributes | Parental Characteristics |
|---|---|---|
| Enjoyment of peer relationships (e.g., smiling, enthusiasm) | Physical appearance | Inductive discipline techniques/moderate level of directiveness |
| Joining ongoing peer activities | Athletic prowess | Emotional expressiveness/warmth |
| Participating in peer activities | Academic ability | Engagement/positive affect during play |
| Initiating peer contacts (e.g., extending invitations to peers) | Language/communication skills | |
| Cooperation/taking turns | | |
| Sharing | | |
| Helping others | | |
| Playing fairly | | |
| Giving affection | | |
| Resolving conflicts/differences | | |

Adapted from Table 1, p. 171 of *Journal of Reading, Writing, and Learning Disabilities*, 1987, 3, La Greca, A. M., Taylor and Francis, Inc., Washington, DC. Reproduced with permission.

they are easily angered and they tend to violate rules (Coie and Dodge 1988; Coie, Dodge, and Coppotelli 1982; Dodge, Coie, and Brakke 1982; Putallaz and Gottman 1983). Children in this group are more likely to attribute hostile intentions to others and to generate aggressive solutions to problematic situations (Dodge and Feldman 1990). Furthermore, rejected status is stable over time and children in this group are believed to be at highest risk for negative future outcomes (Asher 1985; Coie 1985).

In contrast, neglected children tend to be more shy and withdrawn, and more socially anxious. They are extremely nonaggressive and they engage in more solitary play than children in the other groups (Coie and Dodge 1988; Coie, Dodge, and Coppotelli 1982; Coie and Kupersmidt 1983; Dodge 1983; La Greca et al. 1988). This sociometric category seems to be the least stable over time, and may be the most situation-specific. However, it has been suggested that these children may be at higher risk for internalizing disorders than children in other sociometric groups (Rubin 1985).

The brevity of the above review belies the growing complexity and sophistication of the developmental literature in this area. Recent trends in the study of social competence in nonhandicapped children have included: differentiation between distinct types of peer relationships (i.e., peer group status versus friendships); clarification of the heterogeneity within sociometric categories; examination of the direction of causality between sociometric status and social behavior; and investigation of developmental changes in the relationship between social behaviors and peer acceptance (Dunn and McGuire 1992).

## SOCIAL COMPETENCE IN LEARNING-DISABLED CHILDREN

The study of social competence in children with LD began with seminal work by Tanis Bryan in 1974. Since that time, this area has been a focus of steady interest and empirical attention. Although studies have used different definitions of learning disabilities and divergent methods for assessing social status, two conclusions from research in this area have emerged clearly. First, LD children as a group consistently are found to be lower in peer status—less accepted and more rejected—relative to their nondisabled classmates. Second, children with LD are heterogeneous in terms of their social competence and peer acceptance. Not all children with LD are low in peer status and some are considered popular by their peers (see Dudley-Marling and Edmiaston 1985; La Greca and Stone 1990a; Wiener 1987 for reviews of this literature).

These research findings are intriguing and lead us to a number of important questions that can help us understand the phenomenon of low peer acceptance of children with LD.

1. What is the nature of the peer relationship problems in children with LD? Specifically, are children with LD actively rejected by their peers or are they more likely to be ignored or neglected?

2. What factors might underlie the poor peer relationships of children with LD?

3. Which subgroups of children with LD are more prone to peer relationship problems?

The remainder of this section is devoted to reviewing empirical research that relates to these questions.

## Nature of Peer Relationship Problems

Although the developmental literature has documented the importance of distinguishing between children who are rejected and those who are neglected, most studies of children with LD have not differentiated between these two sociometric groups. In an effort to determine the specific nature of the peer relationship problems in children with LD, we examined the sociometric classifications of 57 LD children in the fourth through sixth grades (Stone and La Greca 1990).

The LD group consisted of 38 boys and 19 girls who attended regular classrooms for academic instruction, but who also received up to 12 hours per week of LD resource help. The comparison sample included 490 children (233 boys and 257 girls) who were classmates of the LD children and who did not demonstrate any educational exceptionalities (NLD group).

Sociometric classification was based on the administration of two measures: a rating scale of peer acceptance and a positive peer nomination measure. The rating scale required children to indicate how much they liked to play with each of their same-sex classmates on a 5-point scale. Average scores were computed for each child. For the peer nomination measure, children were asked to indicate the names of the three same-sex classmates they liked the most. The number of positive nominations received by each child was then tabulated. For both measures, scores were standardized by sex within each classroom so that cross-class comparison could be made.

The procedure described by Asher and Dodge (1986) was used to classify children into the following sociometric groups: popular, rejected, neglected, average, and controversial. (The latter group includes children who receive mixed reactions from peers; i.e., many positive and negative nominations.) Seventy-two percent (72%) of the LD children and 65% of the NLD children were assigned to one of the five sociometric groups using this method.

When the sociometric categories were compared, significant differences were found for the LD and NLD groups (see figure 1). LD students were overrepresented in both the rejected and neglected groups, and underrepresented in the popular and average groups. In fact, nearly 75% of the LD children who could be classified were assigned to one of the low peer status groups. These data suggest that children with LD are not characterized by one type of peer relationship problem. On the contrary, the group of low status LD children is heterogeneous, comprised of approximately equal numbers of rejected and neglected children. These results have several implications for intervention, which are discussed in a later section.

### Factors Underlying Poor Peer Relationships

The second question concerns the factors that might contribute to lower peer status in LD children. One approach to this question has been to examine differences between LD and NLD children in specific areas of social functioning. A second approach has been to examine the role that poor academic functioning might play in the low social status of children with LD.

***Aspects of Social Functioning.*** Several different areas of social

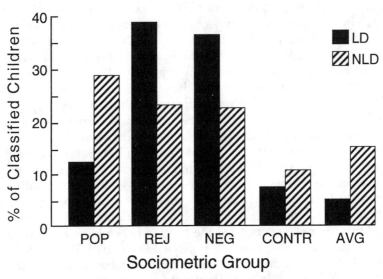

Figure 1. Sociometric status of LD and NLD students. Adapted from Figure 21.1 of La Greca, A. M., and Stone, W. L. 1990. Children with learning disabilities: The role of achievement in their social, personal, and behavioral functioning. In *Learning Disabilities: Theoretical and Research Issues*, eds. H. L. Swanson and B. Keogh. Hillsdale, NJ: Lawrence Erlbaum Associates.

functioning have been studied in an effort to understand the low social status of children with LD. These include: classroom behavior, interaction behaviors, ability to perceive and interpret social cues, understanding of social situations, and communication skills. Most studies have focused on identifying behavioral differences between LD children and NLD children, without examining the relationship between the behavioral deficits and sociometric status directly. As a result, limited conclusions can be drawn about the contribution of a specific deficit to low social status.

With regard to peer interaction behaviors, observations of LD and NLD children have revealed that these groups do not differ in the amount of time they spend interacting, or in the frequency of positive behavior that they exhibit (La Greca 1987). Nevertheless, it is possible that more subtle, qualitative differences in positive social behaviors (e.g., appropriateness for a given situation, skillfulness of execution) may exist between the two groups and may underlie sociometric differences (La Greca and Stark 1986).

Negative classroom behaviors have also been proposed to underlie the low peer status of children with LD. Bender and Smith (1990) conducted a meta-analysis of 25 studies that compared LD and NLD children on teacher ratings and classroom observations. This study revealed that children with LD exhibited less on-task behavior, more off-task behavior, greater distractibility, more conduct disorder, and more shy or withdrawn behavior. It is interesting to note that these behaviors are similar to those in children with attention deficit-hyperactivity disorder (ADHD). Given the substantial diagnostic overlap between children with LD and children with ADHD, it is uncertain whether these classroom behaviors characterize the LD population as a whole, or whether they occur predominantly in the subgroup of LD children who also have ADHD. We return to this issue in a later section.

Two studies evaluated the relationship between specific behaviors and sociometric status in children with LD. Sater and French (1989) found that rejected LD children received higher teacher ratings of inattentive, aggressive, and self-destructive behaviors relative to accepted LD children. Kistner and Gatlin(1989a) compared groups of popular and rejected LD children on teacher ratings and peer assessment measures. Teachers rated the rejected LD children as more inattentive and overactive than the popular LD children. Peers rated the rejected children higher in aggression and withdrawal relative to the popular children. Based on these studies, it seems that both aggressive behavior and passive or withdrawn behavior are correlates of peer rejection in children with LD. Moreover, low peer status also seems to relate to inattention and overactivity.

The verbal and communicative behaviors of children with LD

have also been investigated as potential contributors to low peer status. For example, children with LD have been found to initiate and receive more negative and rejecting verbal statements during social interactions (Bryan et al. 1976). They have also been found to be less effective communicators and less adequate conversational partners (Dudley-Marling 1985; Mathinos 1991). The need for further study of pragmatic skills in naturalistic settings has been emphasized (Dudley-Marling 1985; Vaughn and La Greca 1988).

Another set of factors implicated in the low peer status of children with LD is their social-cognitive skills, or the way they perceive and process social information. Social-cognitive skills include the perception and interpretation of social situations, as well as the ability to generate, evaluate, and select appropriate behavioral responses. Children with LD have been found to perform more poorly on tasks involving role taking (i.e., the ability to take another child's perspective), comprehension of emotions and nonverbal communication, social understanding and problem solving, and social insight (i.e., awareness of one's own social status) (Holder and Kirkpatrick 1991; La Greca 1981; Oliva and La Greca 1988; Stiliadis and Wiener 1989; Toro et al. 1990; Wiener 1987).

Unfortunately, several problems with this literature limit the implications that can be drawn. First, most studies have failed to control for potential differences in cognitive ability or attentional skills between the LD and NLD groups. In fact, when efforts have been made to enhance children's attention to social-processing tasks, no LD/NLD differences in task performance were apparent (Stone and La Greca 1984). Second, the external validity of social-cognitive measure (i.e., relationship to actual social behaviors) has not yet been established. Third, correlations between performance on social-cognitive measures and sociometric status for LD children have generally not been found (Bruck and Hebert 1982; Horowitz 1981). In one study, teacher's ratings of social perception in the natural environment (i.e., the classroom) were related to peer acceptance, whereas children's performance on a laboratory task was not (Stiliadis and Wiener 1989).

***Role of Academic Achievement.*** A second approach to understanding factors underlying the low peer status of children with LD has been to examine the influence of low academic achievement. Academic achievement is related to social acceptance in NLD populations (Dodge, Coie, and Brakke 1982; Gottman, Gonso, and Rasmussen 1975; Green et al. 1980), and most children with LD are characterized, in part, by poor academic achievement. The question that emerges is whether LD/NLD differences in sociometric status are attributable to the poor academic achievement of children with LD.

We investigated this question within the context of a broader study examining social status, self-esteem, and behavioral functioning of children with LD (La Greca and Stone 1990b). In this study, the sociometric status of children with LD was compared to that of low-achieving (LA) and average-achieving (AA) classmates. Students with LD were included only if they could be matched with a same-sex, same-race classmate on the basis of reading achievement scores from the Stanford Achievement Test. Of a total LD sample of 57 children, 32 met the criteria for inclusion in this study (21 boys, 11 girls).

The LA group consisted of 32 same-sex, same-race students whose reading achievement scores fell within one stanine of the LD student's scores. None of the LA students had been formally identified as having academic problems, and none was receiving resource help or academic instruction outside the regular classroom. The AA group consisted of 30 same-sex, same-race classmates of the students with LD whose reading achievement was at or above the 50th percentile.

The groups were compared on three sociometric measures: a peer-rating scale, the number of positive nominations received, and the number of lowest ratings (i.e., "1s") received on the peer rating scale (with 1 indicating "do not like at all"). The results are illustrated in figure 2. Children in the LD group received significantly lower ratings of peer acceptance on the peer rating scale, and obtained significantly fewer positive nominations, relative to children in the LA and

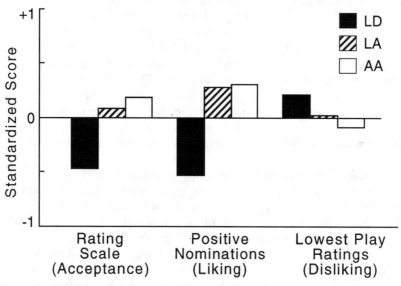

Figure 2. Sociometric ratings of LD, low achieving (LA), and average achieving (AA) students.

AA groups. The LA and AA groups did not differ. No significant group differences were obtained on the measure of lowest play ratings, which represents an index of peer dislike. These results are consistent with those obtained by Bursuck (1989), who also found that children with LD were less accepted than other low-achieving children without LD.

**Conclusions.** It should be apparent from the above review that we still have a long way to go in understanding the factors underlying low peer status in children with LD. At this point several conclusions can be drawn.

1. Low academic achievement alone does not account for the social difficulties of children with LD,
2. Both aggressive and withdrawn behaviors are related to peer rejection in LD children. However, further study is required to determine whether these behaviors are causes or consequences of the peer rejection.
3. Behaviors similar to those seen in children with ADHD (i.e., inattention, overactivity) are also associated with peer rejection in children with LD. Future research should differentiate between LD children with and without ADHD in order to clarify these findings.
4. Direct study of the relationship of classroom behaviors, communication skills, and social-cognitive skills to sociometric status in LD samples is needed.

### Sociometric Status in LD Subgroups

The third question posed earlier asked which particular subgroups of LD children are more prone to peer status problems than others. Although research in this area has been scant, three subgroups of LD children that may be at especially high risk have ben identified: children with concomitant attention problems; females; and children demonstrating particular patterns of cognitive functioning.

**ADHD Subgroup.** The importance of studying this subgroup derives from findings that: (1) children with ADHD experience peer relationship difficulties (Pelham and Milich 1984); and (2) attention deficits are common in children with LD (Eliason and Richman 1988; McKinney 1989). It is, therefore, possible that findings of poor peer relationships among children with LD may be attributed to the ADHD subgroup within the LD population. Unfortunately, only one study could be found that compared the sociometric status of LD boys with and without attention problems (Flicek and Landau 1985). This study found that LD boys with attention deficits were more rejected and less popular than LD boys without attention problems. The attention deficit subgroup was also rated as most aggressive by teachers.

In light of the substantial overlap between these two disorders, it would seem critical for future research to evaluate the presence of ADHD in LD samples, as well as study this LD subgroup in a systematic manner.

*Females.*   Results of several studies have suggested that girls with LD are more rejected and less accepted compared to both NLD girls and LD boys (Bryan 1974; Gottlieb et al. 1986; Hutton and Polo 1976; Kistner and Gatlin 1989b; Scranton and Ryckman 1979). Although gender differences in social status have not been obtained uniformly, no studies have reported LD girls to be more socially adept than NLD girls or LD boys.

Investigations of gender differences are complicated by the lower prevalence of learning disabilities among girls than boys; as a result, it can be extremely difficult to obtain adequate samples of girls with LD. Collaborative research that brings together the resources of several school districts or multiple investigators may be needed to obtain an adequate database for understanding the social difficulties encountered by many girls with LD.

*Cognitive patterns.*   Several different approaches have been used to derive subgroups of LD children on the basis of the patterns exhibited on standardized tests of intelligence. Landau, Milich, and McFarland (1987) formed three groups on the basis of the discrepancy between Verbal (V) and Performance (P) IQ scores on the Wechsler Intelligence Scale for Children—Revised (WISC-R): V > P; V = P; and V < P. These authors found that LD children fitting the V = P or V < P profiles were less popular than their NLD classmates, with the V = P evidencing more peer rejection as well. Children in the V > P group fared better with respect to peer status, leading the authors to hypothesize that a relative strength in verbal functioning may serve to mitigate the development of low social status in children with LD.

In contrast, it is interesting to note that other investigators have proposed that children with nonverbal learning disabilities (i.e., V > P) are at elevated risk for social difficulties (Rourke 1989; Rourke and Fuerst 1992; Semrud-Clikeman and Hynd 1990). However, the peer status of children exhibiting nonverbal learning disabilities has not yet been investigated directly.

Wiener (1980) used subtest scores on the WISC-R to categorize children as having conceptual, spatial, or sequential disabilities. Results of this study revealed that children displaying conceptual and spatial deficits exhibited more peer relationship problems than children with sequential disabilities. The author hypothesized that social perceptual and social cognitive difficulties might be associated with conceptual and spatial deficits and might underlie the social difficulties of LD children in these subgroups.

In summary, research investigating social competence among LD subgroups is in the infancy stage of development. It seems that girls with LD and LD boys who have concomitant ADHD represent subgroups at elevated risk for social difficulties. However, further study of gender differences, ADHD subgroups, and cognitive subtypes is clearly warranted.

## Hypotheses Accounting for Low Social Competence in LD Children

A number of different hypotheses have been advanced to explain the social difficulties of children with LD (see Wiener 1987). These hypotheses have been classified into two main categories (Vaughn and Hogan 1990). Within the first category, social deficits are viewed as resulting from the same underlying processing and cognitive difficulties that interfere with learning. Within the second category, low peer status is viewed as secondary to learning problems or their concomitants.

***Social Deficits as Primary.*** One hypothesis within this category is that LD children have a psychological processing deficit that affects their social perception, social cognition, and pragmatic language skills. This hypothesis predicts an association between peer acceptance and aspects of social information processing (Wiener 1987).

A second hypothesis is that LD children are inactive learners in the classroom as well as in social situations, and poor learning strategies account for the low peer status. This hypothesis predicts an association between peer status and: (1) strategies used in social situations; and (2) attributions for social success and failure in the social domain (Wiener 1987).

Support for the primacy of social deficits is limited at the present time. As we have discussed, social-cognitive skills and social interaction strategies have rarely been associated with sociometric status in LD populations. However, some indirect evidence for this position comes from a prospective study conducted by Vaughn and Hogan (1990). These authors found that kindergarten children who were later identified as LD received lower peer acceptance ratings than their classmates as early as two months after beginning formal schooling. These findings suggest that these children were perceived differently than their peers even before their learning problems were identified.

***Social Deficits as Secondary.*** There are several variants of this position. One hypothesis is that LD children obtain low peer status because they lack abilities valued by their peers, such as academic ability. This hypothesis predicts that: (1) LD children and low-achieving children without LD should not differ in peer status; and (2) LD children with other valued attributes should fare better on measures of peer status (Wiener 1987). Our review has indicated that low academic achievement alone does not account for low peer status in LD children, because children with LD were found to be less accepted than low achievers (La Greca and Stone 1990b). However, there is some evidence that LD children who are physically attractive, or who have greater intellectual or athletic abilities may constitute a more accepted subgroup (Siperstein, Bopp, and Bak 1978; Siperstein and Goding 1983).

Another hypothesis is that children with LD receive differential treatment from teachers, parents, and peers, which leads to low sociometric status. Evidence for differential treatment of LD children by teachers has been obtained (Siperstein and Goding 1983, 1985). Moreover, a recent study has found that LD children who were in classes where they were accepted by their general education teachers were as well liked and no more rejected than students from other achievement groups (Vaughn et al. in press). However, a causal relationship between differential treatment and low peer status has not yet been demonstrated.

Other hypotheses that fall within this category are: (1) LD children develop poor self-esteem as a result of their school difficulties, and their self-concept subsequently affects the quality of their peer interactions; and (2) LD children have less exposure to classmates and fewer opportunities to interact because they leave the classroom to receive resource or remedial help. These hypotheses have received little empirical attention.

In summary, limited support is available for both categories of hypotheses described above. As Wiener (1987) has suggested, the most productive approach to understanding social deficits in children with LD might require integration of the two viewpoints. That is, specific characteristics or deficits of children with LD may affect the quality of their social interactions, which may then lead to differential treatment from others.

## IMPLICATIONS FOR INTERVENTION

A number of important implications for social skills intervention with LD children can be drawn from the above discussion. The first is that a comprehensive assessment of LD children should be conducted prior to initiating any intervention program. Children with LD represent a heterogeneous population. Not all children with LD have social difficulties, and not all children with social difficulties have the same type of problem. It is important to differentiate those children actively rejected from those who may be neglected or ignored because these two subgroups are likely to require different types of intervention.

Assessment of children's social networks and friendships may also be important. There is some evidence in the developmental literature that reciprocal friendships may attenuate the negative effects of rejected status (Howes 1988).

Second, intervention programs should be tailored to the specific needs of each child. For example, intervention goals for rejected children might include reducing socially aversive behaviors, controlling acting-out behaviors, and learning acceptable peer behaviors. On the other hand, neglected children may experience more social anxiety and may require interventions geared toward reducing anxiety or socially related fears. Children who have concomitant attention deficits may require more comprehensive interventions that include contingency management training for parents and teachers (Pelham and Bender 1982).

Third, the behaviors selected for intervention should be socially valid (Furman 1980). Intervention programs should focus on behaviors important for peer acceptance; nonsocial behaviors as well as interpersonal behaviors should be considered. For example, if athletic abilities are important for peer acceptance, as some studies suggest, then providing additional opportunities for sports practice may help mitigate low social status for high-risk children. The development of nonacademic areas of expertise may enable children with LD to participate in peer activities from a position of strength and skill, rather than from one of failure and frustration.

Fourth, training should involve significant others in the child's environment. The contextualist model emphasizes the reciprocal nature of peer relationships, and emphasizes the importance of changing the attitudes and behaviors of teachers and peers as well as the behaviors of the target children (Forman 1987). For example, by involving nonhandicapped peers in intervention, they become more aware of positive behavioral changes and may be more committed to maintaining and promoting these changes (Vaughn and La Greca 1988). Methods of involving peers in training include cooperative learning tasks (Anderson 1985), peer tutoring (Eiserman 1988), peer-mediated social initiations (Strain, Odom, and McConnell 1984), and peer pairing (Fox 1989; Vaughn, Lancellota, and Minnis 1988).

The relationship between parent behaviors and social status reported in the developmental literature also suggests the importance of offering parent training or teaching parent-child interaction skills as an adjunct to direct intervention with the child.

Fifth, it is critical that social interventions incorporate procedures to facilitate the transfer of learning from the intervention setting to naturalistic settings. One common pitfall of many intervention programs is that the skills learned in the intervention setting fail to generalize. There are multiple ways to promote skill generalization, such as: varying the setting, the trainers, the materials and the tasks; teaching a variety of different behavioral responses; teaching behaviors that will be supported by the natural environment; training and rehearsing skills in natural settings; fading training consequences to approximate natural contingencies; and using peers as change agents (Michelson and Mannarino 1986).

A recent review of 22 studies employing social intervention for children with LD revealed positive effects for 14 studies (McIntosh, Vaughn, and Zaragoza 1991). The following components characterized successful interventions: inclusion of LD subjects with demonstrated social skills difficulties; use of cognitive behavior modification or metacognitive strategies; provision of individual or small group instruction; and longer duration of training.

## CONCLUSION

This chapter has examined the social competence of children with LD by reviewing their peer status with particular attention to three issues: the type of peer problems exhibited; the factors underlying low peer status; and the existence of subgroups at elevated risk for social difficulties. It is clear from the literature that children with LD are at high risk for peer acceptance problems. However, the type of social difficulty may vary from one child to the next, with some children experiencing rejection while others experience neglect. We have seen that low academic achievement alone does not account for the low peer status of LD children, though aggressive and withdrawn behavior, inattention, and overactivity are associated with peer rejection in this population. Certain LD subgroups, especially girls and children with concomitant attention deficits, seem to be at particular risk for peer relationship difficulties.

As research methodology in this area continues to improve, more complete answers to the questions posed in this chapter should be forthcoming. Further research devoted to examining specific subgroups of LD children and studying the relationship between specific behaviors and sociometric status directly is sorely needed. Our ultimate objective should be to enable LD children to partake fully in the rich opportunities that peer relationships afford.

## REFERENCES

Anderson, M. A. 1985. Cooperative group tasks and their relationship to peer acceptance and cooperation. *Journal of Learning Disabilities* 18:83–86.

Asher, S. R. 1985. An evolving paradigm in social skills training research with children. In *Children's Peer Relations: Issues in Assessment and Intervention*, eds. B. H. Schneider, K. H. Rubin, and J. E. Ledingham. New York: Springer-Verlag.

Asher, S. R., and Dodge, K. A. 1986. Identifying children who are rejected by their peers. *Developmental Psychology* 22:444–49.

Bender, W. N., and Smith, J. K. 1990. Classroom behavior of children and adolescents with learning disabilities: A meta-analysis. *Journal of Learning Disabilities* 23:298–305.

Bruck, M., and Hebert, M. 1982. Correlates of learning disabled students' peer-interaction patterns. *Learning Disability Quarterly* 5:353–62.

Bryan, T. 1974. Peer popularity of LD children. *Journal of Learning Disabilities* 7:31–35.

Bryan, T., Wheeler, R., Felcan, J., and Henek, T. 1976. "Come on, Dummy": An observational study of children's communications. *Journal of Learning Disabilities* 9:53–61.

Bursuck, W. 1989. A comparison of students with learning disabilities to low achieving and higher achieving students on three dimensions of social competence. *Journal of Learning Disabilities* 22:188–94.

Coie, J. D. 1985. Fitting social skills intervention to the target group. In *Children's Peer Relations: Issues in Assessment and Intervention*, eds. B. H. Schneider, K. H. Rubin, and J. E. Ledingham. New York: Springer-Verlag.

Coie, J. D., and Dodge, K. A. 1988. Multiple sources of data on social behavior and social status in the school: A cross-age comparison. *Child Development* 59:815–29.

Coie, J. D., and Kupersmidt, J. 1983. A behavioral analysis of emerging social status in boys' groups. *Child Development* 54:1400–1416.

Coie, J. D., Dodge, K. A., and Coppotelli, H. 1982. Dimensions and types of social status: A cross-age perspective. *Developmental Psychology* 18: 557–70.

Coie, J. D., Dodge, K. A., and Kupersmidt, J. 1990. Peer group behavior and social status. In *Peer Rejection in Childhood*, eds. S. R. Asher and J. D. Coie. Cambridge: Cambridge University Press.

Cowen, E. L., Pedersen, A., Babigian, H., Izzo, L. D., and Trost, M. D. 1973. Long-term follow-up of early detected vulnerable children. *Journal of Consulting and Clinical Psychology* 41:438–46.

Dodge, K. A. 1983. Behavioral antecedents of peer social status. *Child Development* 54:1386–1399.

Dodge, K. A., and Feldman, E. 1990. Issues in social cognition and sociometric status. In *Peer Rejection in Childhood*, eds. S. R. Asher and J. D. Coie. Cambridge: Cambridge University Press.

Dodge, K. A., Coie, J. D., and Brakke, N. P. 1982. Behavior patterns of socially rejected and neglected preadolescents: The roles of social approach and aggression. *Journal of Abnormal Child Psychology* 10:389–409.

Dodge, K. A., Pettit, G. S., McClaskey, C. L., and Brown, M. M. 1986. Social competence in children. *Monographs of the Society for Research in Child Development* 51 (Serial No. 213).

Dudley-Marling, C. 1985. The pragmatic skills of learning disabled children: A review. *Journal of Learning Disabilities* 18:193–99.

Dudley-Marling, C. C., and Edmiaston, R. 1985. Social status of learning disabled children and adolescents: A review. *Learning Disability Quarterly* 8:189–204.

Dunn, J., and McGuire, S. 1992. Sibling and peer relationships in childhood. *Journal of Child Psychology and Psychiatry* 33:67–105.

Eiserman, W. D. 1988. Three types of peer tutoring: Effects on the attitudes of students with learning disabilities and their regular class peers. *Journal of Learning Disabilities* 21:249–52.

Eliason, M. J., and Richman, L. C. 1988. Behavior and attention in LD children. *Learning Disabilities Quarterly* 11:360–69.

Flicek, M., and Landau, S. 1985. Social status problems of learning disabled and hyperactive/learning disabled boys. *Journal of Clinical Child Psychology* 14:340–44.

Forman, E. A. 1987. Peer relationships of learning disabled children: A contextualist perspective. *Learning Disabilities Research* 2:80–90.

Fox, C. L. 1989. Peer acceptance of learning disabled children in the regular classroom. *Exceptional Children* 56:50–59.

Furman W. 1980. Promoting social development. In *Advances in Clinical Child Psychology*, Vol. III, eds. B. B. Lahey and A. E. Kazdin. New York: Plenum.

Furman, W. 1982. Children's friendships. In *Review of Human Development*, eds. T. M. Field, A. Huston, H. C. Quay, L. Troll, and G. E. Finley. New York: Wiley.

Furman, W., and Robbins, P. 1985. What's the point? Issues in the selection of treatment objectives. In *Children's Peer Relations: Issues in Assessment and Intervention*, eds. B. H. Schneider, K. H. Rubin, and J. E. Ledingham. New York: Springer-Verlag.

Gottlieb, B. W., Gottlieb, J., Berkell, D., and Levy, L. 1986. Sociometric status and solitary play of LD boys and girls. *Journal of Learning Disabilities* 19: 619–22.

Gottman, J. M., Gonso, J., and Rasmussen, B. 1975. Social interaction, social competence, and friendship in children. *Child Development* 46: 709–718.

Green, K. D., Forehand, R., Beck, S. J., and Vosk, B. 1980. An assessment of the relationship among measures of children's social competence and children's academic achievement. *Child Development* 51:1149–1156.

Gresham, F. M. 1983. Social validity in the assessment of children's social skills: Establishing standards for social competency. *Journal of Psychoeducational Assessment* 1:299–307.

Gresham, F. M., and Elliott, S. N. 1989. Social skills assessment technology for LD students. *Learning Disability Quarterly* 12:141–52.

Gresham, F. M., and Reschly, D. J. 1988. Issues in the conceptualization, classification, and assessment of social skills in the mildly handicapped. In *Advances in School Psychology* Vol. VI, ed. T. R. Kratochwill. Hillsdale, NJ: Lawrence Erlbaum Associates.

Hartup, W. W. 1983. Peer relations. In *Handbook of Child Psychology*, Vol. IV, ed. P. H. Mussen. New York: Wiley.

Holder, H. B., and Kirkpatrick, S. W.. 1991. Interpretation of emotion from facial expressions in children with and without learning disabilities. *Journal of Learning Disabilities* 24:170–77.

Horowitz, E. C. 1981. Popularity, decentering ability, and role-taking skills in learning disabled and normal children. *Learning Disability Quarterly* 4:23–30.

Howes, C. 1988. Peer interaction of young children. *Monographs of the Society for Research in Child Development* 53 (Serial No. 217).

Hutton, J. B., and Polo, L. 1976. A sociometric study of learning disability children and type of teaching strategy. *Group Psychotherapy, Psychodrama, and Sociometry* 29:113–20.

Kistner, J. A., and Gatlin, D. 1989a. Correlates of peer rejection among children with learning disabilities. *Learning Disability Quarterly* 12:133–40.

Kistner, J. A., and Gatlin, D. F. 1989b. Sociometric differences between learning-disabled and nonhandicapped students: Effects of sex and race. *Journal of Educational Psychology* 81:118–120.

La Greca, A. M. 1981. Social behavior and social perception in learning-disabled children: A review with implications for social skills training. *Journal of Pediatric Psychology* 6:395–416.

La Greca, A. M. 1987. Children with learning disabilities: Interpersonal skills and social competence. *Reading, Writing, and Learning Disabilities* 3:167–85.

La Greca, A. M., and Stark, P. 1986. Naturalistic observations of children's social behavior. In *Children's Social Behavior*, eds. P. S. Strain, M. J. Guralnick, and H. M Walker. New York: Academic Press.

La Greca, A. M., and Stone, W. L. 1990a. Children with learning disabilities: The role of achievement in their social, personal, and behavioral functioning. In *Learning Disabilities: Theoretical and Research Issues*, eds. H. L. Swanson and B. Keogh. Hillsdale, NJ: Lawrence Erlbaum Associates.

La Greca, A. M., and Stone, W. L. 1990b. LD status and achievement: Confounding variables in the study of children's social status, self-esteem, and behavioral functioning. *Journal of Learning Disabilities* 23: 483–90.

La Greca, A. M., Dandes, S., Wick, P., Shaw, K., and Stone, W. L. 1988. The development of the Social Anxiety Scale for Children (SASC): Reliability and concurrent validity. *Journal of Clinical Child Psychology* 17:84–91.

Landau, S., and Milich, R. 1990. Assessment of children's social status and peer relations. In *Through the Eyes of the Child: Obtaining Self-reports from Children and Adolescents*, ed. A. M. La Greca. Boston: Allyn & Bacon.

Landau, S., Milich, R., and McFarland, M. 1987. Social status differences among subgroups of LD boys. *Learning Disability Quarterly* 10:277–82.

MacDonald, K., and Parke, R. D. 1984. Bridging the gap: Parent-child play and peer interactive competence. *Child Development* 55:1265–1277.

Mathinos, D. A. 1991. Conversational engagement of children with learning disabilities. *Journal of Learning Disabilities* 24:439–46.

McConnell, S. R., and Odom, S. L. 1986. Sociometrics: Peer-referenced measures and the assessment of social competence. In *Children's Social Behavior: Development, Assessment, and Modification*, eds. P. S. Strain, M. J. Guralnick , and H. M. Walker. Orlando, FL: Academic Press.

McIntosh, R., Vaughn, S., and Zaragoza, N. 1991. A review of social interventions for students with learning disabilities. *Journal of Learning Disabilities* 24:451–58.

McKinney, J. D. 1989. Longitudinal research on the behavioral characteristics of children with learning disabilities. *Journal of Learning Disabilities* 22: 141–65.

Michelson, L., and Mannarino, A. 1986. Social skills training with children: Research and clinical application. In *Children's Social Behavior*, eds. P. S. Strain, M. J. Guralnick,, and H. M. Walker. Orlando, FL: Academic Press.

Oliva, A. H., and La Greca, A. M. 1988. Children with learning disabilities: Social goals and strategies. *Journal of Learning Disabilities* 21:301–306.

Parke, R. D., MacDonald, K. B., Burks, V. M., Bhavnagri, N., Barth, J. M., and Beitel, A. 1989. Family and peer system: In search of the linkages. In *Family Systems and Life-span Development*, eds. K. Kreppner and R. M. Lerner. Hillsdale, NJ: Lawrence Erlbaum Associates.

Parker, J. G., and Asher, S. R. 1987. Peer relations and later personal adjustment: Are low-accepted children at risk? *Psychological Bulletin* 102:357–89.

Pelham, W., E., and Bender, M. E. 1982. Peer relationships in hyperactive children: Description and treatment. In *Advances in Learning and Behavioral Disabilities*, Vol. I, eds. K. Gadow and I. Bailer. Greenwich, CT: JAI Press.

Pelham, W. E., and Milich, R. 1984. Peer relations in children with hyperactivity/attention deficit disorder. *Journal of Learning Disabilities* 17:560–67.

Putallaz, M. 1987. Maternal behavior and children's sociometric status. *Child Development* 58:324–40.

Putallaz, M., and Gottman, J. M. 1983. Social relationship problems in children: An approach to intervention. In *Advances in Clinical Child Psychology*, Vol. VI, eds. B. B. Lahey and A. E. Kazdin. New York: Plenum.

Putallaz, M., and Heflin, A. H. 1990. Parent-child interaction. In *Peer Rejection in Childhood*, eds. S. R. Asher and J. D. Coie. Cambridge: Cambridge University Press.

Roff, M., Sells, S. B., and Golden, M. M. 1972. *Social Adjustment and Personality Development in Children*. Minneapolis: University of Minnesota Press.

Rourke, B. P. 1989. *Nonverbal Learning Disabilities: The Syndrome and the Model*. New York: Guilford.

Rourke, B. P., and Fuerst, D. R. Psychosocial dimensions of learning disability subtypes: Neuropsychological studies in the Windsor laboratory. *School Psychology Review*.

Rubin, K. H. 1985. Socially withdrawn children: An "at risk" population? In *Children's Peer Relations: Issues in Assessment and Intervention*, eds. B. H. Schneider, K. H. Rubin, and J. E. Ledingham. New York: Springer-Verlag.

Sater, G. M., and French, D. C. 1989. A comparison of the social competencies of learning disabled and low achieving elementary-aged children. *Journal of Special Education* 23:29–42.

Scranton T. R., and Ryckman, D. B. 1979. Sociometric status of learning disabled children in an integrative program. *Journal of Learning Disabilities* 12:49–54.

Semrud-Clikeman, M., and Hynd, G. W. 1990. Right hemispheric dysfunction in nonverbal learning disabilities: Social, academic, and adaptive functioning in adults and children. *Psychological Bulletin* 107:196–209.

Siperstein, G., and Goding, M. J. 1983. Social integration of learning disabled children in regular classrooms. *Advances in Learning and Behavioral Disabilities* 2:227–63.

Siperstein, G. N, and Goding, M. J. 1985. Teachers' behavior toward LD and non-LD children: A strategy for change. *Journal of Learning Disabilities* 18:139–44.

Siperstein, G., Bopp, M. J., and Bak, J. J. 1978. Social status of learning disabled children. *Journal of Learning Disabilities* 11:98–102.

Stiliadis, K., and Wiener, J. 1989. Relationship between social perception and peer status in children with learning disabilities. *Journal of Learning Disabilities* 22:624–29.

Stone, W. L., and La Greca, A. M. 1984. Comprehension of nonverbal communication: A reexamination of the social competencies of learning-disabled children. *Journal of Abnormal Child Psychology* 12:505–518.

Stone, W. L., and La Greca, A. M. 1990. The social status of children with learning disabilities: A reexamination. *Journal of Learning Disabilities* 23:32–37.

Strain, P. S., Odom, S. L., and McConnell, S. 1984. Promoting social reciprocity of exceptional children: Identification, target behavior selection, and intervention. *RASE* 5:21–28.

Toro, P A., Weissberg, R. P., Guare, J., and Liebenstein, N. L. 1990. A comparison of children with and without learning disabilities on social problem-solving skill, school behavior, and family background. *Journal of Learning Disabilities* 23:115–20.

Vaughn, S., and Hogan, A. 1990. Social competence and learning disabilities: A prospective study. In *Learning Disabilities: Theoretical and Research Issues*, eds. H. L. Swanson and B. Keogh. Hillsdale, NJ: Lawrence Erlbaum Associates.

Vaughn, S. R., and La Greca, A. M. 1988. Social interventions for learning disabilities. In *Learning Disabilities: State of the Art and Practice*, ed. K. A. Kavale. Boston: College-Hill Press.

Vaughn, S., Lancellota, G. X., and Minnis, S. 1988. Social strategy training and peer involvement: Increasing peer acceptance of a female LD student. *Learning Disabilities Focus* 4:32–37.

Vaughn, S., McIntosh, R., Schumm, J., Haager, D., and Callwood, D. In press. Social status and peer acceptance revisited. *Learning Disabilities: Research and Practice*.

Wiener, J. 1980. A theoretical model of the acquisition of peer relationships of learning disabled children. *Journal of Learning Disabilities* 13:42–47.

Wiener, J. 1987. Peer status of learning disabled children and adolescents: A review of the literature. *Learning Disabilities Research* 2:62–79.

# Chapter • 10

## Diagnosis and Treatment of Depressive Disorders in Children with Learning Disabilities

*Paramjit T. Joshi*

Depressive disorders in children have become increasingly apparent in the last decade and contribute significantly to serious psychiatric disturbance in childhood and adolescence (Rutter et al. 1970; Carlson and Strober 1978). In fact, Shaffer and Fisher (1981) have suggested that the incidence of depressive disorders in children may be increasing. The diagnostic criteria of depressive disorders in children and adolescents are based on distinct clinical phenomena similar to adult affective disorders, as described in the DSM III-R (American Psychiatric Association 1987). This description allows uniformity in identifying affective disorders in prepubertal children and adolescents. Debate continues about the effect of developmental variations on clinical presentations of depressive disorders in children and adolescents (Ringdahl 1980). The issue becomes especially pertinent when examining children and adolescents who are both learning disabled and have a depressive disorder.

Three depressive disorders have been described in adults, children, and adolescents: (1) adjustment disorder with depressed mood (ADDM), (2) dysthymic disorder (DD), and (3) major depressive disorder (MDD).

## ADJUSTMENT DISORDER WITH DEPRESSED MOOD

Adjustment disorder with depressed mood (ADDM) is the most benign of the three depressive disorders. By definition, it occurs in the presence of an identifiable stressful event, with the child adjusting to that stress in a maladaptive way with depressive symptoms, such as low mood, tearfulness, and hopelessness. The severity of the depressive symptoms seem to be incongruent with the intensity and severity of a given stressor. The disorder usually occurs within three months of stressor onset, does not last for more than six months, and is associated with a return to a normal affective state.

DSM III-R criteria for ADDM are (American Psychiatric Association 1987) the following:

1. A reaction to an identifiable psychosocial stressor or multiple stressors occurring within three months of the onset of the stressor.
2. Maladaptive nature of the reaction as indicated by either of the following:
   a. Impairment in school functioning, social activities, or relationships with others.
   b. Symptoms exceeding normal and expectable reactions to the stressor.
3. The disturbance is not merely one instance of a pattern of overreaction to stress or an exacerbation of one of the other mental disorders.
4. The maladaptive behavior persists no longer than six months.
5. The disturbance does not meet the criteria for any specific mental disorder and does not represent uncomplicated bereavement.

In children and adolescents, common stressors are separation/divorce of parents, death of a loved one, move to a new neighborhood, change of school, abuse, and other psychosocial stressors. These may be single or multiple. Rutter (1981) noted that adjustment disorders rarely are precipitated by highly traumatic or catastrophic events. Several other variable and mediating factors, such as developmental and cognitive maturity, temperamental vulnerabilities, and the adequacy of support systems and coping skills may influence the response of a child or adolescent to a given stressor. Therefore, it is difficult to predict any youngster's response to a stressor. ADDM cannot be diagnosed if another specific mental disorder is present. It should be distinguished from uncomplicated bereavement, a dysphoria that seems appropriate in severity and duration to the stressor.

Kovacs (1992) followed children longitudinally for several years (mean time 7.4 years) and found that 97% of children with an adjustment disorder recovered, with a mean episode length of 8.86 months. Kovacs noted that this length of time was somewhat longer than the six months described in the DSM III-R criteria for an adjustment disorder. In the same study, Kovacs also noted that children who develop ADDM recover faster than children who have adjustment disorders where other symptoms of misbehavior and conduct were present. Development of major depressive disorder in this group of children was not higher than in a control group followed for a similar length of time. Therefore, Kovacs concluded that there are no long-term consequences to ADDM. There are no reports in the literature describing this depressive disorder specifically in learning-disabled children and adolescents. However, our clinical experience suggests that children and adolescents with learning disabilities who have ADDM and adequate support systems both at home and school fare better than those whose psychosocial problems interfere in their recovery.

## DYSTHYMIC DISORDER

Dysthymic disorder (DD), also listed as depressive neurosis in the DSM III-R, is the most chronic and complicated of the three depressive disorders. Symptoms of depression usually last for more than a year. The symptoms of dysthymic disorder are somewhat similar to those seen in MDD, such as appetite and sleep changes, fatigue and low energy, indecisiveness and poor concentration, along with feelings of helplessness and hopelessness. However, the severity of the symptoms is not of the same magnitude as seen in MDD. To meet the DSM III-R criteria the child or adolescent must exhibit depressive symptoms for more than two months. It has often been suggested that an episode of major depression can be superimposed upon an underlying dysthymic disorder, sometimes known as "double depression." Most patients have a complicated course, and the prognosis is hard to determine.

DSM III-R criteria for dysthymic disorder are the following:

1. Depression or irritability for most of the day, more days than not, as reported by the patient's subjective account or others' objective observations, lasting a year in children and adolescents (two years in adults)
2. The presence of at least two of the following conditions while depressed or irritable:
   a. Poor appetite or overeating
   b. Insomnia or hypersomnia
   c. Low energy or fatigue
   d. Low self-esteem

       e.  Poor concentration or difficulty making decisions

       f.  Feelings of hopelessness

3.  During the one-year period, symptoms of depression or irritability should be present for more than two months.

4.  Absence of an unequivocal major depressive episode during the one-year period of the disturbance

5.  Absence of an unequivocal manic or hypomanic episode

6.  Absence of symptoms such as schizophrenia or delusional disorder superimposed on a chronic psychotic disorder

7.  Absence of an organic etiology initiating or maintaining the symptoms; for example, thyroid disease or steroid use.

No specific reports exist in the literature describing the clinical presentation of DD in learning-disabled children and adolescents. Despite the similarities between MDD and DD, Kovacs (1988), has postulated that the two conditions should be treated as distinct clinical entities, because the temporal aspects of their recovery are different. In previous studies, these authors have described two thirds of the children with DD as being at risk for MDD, but only one third of the children with MDD are at risk for having a concurrent DD (Kovacs 1984; Kovacs et al. 1984).

## MAJOR DEPRESSIVE DISORDER

The remainder of this chapter focuses on major depressive disorders, especially in learning-disabled children. According to the United States Department of Education, approximately 5% of children and adolescents have learning disabilities. Diagnosis of depressive disorders in children is more difficult to ascertain and diagnose than in adults. Children often are unable to describe their affective state orally; therefore, diagnosis cannot always rest on their oral reports. Although there are no separate criteria for major depressive disorder in learning-disabled children, it is even more difficult to diagnose them because of their cognitive and developmental limitations. Because they experience many stressors, especially at school, it can be difficult to ascertain whether the symptoms represent an adjustment disorder with depressed mood.

DSM III-R diagnostic criteria for a major depressive episode are the following:

1.  Depression or pervasive anhedonia for more than 2 weeks

2.  Five out of the following features also for more than 2 weeks:

       a.  Depressed mood (However, irritability is the most common affective state seen in children and adolescents.)

b. Appetite disturbances, usually a decrease in appetite with weight loss, and occasionally an increase in appetite, with a craving for carbohydrates (At times there is no change in appetite or weight per se, but the child or adolescent may not enjoy eating and may lose interest in the pleasure derived from eating.)

c. Sleep disturbances, often associated with children who are depressed, are the same as seen in adults; namely, trouble settling for bed, difficulty falling asleep, middle of the night wakening, and sometimes early morning awakening (At times children and adolescents report being awakened by bad dreams and/or nightmares. If this is a change in the usual pattern of sleep, it should raise suspicion of a possible mood disorder.)

d. Motor agitation or retardation is seen in children or adolescents as motor restlessness, fidgetiness, and trouble sitting still (Conversely, the child or adolescent may become motorically retarded, moving and talking slowly.)

e. Loss of interest in usual activities is one most readily observed by parents and others close to the patient, because youngsters will either cease their usual activities or not want to be around their friends and family. Children and adolescents who belong to clubs, sports teams, or other group activities will show less enthusiasm and interest, often giving up the activity all together.

f. Loss of energy and lethargy are often evident in children and adolescents in the midst of a depressive episode. They feel tired, napping in the middle of the day, or just lying around. They are easily exhausted and complain of low energy.

g. Self-reproach and guilt, often seen in adults, can be a symptom of depression in children and adolescents. However, because guilt is a more abstract and sophisticated concept of psychological development, it is often not present in very young children.

h. Impaired concentration usually translates into difficulty in school, resulting in a decline in school performance. Academic grades may plummet, or students may have to work much harder to maintain academic performance. They describe their minds as wandering or at times being "just blank." This symptom is noticed by both parents and teachers.

i. Recurrent thoughts of death and suicide can occur in young children. Failing to ask about such thoughts is an error because most children are aware of death, even if at a simple, concrete psychological level.

3. There are exclusionary criteria for the diagnosis of a major depressive episode; that is, presence of schizophrenia, organic disorder, and uncomplicated bereavement.

The DSM III-R states that certain other features, such as symptoms of separation-anxiety, social withdrawal, and oppositional behavior may be more common in children and adolescents with MDD.

Impaired cognitive functioning has been reported in adults with major depressive disorder (McAllister 1981; Fogel and Sparadeo 1985; Colby and Gotlib 1988). This impairment, sometimes referred to as a pseudodementia, usually dissipates as the patient recovers. Evidence of this in children and adolescents is sparse because of the small samples of most studies and lack of data. However, Brumback and colleagues (Brumback, Staton, and Wilson 1980; Brumback, Jackoway, and Weinberg 1980) have demonstrated cognitive impairment in children diagnosed with MDD. This raises concerns about the childrens' school performance, which may be adversely affected as a result of MDD. Therefore, children who are learning disabled and doing poorly in school may become further compromised in their cognitive skills when afflicted with MDD. This has definite implications in providing appropriate educational and psychiatric services. It is, therefore, crucial that educators be familiar with the signs and symptoms of major depressive disorders in children and adolescents to enable them to become effective advocates for their students.

Several investigators have identified depressive symptoms, behavioral difficulties, hyperactivity, and attentional problems in learning-disabled children (Ollendick and Yule 1990; Rourke, Young, and Leenaars 1989; Ritter 1989; Hoyle and Serefica 1988; Jensen, Burke, and Garfinkel 1988; Bruck 1986; Epstein, Cullinan, and Lloyd 1986; Margalit and Raviv 1984; Paget and Reynolds 1984; Bryan, Sonnefeld, and Greenberg 1981). In 1985, Livingston reviewed the literature on the association between MDD and LD and questioned the cause-and-effect relationship between the two conditions. He wondered if the two conditions exacerbated each other and also hypothesized a possible common brain abnormality causing the two to co-occur. Livingston (1985) raised three important questions, related to depressive illness and learning difficulties.

1. "Does depression cause or worsen learning problems?" (p. 518). As Livingston stated, "there is a temporal relationship between the onset of MDD and the onset or worsening of impaired learning, and that resolution or successful treatment of MDD is associated with improvement in school performance" (p. 518).

Brumback and Weinberg (1977) in fact, included school performance impairment as a criteria for MDD. Although no studies
show this phenomenon in very young children, it has been
demonstrated in college students (Whitney, Cadoret, and
McClure 1971). Cognitive improvement associated with treatment of MDD with tricyclic antidepressants in children was
shown by Staton, Wilson, and Brumback (1981).

2. "Do learning disabilities put children at greater risk for
   depression?" (p. 519).

   Again, Livingston (1985) hypothesized that MDD was more
   prevalent in children with learning disabilities when compared to controls, or even to children with other psychiatric
   or social problems. In a study examining 100 hospitalized
   children, age range 9 to 12 years, Kashani, Cantrell, and
   Shekim (1982) reported that 62% of the 13 children who met
   DSM III criteria for MDD, were also diagnosed as having
   learning disabilities. However, only 22% of the 87 nonde-
   pressed children met criteria for LD. Kashani concluded that
   perhaps some children were predisposed to have both conditions, thereby lending credence to the hypothesis put forward by Livingston.

3. "Is there some particular brain dysfunction that puts children at increased risk for both MDD and LD?" (p. 519).

   Studies in adults have suggested a relationship between
   MDD and right hemispheric dysfunction (Yozewitz, Bruder,
   and Sutton 1979; Silberman, Weingartner, and Silberman
   1983). Robinson et al. (1984) have demonstrated an increased
   incidence of depression in left hemispheric poststroke
   patients and a higher incidence of manic-like symptoms in
   those patients with a right hemispheric stroke. This might
   lead us to believe that, in fact, there is a relationship of specific brain dysfunction and MDD. Rutter (1982) wrote about
   nonspecific psychiatric vulnerabilities in children who had
   experienced a brain insult/injury or dysfunction. Similarly,
   Brumback and associates (Brumback, Staton, and Wilson
   1980; Brumback and Staton 1983) described an association
   between brain dysfunction and MDD in children.

## DIAGNOSIS

Diagnosis of depressive disorders in adults, children, and adolescents
is based on the history and examination of the mental state. It is
important to take a complete history, which should include a detailed
family history because it is extremely valuable in identifying children

and adolescents at risk for developing MDD, and a comprehensive mental status examination. However, even with a good history and examination, it sometimes remains unclear if the patient has a major depression. Diagnosis is even more difficult with very young, prepubertal children who are unable to describe their mood states. It is helpful to obtain information from a number of sources: for example, parents, grandparents, the classroom teacher, day-care provider, or babysitter. Questions should be asked about changes in mood, behavior, and interactions with adults and peers; lack of interest in activities; lethargy; lack of motivation; decrease in concentration; and excessive tearfulness or irritability. Young children rarely can participate in a formal mental state examination. Often they do not understand the meaning of words such as mood, sad, or blue; but they can understand a *sad face* or a *smiling face* and they can point to the one that best depicts the way they feel.

Diagnosis can be aided by the use of questionnaires designed to measure depressive symptoms in children and adolescents. Among these are the Beck Depression Scale (Beck, Ward, and Mendelson 1961), the Children's Depression Inventory (Kovacs 1981), and the Johns Hopkins Depression Checklist (HDCL) for children (Joshi, Capozzoli, and Coyle 1990). Unlike the latter, the first two are subjective rating scales relying on self-report from the patients with no input from the parents. Kazdin, French, and Onis (1983) have shown that there is less than 100% concordance between self-rating and parents' evaluation of their child's depressive symptoms. It is important to keep in mind that parents usually have access to different information about depressive symptoms in their children. Parents are usually less aware of their children's affective state which is "internalized," and more aware of and accurate in describing behaviors such as overt irritability, oppositionality, and disruptiveness. Furthermore, children's self-rating may be much more sensitive to and affected by immediate life circumstances than are those of adults, and therefore, more valuable over time. Although the prevalence of serious depression in children and adolescents is approximately 1% to 2% (Kashani and Simonds 1979), reports of up to 33% have been reported in the literature using the Beck Depression Scale (Albert and Beck 1975). The Johns Hopkins Depression Checklist (Joshi et al. 1990), which is a 38-item checklist, has been normalized on a large normal population age 5–13 years. Unlike the subjective scales, the HDCL is an objective measure, completed by the parents. It has been shown to be sensitive to change over time when used in depressed in-patients (Joshi et al. 1990). Structured and semistructured interviews, such as the Kiddie Schedule for Affective Disorders and Schizophrenia (K-SADS) (Chambers, Puig-Antich, and Hirsh 1985), Diagnostic Inter-view for Children and Adolescents–Revised (DICA-R) (Herjanic and Reich 1982) and the Diagnostic Interview Schedule for

Children (DISC) (Costello et al. 1984) are also used for clinical and research purposes to identify depressed children and adolescents.

In addition to the various available diagnostic instruments, clinicians often rely on other methods to help support clinical impressions. Some of these methods include cognitive and projective testing; that is, responses to Rorschach cards or the Thematic Apperception Test (TAT) stories. Themes indicative of depression, self-blame, hopelessness/helplessness, abandonment, and self-harm or suicide are often prevalent. Scores on the cognitive tasks related to memory and concentration are often effected; however, our experience has been that scores usually return to baseline after the child gets well. These lowered scores might suggest the "pseudodementia" reported in adults. Children's artwork is reflective of their mental states. In our experience, depressed children typically draw ill-defined figures, with decreased intensity of lines. The pictures are disorganized and lack color. Marked improvement is seen in artwork once a child becomes euthymic. Because drawing is common activity of most young children, it could be clinically helpful to follow a child's artwork.

Several biological markers, such as cortisol secretion and sleep EEG changes, have been associated with depression in adults (Berger et al. 1984; Mason 1968; APA Task Force Report 1987). The one studied fairly extensively in children is cortisol secretion (Dexamethasone Secretion Test [DST]). As in most adult studies of DST, the results in children and adolescents are equally inconclusive (Doherty et al. 1986; Casat, Arana, and Powell 1989; Naylor, Greden, and Alessi 1990; Birmaher et al. 1992a, b). None of these biological tests currently is being administered routinely to children with MDD. In most instances, they are part of a research design and are still being investigated as to their usefulness.

### TREATMENT

Treatment of learning-disabled children with MDD can be more complex than treatment for those who are without a learning disability. Three aspects of treatment should be emphasized: (1) education about the illness once the patient has been diagnosed with MDD; (2) pharmacotherapy; and (3) supportive therapy.

### Education

Education involves open discussion with the child and his or her parents about the general nature of the disorder, its presentation, prognosis, and specific aspects as they apply to the particular child, keeping in mind the child's specific deficits and disabilities. Because MDD is episodic, the patient and family should be able to recognize recurrences and seek treatment in a timely fashion. The child or adolescent and the parents often can be referred to helpful readings, seminars, and other materials on the disorder available from the American Academy of Child and Adolescent Psychiatry.

## Pharmacotherapy

Pharmacotherapy includes the use of antidepressants, mood stabilizers, and anticonvulsants. Treatment of depression with tricyclics was first noted in 1969 by Lucas and Pasley. There was controversy and debate at the time about the nosology and whether depression in fact was a distinct clinical entity in children and adolescents. In the last decade, there has been increasing clarity; several studies have described depressive phenomena in children and adolescents. With the advent of diagnostic criteria, studies examining the efficacy of the use of antidepressants appeared. Although most open studies have shown antidepressants to be effective in the treatment of MDD in the young, most of the rigorous, double-blind, placebo-controlled studies repeatedly have been unable to demonstrate any superiority of antidepressants to placebos (Weinberg et al. 1973; Puig-Antich et al. 1978; Preskorn, Weiler, and Weller 1982; Petti and Law 1982; Kashani, Shekim, and Reid 1984; Geller et al. 1992). Most of the patients in these studies had a chronic, unremitting course of depressive illness, with a high degree of comorbidity. In adults, however, the same drugs have been shown to be efficacious in the treatment of depression, although not to the same degree as in those with a high degree of co-morbidity (Hamilton 1979; Keller et al. 1990: Liebowitz, Hollander, and Schneider 1990). Perhaps studies with depressed youngsters who have fewer co-morbid conditions may reveal more promising results.

The groups of antidepressants used in the treatment of depression in children and adolescents have been tricyclic antidepressants, monoamine oxidase inhibitors, fluoxetine, lithium, and anticonvulsants.

***Tricyclic Antidepressants.*** The most commonly prescribed tricyclics are imipramine (Tofranil), desipramine (Norpramine), and nortriptyline (Pamelor or Aventyl). One of the serious side effects of the tricyclic antidepressants is cardiotoxicity, so it is important to assess baseline cardiac status, including an EKG, and pulse and blood pressure recordings in both the prone and supine positions. It is important to discuss the use of tricyclics with the parents, and to discuss with the child or adolescent potential untoward side effects. Several studies have demonstrated lengthening of the PR and QRS intervals at doses of 5 mg/kg of imipramine (Puig-Antich, Ryan, and Rabinovich 1985; Biederman et al. 1989; Schroeder et al. 1989). Although not mandatory, informed consent is desirable. The use of therapeutic blood levels is becoming part of the normal practice when administering tricyclic antidepressants to children and adolescents. The guidelines are the same as in adults; that is, levels between 150–250 ng/ml of desipramine or a combination of desipramine and imipramine or, in the case of nortriptyline, a level between 50–150 ng/ml. The advantages of obtaining blood levels is two-fold—to guide dosing regimen and to determine compliance. Other annoying side effects are mouth dryness, constipation, postural dizziness, and, occasionally, weight gain.

*Monoamine Oxidase Inhibitors (MAOIs).* The monoamine oxidase inhibitors are infrequently used in the treatment of major depression in children and adolescents. Only one study in the literature describes the efficacy of MAOIs in adolescents (Ryan, Puig-Antich, and Rabinovich 1988). Scientific studies and the use of MAOIs in the young may be limited by potentially life-threatening side effects of hypertensive crises in patients who do not follow a tyramine-free diet. These dietary restrictions can be difficult to monitor in children and adolescents, especially those who have problems with compliance and reliability. In light of some of the newer antidepressants with potentially less serious side effects, the MAOIs are no longer one of the first antidepressants considered in the treatment of depression in children and adolescents.

*Fluoxetine.* Fluoxetine (Prozac) is a newer antidepressant that has received much publicity, both in the lay press and in scientific publications. It is a selective serotonin re-uptake inhibitor (SSRI), which has been shown to be efficacious in the treatment of major depression and obsessive-compulsive disorder in adults. In children and adolescents, there are two reports of its use in the treatment of major depression (Joshi et al. 1989; Simeon, Dinicola, and Ferguson 1990). Fluoxetine has a long half-life and dosing should be done more slowly; for example, 10 mg/day or every other day. It tends to have a cumulative effect over time, and there are reports of patients who were being treated for obsessive-compulsive disorder becoming disinhibited, impulsive, hyperactive, and self-destructive at higher doses (King, Riddle, and Chappell 1991). The advantages of fluoxetine are its minimal cardiac, anticholinergic, and antihistaminic side effects.

*Lithium.* Lithium, a naturally occurring salt, has been used in children and adolescents for a variety of disorders and symptoms, from the treatment of bipolar disorders (Youngerman and Canino 1978), organic mood disorders (Joshi, Capozzoli, and Coyle 1985), management of aggression (Lena 1980; Jefferson, Greist, and Ackerman 1983), and as an adjunct to tricyclic antidepressants in the treatment of major depression (Strober 1989). Because lithium is excreted through the kidneys and has a tendency to concentrate in the thyroid, it is important to obtain baseline thyroid functions and an estimate of renal clearance and kidney functions. Dosing of lithium in children and adolescents follows the same guidelines as in adults. In the very young, our practice is to start on a low dose of 150 mg twice daily, monitoring to obtain therapeutic blood levels of between 0.7–1.2 meq/l. The side effects should be discussed with the parents, as in starting any medication. The annoying and early side effects are usually gastrointestinal, including nausea, abdominal cramps, and diarrhea. These usually tend to subside in the first few days of treatment and are sometimes alleviated by prescribing the coated lithium preparation—lithobid. Some of the later side effects include hand tremors, which can be extremely embarrassing to a school-aged child who finds it difficult to write. This can be especially annoying to a learning-disabled child in whom other disabilities get exacerbated. Polyuria and polydipsia are signs of nephrogenic diabetes insipidus that can cause an emergence of enuresis, which again can result in embarrassment and, later, noncompliance in a school-aged child. Toxicity results in cardiac arrhythmias at levels above 1.2 meq/l with impairment in cognitive functioning, lethargy, and stupor. Monitoring of lithium in children and adolescents should be done carefully and frequently to avoid untoward side effects.

***Anticonvulsants.*** The most commonly used anticonvulsant in the treatment of depression and manic depressive illness in children and adolescents is carbamazepine (Tegretol). In adults, it has been shown to be prophylactic in mania and depression in patients resistant to lithium (Post, Uhde, and Ballenger 1983; Potter 1983). Several reports have shown carbamazepine to decrease impulsiveness, agitation, and affective lability in children and adolescents (Remschmidt 1976; Yatham and McHale 1988; Kafantaris, Campbell, and Pardonn-Gayol 1992). The usual dose ranges from 300–800 mg/day in divided doses, with a plasma level of 6–12 ug/ml. Discussion with the family of potential side effects, such as allergic skin rash, initial lethargy and drowsiness, dysarthria, and ataxia is important. Other side effects include a decrease in the white cell count. Therefore, before starting treatment with carbamazepine, it is important to obtain baseline blood counts, including differential and platelet counts. Work-up should also include electrolytes, liver function tests, and an EKG. Carbamazepine has been used in combination with the tricyclic antidepressants and with lithium. Combination with the MAOIs can result in alarming and toxic plasma levels of carbamazepine and is not recommended (Rudorfer and Potter 1987).

## Supportive Treatment

Supportive treatment includes teaching about the illness to families and patients, especially adolescents. Denial of depressive illness is a common occurrence, not only with young patients but also with their families. Many times patients and their families feel stigmatized and need supportive counseling to help with their feelings of inadequacy, anger, and despair. This can be done in supportive individual therapy, family therapy, or sometimes by referring them to support groups especially formed for those suffering from a major depressive disorder. Several groups have been formed for all ages and their families to discuss the effects of having a depressive disorder in themselves or their loved ones. Supportive treatment in the young may also include talking with school counselors and the child's teacher to acquaint them with the signs and symptoms of the disorder, and to get them involved in helping the child in school.

Another intervention might be to refer the young patient's ill parent for treatment for a condition that previously may have gone unidentified. There is evidence of strong family histories in children and adolescents with depressive disorders, so other family members may need psychiatric intervention and appropriate treatment. Treatment also includes helping children see themselves in context with their friends, school, and future goals and aspirations. It is important to help adolescents gradually take responsibility for their own care as they get ready to move into the adult world and away from the confines of their immediate families.

Diagnosis and treatment of depressive disorders are becoming broader as we become more skilled in identifying children and adolescents at risk and those who already suffer from these disorders. In learning-disabled youngsters, there are other mediating factors related to their specific learning disability, which makes it even more important to identify the disorder correctly and initiate treatment efficiently. We continue to make important strides in the field of depressive disorders and it is to be hoped that the next decade will answer yet unanswered questions.

## REFERENCES

Albert, N., and Beck, A. T. 1975. Incidence of depression in early adolescence: A preliminary study. *Journal of Youth and Adolescence* 4:301–307.
American Psychiatric Association. 1987. *Diagnostic and Statistical Manual of Mental Disorders—DSM III-R*, 3rd. ed. Washington, DC: American Psychiatric Association.
APA Task Force on Laboratory Tests in Psychiatry. 1987. The dexamethasone suppression test: An overview of its current status in psychiatry. *American*

*Journal of Psychiatry* 144:1253–1262.

Berger, M., Pirke, K. M., Doerr, P., Kreicg, J. C., and Zersten, V. 1984. The limited utility of the dexamethasone suppression test for the diagnostic process in psychiatry. *British Journal of Psychiatry* 145:372–82.

Biederman, J., Baldessarinai, R. J., Wright, V., Keen, D., Harmatz, J. S., and Goldbatt, A. 1989. A double-blind placebo controlled study of desipramine in the treatment of ADD: II. Serum drug levels and cardiovascular findings. *Journal of the American Academy of Child and Adolescent Psychiatry* 28:903–911.

Birmaher, B., Ryan, N. D., Dahl, R. E., Rabinovich, H., Ambrosini, R. J., Williamson, D., Novacenko, H., Nelson, B., Puig-Antich, J., and Lo, E. S. 1992a. Dexamethasone suppression test in children with major depressive disorder. *Journal of the American Academy of Child and Adolescent Psychiatry* 31:291–97.

Birmaher, B., Dahl, R. E., Ryan, N. D., Rabinovich, H., Ambrosini, P. J., Al-Shabbout, M., Novacenko, H., Nelson, B., and Puig-Antich, J. 1992b. The dexamethasone suppression test in adolescent outpatients with major depressive disorder. *American Journal of Psychiatry* 149:1040–1045.

Beck, A. T., Ward, C. H., and Mendelson, M. 1961. An inventory for measuring depression. *Archives of General Psychiatry* 4:561–71.

Bruck, M. 1986. Social and emotional adjustments of learning disabled children: A review of the issues. In *Handbook of Cognitive, Social, Neuropsychological Aspects of Learning Disabilities*, ed. S. Ceci. Hillsdale, NJ: Lawrence Erlbaum Associates.

Brumback, R. A., and Staton, R. D. 1983. Learning disabilities and childhood depression. *American Journal of Orthopsychiatry* 53:269–81.

Brumback, R. A., and Weinberg, W. 1977. Childhood depression: An explanation of a behavior disorder of children. *Perception and Motor Skills* 44: 911–916.

Brumback, R. A., Jackoway, M. K., and Weinberg, W. A. 1980. Relation of intelligence to childhood depression in children referred to an educational diagnostic center. *Perception and Motor Skills* 50:11–17.

Brumback, R. A., Staton, R. D., and Wilson, H. 1980. Neuropsychological study of children during and after remission of endogenous depressive episodes. *Perception and Motor Skills* 50:1163–1167.

Bryan, T. H., Sonnefeld, L. J., and Greenberg, F. Z. 1981. Children's and parents' views of integration tactics. *Learning Disability Quarterly* 4:170–79.

Carlson, G. A., and Strober, M. 1978. Manic-depressive illness in early adolescence. *Journal of the American Academy of Child and Adolescent Psychiatry* 17:138–53.

Casat, C. D., Arana, G. W., and Powell, K. 1989. The DST in children and adolescents with major depressive disorder. *American Journal of Psychiatry* 146:503–507.

Chambers, W. J., Puig-Antich, J., and Hirsh,M. 1985. The assessment of affective disorders in children and adolescents by semi-structured interview. *Archives of General Psychiatry* 42:696–702.

Colby, C.A., and Gotlib, I. H. 1988. Memory deficits in depression. *Cognitive Therapy and Research* 12(6):611–27.

Costello, A. J., Edelbrook, C. S., Kalas, R., Dulcan, M. D., and Klaric, S. H. 1984. *Development and Testing of the NIMH Diagnostic Interview Schedule for Children in a Clinical Population* (Contract #RSP-DB-81/0027). Rockville, MD: Center for Epidemiologic Studies, NIMH.

Doherty, M. B., Madansky, D., Kraft, J., Caterake, L. L., Rosenthal, P. A., and Coughlin, B. F. 1986. Cortisol dynamics and test performance of the dexamethasone suppression test in 97 psychiatrically hospitalized children age 3–16 years. *Journal of the American Academy of Child and Adolescent Psychiatry* 25:400–408.

Epstein, M. H., Cullinan, D., and Lloyd, J. W. 1986. Behavior problem patterns among the learning disabled: III-Replication across age and sex. *Learning Disability Quarterly* 9:43–54.

Fogel, B. S., and Sparadeo, F. R. 1985. Cognitive deficits accentuated by depression. *Journal of Nervous and Mental Disorders* 173(2):120–24.

Geller, B., Cooper, T. B., Graham, D. L., Fetner, H. H., Marsteller, F. A., and Wells, J. M. 1992. Pharmacokinetically designed double-blind, placebo controlled study of nortriptyline in 6 to 12 year olds with major depressive disorder. *American Journal of the Academy of Child and Adolescent Psychiatry* 31:34–44.

Hamilton, M. 1979. Mania and depression: Classification, description, and course. In *Psychopharmacology of Affective Disorders*, eds. E. S. Paykel and A. Coppen. New York: Oxford University Press.

Herjanic, B., and Reich, W. 1982. Development of a structured psychiatric interview for children: Agreement between child and parent on individual symptoms. *Journal of Abnormal Child Psychology* 10:307–324.

Hoyle, , S. G., and Serafica, F. C. 1988. Peer status of children with and without learning disabilities—A multimethod study. *Learning Disability Quarterly* II:322–30.

Jenson, J. B., Burke, N., and Garfinkel, B. D. 1988. Depression and symptoms of attention deficit disorder with hyperactivity. *Journal of the American Academy of Child and Adolescent Psychiatry* 27(6):742–47.

Jefferson, J. W., Greist, J. H., and Ackerman, D. L. 1983. *Lithium Encyclopedia for Clinical Practice*. Washington, DC: American Psychiatric Press.

Joshi, P. T., Capozzoi, J. A., and Coyle, J. T. 1985. Effective management with lithium of a persistent, post-traumatic hypomania in a 10 year old child. *Journal of Developmental and Behavioral Pediatrics* 6(6):352–54.

Joshi, P. T., Capozzoli, J. A., and Coyle, J. T. 1990. The Johns Hopkins Depression Scale: Normative data and validation in child psychiatry patients. *Journal of the American Academy of Child and Adolescent Psychiatry* 29(2):283–88.

Joshi, P. T., Capozzoli, J. A., Walkup, J. T., DeTrinis, R. B., and Coyle, J. T. 1990. Hopkins Depression Checklist: Follow up study. Paper presented at the 37th annual meeting of the American Academy of Child and Adolescent Psychiatry, Chicago, October.

Joshi, P. T., Walkup, J. T., Capozzoli, J. A., DeTrinis, R. B, and Coyle, J. T. 1989. The use of fluoxetine in the treatment of major depressive disorder in children and adolescents. Paper presented at the 36th annual meeting of the American Academy of Child and Adolescent Psychiatry, New York, October.

Kafantaris, V., Campbell, M., and Pardonn-Gayol, M. V. In press. Carbamazepine in hospitalized aggressive conduct disordered children: A pilot study. *Psychopharmacological Bulletin*.

Kashani, J. H., and Simonds, J. F. 1979. The incidence of depression in children. *American Journal of Psychiatry* 136:1203–1205.

Kashani, J. H., Cantwell, D. P., and Shekim, W. O. 1982. Major depressive disorder in children admitted to an inpatient community mental health center. *American Journal of Psychiatry* 139:671–72.

Kashani, J. H., Shekim, W. O., and Reid, J. C. 1984. Amitriptyline in children with MDD: A double-blind crossover pilot study. *Journal of the American Academy of Child and Adolescent Psychiatry* 23:348–51.

Kazdin, A. E., French, N. H., and Unis, A. S. 1983. Assessment of childhood depression: Correspondence of child and parent ratings. *Journal of the American Academy of Child and Adolescent Psychiatry* 22:157–64.

Keller, M. B., Lavori, P. W., Endicott, J., Coryell, W., and Klerman, G. L. 1990. Diagnostic and course of illness variables pertinent to refractory depression. In *APA Annual Review of Psychiatry*, eds. A. Tasman, C. Kaufman, and S. Goldfinger. Washington, DC: American Psychiatric Press.

King, R. A., Riddle, M. A., and Chappell, P. B. 1991. Emergence of self-destructive phenomenon in children and adolescents during fluoxetine treatment. *Journal of the American Academy of Psychiatry* 30: 179–86.

Kovacs, M. 1981. Rating scales to assess depression in school aged children. *Acta Paedopsychiatrica (Basel)* 46:305–315.

Kovacs, M. 1985. The Children's Depression Inventory (CDI). *Psychopharmacological Bulletin* 21:995–98.

Kovacs, M. 1992. A prospective study of DSM III Adjustment disorders in childhood. Paper presented at the Institute on Long Term Outcome of Childhood Disorders at the annual meeting of the American Academy of Child and Adolescent Psychiatry, Washington, DC.

Kovacs, M., Feinberg, T. L., Crouse-Novak, M. A., Paulauskas, S. L., and Finkelstein, R. 1984. Depressive disorders in childhood. I. A longitudinal prospective study of characteristics and recovery. *Archives of General Psychiatry* 41:229–37.

Kovacs, M., Paulauskas, S., Gatsonis, C., and Richards, C. 1988. Depressive disorders in childhood. III. A longitudinal study of comorbidity with and risk for conduct disorders. *Archives of General Psychiatry* 46:776–82.

Kovacs, M., Pollack, M., and Finkelstein, R. 1984. Depressive disorders in childhood. II. A longitudinal study of the risk for a subsequent major depression. *Archives of General Psychiatry* 41:643–49.

Lena, B. 1980. Lithium treatment of children and adolescents. In *Handbook of Lithium Therapy*, ed. F. N. Johnson. Lancaster: MAP Press.

Liebowitz, M. R., Hollander, E., and Schneider, F. 1990. Anxiety and depression: Discrete diagnostic entities? *Clinical Psychopharmacology* 10:61S–66S.

Livingston, R. 1985. Depressive illness and learning difficulties: Research needs and practical implications. *Journal of Learning Disabilities* 18(9):518–20.

Lucas, A., and Pasley, F. 1969. Psychoactive drugs in the treatment of emotionally disturbed children: Haloperidol and diazepam. *Comprehensive Psychiatry* 10:376–86.

Margalit, M., and Raviv, A. 1984. Learning disabilities' expressions of anxiety in terms of minor somatic complaints. *Journal of Learning Disabilities* 17: 226–28..

Mason, J. W. 1968. A review of psychoendocrine research on the pituitary-adrenal cortical system. *Psychosomatic Medicine* 30:576–607.

McAlister, T. W. 1981. Cognitive functioning in the affective disorders. *Comprehensive Psychiatry* 22(6):572–88.

Naylor, M. W., Greden, J. F., and Alessi, N. E. 1990. Plasma dexamethasone levels in children given the dexamethasone suppression test. *Biological Psychiatry* 27:592–600.

Ollendick, T. H., and Yule, W. 1990. Depression in British and American children and its relation to anxiety and fear. *Journal of Consulting and Clinical Psychology* 58(1):126–29.

Paget, K. D., and Reynolds, C. R. 1984. Dimensions, levels and reliabilities on the revised children's Manifest Anxiety Scale with learning disabled children. *Journal of Learning Disabilities* 17:137–41.

Petti, T. A., and Law, W. 1982. III. Imipramine treatment of depressed children: A double-blind pilot study. *Journal of Clinical Psychopharmacology* 2:107–110.

Post, R. M., Uhde, T. W., and Ballenger, J. C. 1983. Prophylactic efficacy of Carbamazepine in manic-depressive illness. *American Journal of Psychiatry* 140:1602–1604.

Potter, H. W. 1983. Schizophrenia in children. *American Journal of Psychiatry* 12:1253.

Preskorn, S. H., Weller, E. B., and Weller, R. A. 1982. Plasma levels of imipramine and metabolites in 68 hospitalized children. *Journal of Clinical Psychiatry* 43:450–53.

Puig-Antich, J., Blau, S., Marx, N., Greenhill, L. L, and Chambers, W. 1978. Prepubertal major depressive disorder: A pilot study. *Journal of the American Academy of Child and Adolescent Psychiatry* 17:695–707.

Puig-Antich, J., Ryan, N. D., and Rabinovich, H. 1985. Affective disorders in childhood and adolescence. In *Diagnosis and Psychopharmacology of Childhood and Adolescent Disorders*, ed. J. M Wiener. New York: Wiley.

Remschmidt, H. 1976. The psychotropic effect of carbamazepine in non-epileptic patients. In *Epileptic Seizures Behavior Pain*, ed. W. Birkmayer. Berne: Hans Huber.

Ringdahl, I. C. 1980. Depressive reactions in children and adolescents. *Psychosomatics* 21:930–38.

Ritter, D. R. 1989. Social competence and problem behavior of adolescent girls with learning disabilities. *Journal of Learning Disabilities* 22(7):460–61.

Robinson, R. G., Kubos, K. L., Starr, L. B., Rao, K., and Price, T. R. 1984. Mood disorders in stroke patients: Importance of location of lesion. *Brain* 107: 81–93.

Rourke, B. P., Young, G. C., and Leenaars, A. A. 1989. A childhood learning disability that predisposes those afflicted to adolescent and adult depression and suicide risk. *Journal of Learning Disabilities* 22(3):169–73.

Rudorfer, M. V., and Potter, W. Z. 1987. Pharmacokinetics and antidepressants. In *Psychopharmacology: The Third Generation of Progress*, ed. H. Y . Meltzer. New York: Raven Press.

Rutter, M. 1981. Stress, coping and developing: Some issues and some questions. *Journal of Child Psychology and Psychiatry* 22:323–56.

Rutter, M. 1982. Syndromes attributed to minimal brain dysfunction in childhood. *American Journal of Psychiatry* 139:21–23.

Rutter, M., Graham, P., Chadwick, O. F. D., and Yule, W. 1976. Adolescent turmoil: Facts or fiction. *Journal of Child Psychology and Psychiatry* 17:35–56.

Rutter, M., Tizard, J., and Whitmore, K. (eds.) 1970. *Education, Health and Behaviour*. London: Longman.

Ryan, N. D., Puig-Antich, J., and Rabinovich, H. 1988. MAOIs in adolescent major depression unresponsive to tricyclic antidepressants. *Journal of the American Academy of Child and Adolescent Psychiatry* 27:755–58.

Schroeder, J. S., Mullin, A. V., Elliot, G. R., Stein, H., Nichols, M., Gordon, A., and Paulos, M. 1989. Cardiovascular effects of desipramine in children. *Journal of the American Academy of Child and Adolescent Psychiatry* 28:376–79.

Shaffer, D., and Fisher, P. 1981. The epidemiology of suicide in children and young adolescents. *Journal of the American Academy of Child and Adolescent Psychiatry* 20:545–65.

Silberman, E. K., Weingartner, H., and Stillman, R. 1983. Altered lateralization of cognitive processes in depressed women. *American Journal of Psychiatry* 140:1340–1344.

Simeon, J. G., Dinicola, V. F., Ferguson, B. H. 1990. Adolescent depression: A placebo controlled fluoxetine treatment study and follow-up. *Progress in Neuropsychopharmacology and Biological Psychiatry* 14:791–95.

Staton, D., Wilson, H., and Brumback, R. 1981. Cognitive improvement associated with tricyclic antidepressant treatment of childhood major depressive illness. *Perceptual and Motor Skills* 53:219–34.

Strober, M. 1989. Effects of imipramine, lithium and fluoxetine in the treatment of adolescent major depression. Washington, DC: National Institutes of Mental Health, New Clinical Drug Evaluation Unit (NCDEU) Annual Meeting (Abstract).

Whitney, W., Cadoret, R. J., and McClure, J. 1971. Depressive symptoms and academic performance in college students. *American Journal of Psychiatry* 128:766–70.

Weinberg, W., Rutman, J., Sullivan, L., Penick, E. C., and Dietz, S. G. 1973. Depression in children referred to an educational diagnostic center: Diagnosis and treatment. *Journal of Pediatrics* 83:1065–1072.

Yatham, L. N., and McHale, P. A. 1988. Carbamazepine in the treatment of aggression: A case report and review of the literature. *Acta Psychiatry Scandinavia* 78:188–90.

Youngerman, J., and Canino, I. A. 1978. Lithium carbonate use in children and adolescents. *Archives of General Psychiatry* 35:216.

Yozewitz, A., Bruder, G., and Sutton, S. 1979. Evidence for right hemisphere dysfunction in affective psychosis. *British Journal of Psychiatry* 135:224–27.

# Chapter • 11

## CONDUCT DISORDER VERSUS OPPOSITIONAL DEFIANT DISORDER
### *Endpoint of Learning Disabilities*

*Pasquale J. Accardo*

### CRYSTALLIZATION

Any discussion of the relationship between behavior disorders (BD) and learning disabilites (LD) requires that serious consideration be paid to a tertium quid—attention deficit hyperactivity disorder (ADHD). In its various guises, ADHD frequently is confused with and misdiagnosed as a behavioral disorder or, less often, as a learning disability.

From the viewpoint of child psychiatry, the behavior disorder syndromes of conduct disorder (CD) and oppositional defiant disorder (ODD) have long been considered purer entities—less tainted by any suggestion of organic etiology. From the perspective of special education, the definition of learning disabilities specifically excludes the impact of behavioral factors. Thus, the "unmotivated" student does not receive a diagnosis of learning disability. From the points of view of child psychiatry and special education, behavior disorder and learning disability are clearly defined operational constructs, whereas attention deficit hyperactivity disorder is seen as a confusing interloper.

This work was supported in part by grants from Columbian Charities of Missouri and the Knights of Columbus.

Within the past several years, leading pediatric journals have published articles suggesting that ADHD is nonexistent and that the behaviors purportedly composing this pseudosyndrome are variants of normal or simply the logical outcome of specific parenting deficits (Burke and McGee 1990; Carey 1988, 1992).

In fact, all of these assumptions about BD, LD, and ADHD are untrue, and any attempt to assess the association of BD with LD and/or ADHD will require at least a summary prologue of the sources of confusion that need correction.

First, far from being clearly defined and self-evident, there is significant doubt as to the objective existence of such conditions as oppositional defiant disorder and conduct disorder (Malmquist 1990). The process used to justify these labels can ultimately be used to justify any labeling of deviant behavior (Szasz 1961).

Second, although learning disabilities have definable diagnostic criteria to support their objective existence, the absence of a generally accepted subtyping schema leaves this group of developmental disabilities rather nebulous at the boundaries and somewhat disorganized internally. The serious design weaknesses implicit in most learning disabilities research is highlighted in the *Report to the U.S. Congress* of the Interagency Committee on Learning Disabilities (1988). This state of confusion may be multiplied further by attempts to address the issue of whether language-based learning disabilities are separate from other learning disabilities and from pure language disorders.

Third, child psychiatry's attempt to classify ADHD as a poor relation to oppositional defiant disorder and conduct disorder has been upset by striking evidence of a specific organic etiology. The classic report of Zametkin et al. (1990) has acted as a catalyst in a supersaturated solution, with the resultant crystallization leaving everyone scurrying for cover.

And lest credit not be given where due, the interpretation of ADHD as a specific diagnosable neurobehavioral syndrome has been a quietly persistant tradition in developmental pediatrics since the time of Still (Accardo and Whitman 1991; Capute and Accardo 1991). Until the past several years, the prevalent attitude has been to consider ADHD as an emotional diagnosis—a disruptive behavior disorder—rather than a neurodevelopmental diagnosis. The placement of ADHD, LD, and developmental language disorders on the spectrum of mildly handicapping, chronic central nervous system conditions (figure 1) may be a recent phenomenon, but it is one with very deep roots.

## DISRUPTIVE BEHAVIOR DISORDERS

The *Diagnostic and Statistical Manual*, third edition, revised (DSM III-R,

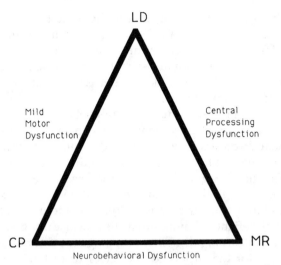

Figure 1. Developmental Pediatrics interprets the symptomatology of attention deficit hyperactivity disorder as milder variations of the attentional, cognitive, and motor dysfunctions observed in the classic brain dysfunction syndromes. (Modified from Capute 1991.)

American Psychiatric Association 1987), has a category called disruptive behavior disorders that includes conduct disorder, oppositional defiant disorder, and attention deficit hyperactivity disorder. These diagnoses are grouped together because their component behaviors are understood to disrupt the child's environment. Acting out, bad, or externalizing behaviors are merely behaviors that bother and irritate others. The relativism implicit in such discriminatory judgments should, in all but the most extreme cases, be considered worrisome.

The items that make up the diagnostic checklist for CD are antisocial behaviors—behaviors that violate societal rules and assault the basic rights of others. The incidence of CDs, if one includes the predelinquent phase, is on the order of ten to fifteen percent (Barkley 1990; Hendren 1990; Kaplan 1988; Lewis 1990; Quay 1985). The child needs to exhibit only three of the thirteen behaviors listed in column one of table I. Because norms can vary from one subpopulation to another and change drastically in a short period of time, these criteria remain subjective. (Was "date rape" rape before there was a conceptualization of "date rape?") The psychiatric diagnosis of CD overlaps to a large extent the legal classification of juvenile delinquincy. A close review of the rationale for "psychiatrifying" this category derived from the juvenile justice system does not inspire confidence in its validity. The little that is gained by lumping a child who tortures animals with a teenager guilty of burglary is surely going to be offset by the resultant terminological confusion. The important thing about a rapist is that he commits rape; that is the issue that needs to be addressed. Classifying him as a CD is a flight into irrelevance. Any hope that the category *conduct disorder* might be salvaged is further undercut by the fact that individual psychotherapy is rarely helpful in the therapy of conduct disorder; the most effective interventions seem to be preventive social programs.

A child qualifies for a diagnosis of ODD (Egan 1991) by exhibiting at least five of the nine behaviors listed in column two, table I. Oppositional disorders have an onset coterminous with the start of formal schooling and have an incidence on the order of five percent. A critical differential diagnostic point is the need to relate the course of the ODD behavior to the timetable of the child's school career and to the parental and teacher reactions to academic underachievement. Oppositional defiant behaviors that disappear during summer vacations suggest a learning disability or a language disorder as the objective substrate for the supposed "behavior disorder." The frequency with which children with ODD are referred for hearing evaluations should make the clinician suspicious of attention deficit disorder as a possible underlying organic causitive factor. Indeed, even without a hearing test, most parents can readily discriminate the child who doesn't hear from the child who doesn't listen. And, with a little training, these parents can further discriminate the child who deliberately tunes them out from the child who erratically seems not to listen. In our clinical experience, the gifted child with a mild to moderate language disorder, learning disability, or an attention deficit disorder without hyperactivity, is at greatest risk to develop an oppositional defiant disorder behavior pattern with the contributing developmental disabilities being missed because the child's cognitive brightness compensates sufficiently to allow him to do well on the typical screening measures of cognitive function.

The child with ADHD exhibits at least eight of the fourteen behaviors listed in column three, table I. Attention deficit disorder with or without hyperactivity has an onset in early childhood with some clinicians considering hyperactive fetal movement patterns (Accardo et al. 1990) and irritable, if not classically colicky, infant behavior as early reflections of this disorder. The incidence is at least three percent of the population, but when milder forms are combined with the various degrees of learning disabilities, it may approach ten percent.

Most studies document a 50 to 75% overlap between ADHD and LD (Accardo, Blondis, and Whitman 1990). Accardo et al. (1991) documented an elevated prevalence of LD in those children with higher dysmorphology scores—with the latter being a classic marker for ADHD. It is also being increasingly accepted that severe language disorder may mimic ADHD, but it remains unclear by what percentage is

TABLE I.    Clinical Criteria for Disruptive Behavior Disorders[a]

| CD | ODD | ADHD |
|---|---|---|
| Robbery | Temper tantrums | Fidgety |
| Armed robbery | Argumentativeness | Cannot sit still |
| Burglary | Defiance | Easily distractible, |
| Physical aggression | Instigation | daydreamer |
| Armed aggression | Blames others | Cannot wait turn |
| Cruelty to animals | Touchiness | Impatient |
| Cruelty to people | Anger, resentment | Fails to finish |
| Runaway | Spitefulness, vindictiveness | Short attention span |
| Arson | Obscenities, swearing | Noisy, loud |
| Truancy | | Interrupts |
| Property damage | | Doesn't listen |
| Rape | | Shifts a lot |
| Prevarication | | Disorganized, sloppy |
| | | Daredevil |
| | | Talks excessively, |
| | | tangentially |

[a]The child must exhibit 3 of the 13 behaviors in column one to qualify for a diagnosis of CD, 5 of 9 in column two for a diagnosis of ODD, and 8 of 14 in column three for a diagnosis of ADHD. It is the major contention of this chapter that CD and ODD are very much overdiagnosed, whereas ADHD and associated learning disabilities and language disorders are very much underdiagnosed, and that the latter organic diagnoses explain away many of these so-called "behavior disorders." (Modified from American Psychiatric Association, 1987.)

that overlap. Despite this high incidence of dual diagnoses, most researchers look at the behavioral correlates and outcomes of pure attention deficit hyperactivity and pure learning disability (Johnson and Blalock 1987; Spreen 1988; Weiss and Hechtman 1986). Those researchers predominantly interested in LD use a minimal screening questionnaire for attentional problems, and those researchers whose primary interest is ADHD use a minimal screening for learning problems. The best way to characterize such minimal screening tests is to recognize that their positive screening result for attentional problems would never qualify a child for stimulant medication, and their positive screening result for learning disability would never succeed in obtaining special education services from the school system. Once a child is in a high-risk category (that is, has a diagnosis of either LD or ADHD), such screening measures have no place either in research or in clinical practice. Children who present in clinical practice with one of these two problems, attentional deficits or learning disabilities, do not routinely need to be evaluated for the other disorder, but it should be carefully considered and watched for closely. The development of a "behavioral disorder" pattern in such a child is an excellent marker that one of these two diagnoses has been missed (figure 2).

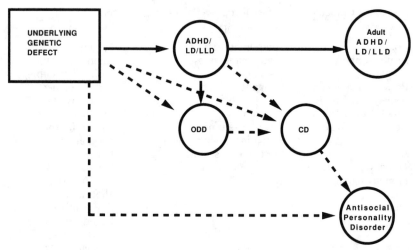

Figure 2.   An exclusively genetic etiology for behavioral disorders remains to be demonstrated. However, most researchers now anticipate that upward of 80% of all ADHD is hereditary in nature, and an occult ADHD (possibly accompanied by an LD and/or a language disorder) should be considered a stronger candidate for the etiology of a "behavior disorder" pattern than a direct genetic factor or adverse child rearing circumstances. (Modified from Whitman 1991.)

## COMORBIDITY

Much of the pilot work investigating the overlap among the above conditions has relied on questionnaires. Such symptom checklists should never be considered sufficient for clinical diagnosis and treatment planning. For example, putting a child on stimulant medication for ADHD solely because of his or her Conners rating scores would be similar to diagnosing a child as mentally retarded solely on the basis of an IQ score.

Consider several behaviors that occur under the diagnostic rubric *conduct disorder*: theft, lying, arson, cruelty to animals. Similar behaviors are often observed in the child with ADHD. One group of researchers would automatically and unthinkingly assign this ADHD child to the category *conduct disorder*. But the fact is that such behaviors are subject to very different interpretations. Take the specific example of aggression. In the CD child, aggression can be characterized as planned, enjoyed, defiant, vicious, remorseless, and hateful, whereas in the child with ADHD, it is better characterized as unplanned, impulsive, remorseful, silly, and stupid (Kirby and Grimley 1986). Similarly the theft, lying, arson, and cruelty to animals that are frequently reported in ADHD children, when carefully investigated as to the specific circumstances of each occurrence, often turn out to be inadvertent expressions of inattention and impulsivity. Too often the referral list of complaints suggests a child with ADHD to be a budding sociopath, when in reality one finds an utterly charming young person whose brake fluid is on empty. There may be no discernible difference with regard to the broken vase or the bruised arm, but the intentionality, the motivation— the etiology—are worlds apart in the two conditions. And there, of course, lies the fundamental weakness in the approach of DSM III-R and all similar instruments. They rely on a phenomenological approach that ignores or at least severely downplays etiology—even when a careful consideration of such etiology is vitally important to diagnosis.

Werry (1988) distinguished the philosophical differences among clinicians categorizing a child who might qualify for a diagnosis of either ADHD or CD. To lean toward a diagnosis of ADHD is, on the one hand, to interpret childhood behavior problems as biologically determined and to classify the child as "sick" and not responsible. To incline, on the other hand, toward a diagnosis of CD is to interpret childhood behavior problems more as the product of adverse child rearing—and yet to continue to hold the child as responsible for his or her bad behavior. In the former case, the medical helping system is called in; in the latter situation, the legal and social engineering systems are called in. In the former situation, the family is more often exonerated from causing the problem, their guilt is relieved, and they are educated to take an active role in treatment; in the latter situation, the family is often viewed as nearly hopeless and removing the child from this deleterious environment is a common treatment recommendation.

The decision to consider a child as having a behavior disorder (such as a CD or an ODD) versus a neurobehavioral syndrome (such as an ADHD) reflects the old nature versus nurture controversy. Most professionals argue that this is not an "either/or" dichotomy but rather a "both/and" situation. Having agreed upon that, they then proceed to act as if one of the two sides of the coin simply did not exist. Two specific points might be noted in support of this contention.

First, there seems to be an almost unreasoning preference on the part of many child psychiatrists to employ a fairly toxic (and occasionally fatal) medication, imipramine (Tofranil), as drug of first choice instead of a relatively benign agent, such as methylphenidate (Ritalin), when treating a teenager or a preteen with ADHD and some few associated depressive features. There seems to be almost a fixation on insisting that the ADHD is in some way a mask for an underlying, occult depressive disorder rather than recognizing that some depressive symptomatology is quite common in untreated and chronically misunderstood ADHD children.

Second, the genetics of behavior is a topic that continues to be glibly misrepresented in many psychiatry textbooks. The greatest failure of genetics to predict behavioral peculiarities is seen in the classic misunderstanding of the behavioral significance of extra Y chromosomes. Early reports of this sex chromosome aneuploidy suggested that the extra Y chromosome would predispose the affected male child toward the development of violent, criminal behavior. Bioethicists worried over whether doctors should tell parents that their newborn baby with a 47XYY karyotype would probably grow up to be a violent, criminal psychopath. The child psychiatry textbooks are careful to point out that this association was eventually disproven. But they remain willfully silent on the rationale behind the original observation and its failure. With every additional Y chromosome, the affected male tends to be taller and to exhibit a lower intelligence quotient. The excess representation of these supermales in the prison population was not because of any increase in violent criminal tendencies, but rather secondary to less intelligent planning of crimes and less intelligent negotiation of the criminal justice system—in other words, to less intelligence. And this lessened intelligence was indeed hereditary (Witkin et al. 1976). The true moral of the story is that "behavior" may not be hereditary, but learning styles, cognitive levels, and other neurobehavioral substrates for behavior are most assuredly genetic. (The philosophical belief in free will as independent of biological determinants would have helped prevent this glaring lapse in simple logical deduction.)

At the time that Werry clarified the above distinctions, the majority of mental health professionals would have preferred a diagnosis of conduct disorder in ambiguous or doubtful cases. Until Lejeune identified the extra chromosome in Down syndrome, many physicians had difficulties in distinguishing the newborn with Down syndrome from the baby with cretinism (congenital hypothyroidism). Since the crystallization of ADHD by Zametkin, it is difficult to return to the self-imposed confusion of Werry's dichotomy. The fact is that a significant portion of much of the childhood behavior that irritates parents and teachers has an organic basis and needs to be addressed from the perspective of biological limitation rather than that of motivational and social psychology (table II). The ancient heuristic principle of Occam's razor (the simplest explanation is the best, and a single explanation is usually the simplest) suggests that much of the psychiatric category of disruptive behavioral disorders may be unnecessary.

Table II.   Etiological Classification for Cephalgia[a]

| Disruptive Behavior Disorders | Supretentorial Cranial Pain |
|---|---|
| 312.00 CD | 001.001 Tension headache |
| 313.81 ODD | 005.009 Somatization |
| 314.01 ADHD | 959.83 Brain tumor |

[a]Hyperactivity associated with ADHD can be considered analogous to headache secondary to brain tumor.

## CONCLUSION

In 1845 the pediatrician Heinrich Hoffmann provided the first description of hyperactive children in his rhymed classic *Der Struwwelpeter*. If one looks carefully at the behaviors his storied urchins exhibited, the group had six of the thirteen conduct disorder behaviors, five of the nine oppositional defiant disorder behaviors, and only four of the fourteen attention deficit hyperactivity disorder behaviors. A revisionist approach to *Struwwelpeter* would suggest that Dr. Hoffmann pioneered in the description of CDs and ODDs. An alternate assessment would be that he perceived, if only dimly, an expanded Strauss syndrome—perhaps even the older "MBD" (table III)—that swallowed up the, for the most part irrelevant, diagnoses of CD and ODD.

Despite an extensive research base to support the organic etiology of ADHD as a neurobehavioral syndrome (often simplistically misinterpreted as "hyporitalinemia"), it has taken many years to arrive at even a minimal consensus. When that minimum was finally achieved, it was not professionals who took the lead in advocating to the federal Department of Education that ADHD be reclassified as a true developmental disorder. Parent groups did so—and this in opposition to many professional organizations who seemed more interested in maintaining the myth of universally dysfunctional families. Prevalence estimates for CD that would have affected almost one out of every two families should have given a clue to the insanity of this imposture. This whole sad history, unfortunately, bears a striking resemblance to the long fought resistance to reframing autism as a heterogenious collection of brain damage syndromes rather than as a disorder caused by poor mothering style.

It will be necessary in the future to jettison those preconceptions that, for whatever reason, espouse, imply, support, or in any way suggest a primarily emotional etiology to disorders of attention and learning. This will involve, in turn, a major overhaul in the working relationship between the school system and the medical profession. The great divorce between the medical and educational models will need to be repaired, and pseudopsychiatric hypotheses will need to be

TABLE III. Expanded Strauss Syndrome[a]

Attention deficit
Impulsivity
Hyperactivity
Inconsistency
Learning disabilitiy
Social learning deficit
Behavior disorders

[a]This conceptualization bears a close resemblance to the old diagnostic categorization, minimal brain dysfunction (MBD).

replaced with firmer medical formulations that can assist educators in their task pragmatically.

## REFERENCES

Accardo, P. J., and Whitman, B. Y. 1991. The misdiagnosis of the hyperactive child. In *Attention Deficit Disorders and Hyperactivity in Children*, Pediatric Habilitation Series, volume 7, eds. P. J. Accardo, T. A. Blondis, and B. Y. Whitman. New York: Marcel Dekker.

Accardo, P. J. Blondis, T. A., and Whitman, B. Y. 1990. Disorders of attention and activity level in a referral population. *Pediatrics* 85: 426–31.

Accardo, P. J., Tomazic, T., Morrow, J., and Whitman, B. Y. 1990. Fetal activity in developmental disabilities. *Pediatric Research* 27: 8A (abstract).

Accardo, P. J., Tomazic, T., Morrow, J., Haake, C., and Whitman, B. Y. 1991. Minor malformations, hyperactivity, and learning disabilities. *American Journal of Diseases of Children* 145: 1184–1187.

American Psychiatric Association. 1987. *Diagnostic and Statistical Manual*, third edition, revised. Washington, DC: American Psychiatric Association.

Barkley, R. 1990. *Attention Deficit Hyperactivity Disorder: A Handbook for Diagnosis and Treatment*. New York: Guilford Press.

Burke, B. L., Jr., and McGee, D. P. 1990. Sports deficit disorder. *Pediatrics* 85:1118.

Capute, A. J. 1991. The "Expanded" Strauss Syndrome: MBD Revisited. In *Attention Deficit Disorders and Hyperactivity in Children*, eds. P. J. Accardo, T. A. Blondis, and B. Y. Whitman. New York: Marcel Dekker.

Capute, A. J., and Accardo, P. J. 1991. A neurodevelopmental perspective on the continuum of developmental disabilities. In *Developmental Disabilities in Infancy and Childhood*, eds. A. J. Capute and P. J. Accardo. Baltimore: Paul H. Brookes Publishing.

Carey, W. B. 1988. A suggested solution to the confusion in attention deficit diagnoses. *Clinical Pediatrics* 27: 348–49.

Carey, W. B. 1992. Temperament issues in the school-aged child. *Pediatric Clinics of North America* 39: 569–84.

Egan, J. 1991. Oppositional defiant disorder. In *Textbook of Child and Adolescent Psychiatry*, ed. J. M. Wiener. Washington, DC: American Psychiatric Press.

Hendren, R. L. 1990. Conduct disorder in childhood. In *Textbook of Child and Adolescent Psychiatry*, ed. J. M. Wiener. Washington, DC: American Psychiatric Press.

Hoffmann, H. 1981. Struwwelpeter. In *Classics of Children's Literature*, eds. J. W. Griffith and C. H. Frey. New York: Macmillan.

Interagency Committee on Learning Disabilities. 1988. *Report to the U.S. Congress*. Washington, DC: U.S. Government Printing Office Publication number 226-487: 39917.

Johnson, D. J., and Blalock, J. W. 1987. *Adults with Learning Disabilities: Clinical Studies*. Orlando, FL: Grune & Stratton.

Kaplan, W. H. 1988. Conduct disorder. In *Handbook of Clinical Assessment of Children and Adolescents*, eds. J. C. Kestenbaum and D. T. Williams. New York: New York University Press.

Kirby, E. A., and Grimley, L. K. 1986. *Understanding and Treating Attention Deficit Disorder*. New York: Pergamon Press.

Lewis, D. D. 1990. Adolescent conduct and antisocial disorders. In *Textbook of*

*Child and Adolescent Psychiatry*, ed. J. M. Wiener. Washington, DC: American Psychiatric Press.

Malmquist, C. P. 1990. Conduct disorder: Conceptual and diagnostic issues. In *Textbook of Child and Adolescent Psychiatry*, ed. J. M. Wiener. Washington, DC: American Psychiatric Press.

Quay, H. C. 1985. Aggression, conduct disorder, and attention problems. In *Attention Deficit Disorder: Identification, Course and Treatment Rationale*, ed. L. M. Bloomingdale. Jamaica, NY: Spectrum Publications.

Spreen, O. 1988. *Learning Disabled Children Growing Up: A Follow-up into Adulthood*. Oxford: Oxford University Press.

Szasz, T. 1961. *The Myth of Mental Illness*. New York: Harper & Row.

Weiss, G., and Hechtman, L. T. 1986. *Hyperactive Children Grown Up: Empirical Findings and Theoretical Considerations*. New York: Guilford Press.

Werry, J. S. 1988. Differential diagnosis of attention deficits and conduct disorder. In *Attention Deficit Disorder: Criteria, Cognition, Intervention*, eds. L. M. Bloomington and J. Sargeant. New York: Pergamon Press.

Whitman, B. Y. 1991. The roots of organicity: Genetics and genograms. In *Attention Deficit Disorders and Hyperactivity in Children*, eds. P. J. Accardo, T. A. Blondis, and B. Y. Whitman. New York: Marcel Dekker.

Witkin, H. A., Mednick, S. A., Schulsinger, F., Bakkestrom, E., Christiansen, K. O., Goodenough, D. R., Hirschhorn, K., Lundsteen, C., Owen, D. R., Philip, J., Rubin, D., and Stocking, M. 1976. Criminality in XYY and XXY men. *Science* 193: 547–55.

Zametkin, A. J., Nordahl, T. E., Gross, M., King, A. C., Semple, W. E., Rumsey, J., Hamburger, S., and Cohen, R. M. 1990. Cerebral glucose metabolism in adults with hyperactivity of childhood onset. *New England Journal of Medicine* 323: 1361–1366.

# Chapter • 12

## Educational Interventions in Learning Disabilities
### Follow-up Studies and Future Research Needs

*Doris Johnson*

Thirty years ago, at a meeting of concerned parents and professionals, the term learning disabilities was proposed for a group of children who were not being served in traditional special education programs (Proceedings from the Fund for Perceptually Handicapped 1963). Both professionals and parents were concerned about those children who were not hearing impaired, mentally deficient, physically handicapped, or emotionally disturbed, but were not learning normally. At that time, some children had been identified and were being served in private schools or clinics, but families who could not afford private tutoring had few options and wanted to obtain help for their children. The services that were available were often for very specific disorders. For example, children with serious reading problems were classified as dyslexic. Some with oral language problems were in programs for developmental aphasia; others were in classes for the brain injured or neurologically impaired. However, none of these terms was broad enough to encompass the entire range of problems. Furthermore, both professionals and parents were concerned about some of the stigmatizing labels. Therefore, the term *learning disability* was proposed by Kirk (1963) and was adopted by the Association for Children with Learning Disabilities (now the Learning Disabilities Association), and later by a division within the Council for Exceptional Children and other groups. Gradually, more programs were begun in schools but widespread services were not available until after the passage of Public Law (PL) 94-142 at which time, a definition for learning disabilities was formulated and services were required for children who met the criteria. Passage of this law also necessitated programs of professional preparation.

As is the case in many fields, the most serious problems were identified first. Hence, many children were placed in self-contained classes. Those with mild-to-moderate conditions were seen in resource rooms or in itinerant programs for one or more hours each day.

The philosophies of education varied according to the theoretical orientation of the educators or specialists. Some early intervention programs included extensive work on perception and perceptual-motor processes (Frostig 1972; Kephart 1971; Strauss and Lehtinen 1947). Others emphasized multisensory instruction for reading and spelling (Orton 1937; Fernald 1943). Some included psycholinguistic training based on the Illinois Test of Psycholinguistic Ability (Kirk, McCarthy, and Kirk 1968). Still others emphasized work in oral language and the relationships between auditory language, reading, and written language (Johnson and Myklebust 1967). Some programs focussed on processing deficits such as memory or sequencing whereas others provided direct instruction in the basic areas of underachievement. Many used theories from applied behavioral analysis while others incorporated concepts from neuropsychology and information processing theories. In certain instances, controversial theories such as motor patterning, special diets, and ocular training were prescribed.

Many of the educational programs were developed primarily for service needs and did not include a plan for research. Consequently, it is difficult to state, with certainty, which procedures were the most effective for specific types of children. In recent years several follow-up studies have been conducted that provide valuable data and insights into the persistent problems of children and adults with learning disabilities (Abbot and Frank 1975; Bruck 1985; Fafard and Haubrich 1981; Finucci, Gottfredson and Childs 1985; Gottesman 1979; Hartzell and Compton 1984; Horn, O'Donnell and Vitulano 1983; Kavale 1988; O'Connor and Spreen 1988; Rawson 1968; Rogan and Hartman 1990; Spekman, Goldberg, and Herman 1992). Even though they are not always well controlled studies, they are useful in planning for the future. As the field has grown and the research base has improved, more controlled intervention studies have been done, but they too, are limited since they generally focus on only one aspect of learning or achievement. Hence, we must address specific interventions as well as broad educational programs.

## FOLLOW-UP STUDIES

One of the problems in reviewing intervention studies in LD is that the terminology has varied over the years. As stated above, the term *learning disability* was first used widely in the 1960s and 1970s. Prior to that time, many students had been identified, but had been classified as dyslexic, aphasic, brain damaged, reading disabled, perceptually handicapped, and other terms. In certain respects, those groups may have been more homogeneous than the current broad population of people with learning disabilities. As the diversity increased, the need for better subject descriptors became even more important.

In an extensive review of longitudinal studies in the areas of learning disability, reading, and attention/hyperactivity, Kavale (1988) cites problems with regard to methodology, including definition of the samples, lack of adequate control groups, failure to account for or control attrition, failure to provide equivalent data at various testing times, and failure to report information other than group means. More details regarding the characteristics of those students who made the most and least progress would have been helpful and is needed in future research. In addition, more information about instruction is essential.

Despite these concerns, the findings discussed below provide some indications of the problems and needs of people with learning disabilities. It should be emphasized, however, that this chapter is not intended to be a comprehensive review. Rather, it is intended to raise issues that should be considered in future prospective studies.

## Academic Achievement

Both empirical studies and individual case reports indicate that learning disabilities persist. Indeed, most definitions now state that they are chronic, life-long conditions. This does not mean, however, that students are unable to make progress. On the contrary, many make significant gains; but even students with high overall ability and good motivation, who have had intensive intervention may have persistent problems in reading, spelling, and/or written language (Rawson 1968; Bruck 1985). Frauenheim and Heckerl (1983) found that 80% of their students with dyslexia who had completed high school still had pronounced reading and writing problems.

In a ten-year follow-up study of 114 learning-disabled students who had been evaluated in a pediatric clinic, Hartzell and Compton (1984) found their subjects had significantly lower levels of school attainment and academic success than their nondisabled siblings. Within their LD group, 35% did not continue past high school, 16% attended junior college, 21% attended college, and 15% graduated from college. These children came from upper middle class families where 74% of the fathers and 53% of the mothers had college educations.

In a study of young adults who had attended the Frostig School in

California, Spekman, Goldberg, and Herman (1992) reported that 90% of the entire group had graduated from high school. They state that this number is higher than percentages reported in other studies of children in both public and private schools. Nevertheless, they found chronic academic deficits. The mean reading score on a measure of single word recognition was grade eight and the mathematics score was lower.

Spreen (1987) reported that significantly more of their LD groups left school at a lower grade than the controls or the general population in the school district. Only one or two out of ten took any college courses as compared to four or five in the control group. They also received lower grades.

Bruck (1985) also found that learning disabilities persisted in their clinical population. However, she said the data on both academic and occupational achievements were encouraging. While the LD subjects had been considered nonreaders as children, at the time of their follow-up, very few were illiterate. Furthermore, her data suggested that continued exposure to literacy tasks can result in progress. Hence, she and others have found that reading and writing instruction in adulthood is warranted, particularly if the people are motivated. Vogel and Adelman (1990) found that when LD college students sought out and used a comprehensive, well-coordinated support system, they graduated at the same rate and in the same time as their nondisabled peers. In addition, their academic failure rate was no higher.

In contrast to the clinical or special school populations described above, Zigmond and Thornton (1985) conducted a follow-up study of 60 learning-disabled and 61 nondisabled students in a large urban school district. The intelligence scores of the LD group were lower than the nondisabled group. The mean IQ for the LD group was 86 (which is significantly lower than some clinical populations), and the mean standard scores for reading and math were 74 and 75, which placed them in the mid-third to fourth grade level. There was little change in either the IQ or academic performance levels at the time of the re-evaluation three years later.

In at least one study, which involved self-report data, Gerber et al. (1990) found that many students with learning disabilities thought their problems had become worse with age. The authors assumed that these feelings may have arisen with increased demands at work. Others report that adults continued to make progress with individualized tutoring.

Thus, the outcomes reflect many factors, including group heterogeneity, type of service, severity of problems, and support systems. Such findings are not unique to learning disabilities. Outcomes for other special populations also vary. Without a doubt some programs are more effective than others. Our task for the future is to determine which procedures and approaches are best for particular learners.

## Grade Repetition

Kavale (1988) stated that it is highly probable that students with learning disabilities will repeat grades. Johnson and Blalock (1987) found that 25 of the 91 adults they tested had repeated at least one grade.

According to Hartzell and Compton (1984), grade repetition did not contribute to a successful academic outcome. However, they found during interviews, that students who had been retained in later grades (e.g., sixth or seventh) were more positive toward their experience than those who had been retained in the early grades. The latter still remembered the experience as a negative one, whereas the older students stated they understood the rationale and had a role in the decision.

Although repetition may occasionally be helpful, before making such a recommendation, we must ask whether more of the same will help. Sometimes students need *different* approaches, not repetition of the same procedures and content. In certain instances, retention can be detrimental to self-esteem. The type of problem, as well as the age, must be considered. For example, children with good auditory receptive language, but poor reading skills may become bored listening to the same content a second time. In contrast, retention may be beneficial for students with more global problems.

## Drop Out Rates

Federal law provides for free and appropriate public education until students are 21 years of age, but many with learning disabilities, as well as those without, leave the educational system before attaining that age. In a follow-up study of 52 students, Levin, Zigmond, and Birch (1985) reported a school-leaving rate of 47% among the LD students and a 36% drop-out rate for other students in the same district. They found that LD students who left school before graduation were often unemployed and poorly equipped academically.

In the Zigmond and Thornton study (1985), there was a significant difference between the LD and non-LD group with regard to drop-out rates from high school. Fifty-four percent of the students with learning disabilities had dropped out, whereas 32% of the non-LD had dropped out before high school graduation. The LD students who remained in high school were more successful on the job than those who dropped out. Therefore, Zigmond and Thornton (1985) concluded that every effort should be made to help students remain in high school and to understand the value of going to school every day.

In contrast, Bruck (1985) found the students in their clinical group were not at risk for dropping out. Perhaps the support systems, motivation, and individualized instruction were different in some of the clinical and public school studies. Johnson and Blalock (1987) found that some who had dropped out of high school later recognized the value of education and wanted tutoring to obtain the GED or to continue their schooling. Thus, in the future it will be necessary to consider the availability of services for those who want intervention.

## EMPLOYMENT

Studies on the employment of adults with learning disabilities also vary. For example, White et al. (1980) found 77% of the LD high school graduates were employed at least part-time 3 to 60 months after leaving school.

Both LD and non-LD graduates in the Zigmond and Thornton Study (1985) were more successfully employed than were the dropouts. The employment for LD graduates (74%) was not significantly different from the employment rate for students without disabilities. The employment rates for both drop-out groups were similar. As stated above, Zigmond and Thornton concluded that it is "worth it" to remain in school. Although basic skills did not increase for students with learning disabilities, their chances of obtaining a job after graduation were better than those who dropped out. The authors felt that those who had remained in school had a better "stick-to-itiveness." It was suggested that employers may be more concerned about dependability, persistence, and attitudes toward work than actual grade-level performance in the basic skills.

Hazazi et al. (1989) conducted a study on employment of 133 students in Vermont, sixty-seven of whom were handicapped. Twenty-four of the handicapped students had been in special classes for the mentally retarded; whereas, forty-three had been in noncategorical classes. Of this latter group, twenty-five had been classified as having a learning disability. Results indicated that nonhandicapped students had better outcomes for post-high school employment. Males were more likely to be employed in both the handicapped and nonhandicapped groups. Rates of unemployment were relatively high in both groups; however, the handicapped students had higher unemployment, lower wages, fewer fringe benefits; they worked fewer hours, and were employed in jobs requiring fewer skills than their nonhandicapped peers. The investigators found the employment was positively linked with paid work experience in high school. Vocational classes were positive for the handicapped but not the non-handicapped.

In the follow-up study at the Frostig school, Spekman, Goldberg, and Herman (1992) reported that 98% of the subjects were financially dependent, whether or not they were living at home. They often were in low-paying and low-status jobs, and were employed part-time, or not at all. Spreen (1987) found that the LD subjects started part-time jobs later in life, had a higher rate of unemployment, and were unemployed more than the control group.

Others report higher employment rates and successful employment in many fields. For example, dyslexics who were taught in a private school using special techniques to overcome their reading disability were employed later in professions such as law, medicine, and business (Rawson 1968). Similarly, Johnson and Blalock (1987) reported that adults evaluated in a clinical setting were employed in many occupations ranging from professional to unskilled labor. Only a small percentage were unemployed. The difference in outcome may be related to overall ability, SES levels, support systems, special services, and motivation. In addition, employment figures may vary with the economic conditions of the locality and the times at which the study was conducted.

The findings from Bruck's study (1985) are more encouraging. She found the LD subjects were not underemployed, and were employed in a wide range of occupations, including social work, accounting, nursing, computer analysis and mechanics. She found occupational achievement was not associated with severity of learning disability. Furthermore, most subjects were satisfied with their jobs, although many hoped for advancement. Only a few were in unskilled jobs.

The group in the Hartzell and Compton (1984) study were too young to draw conclusions about job success. Both the LD students and their siblings had the same entry level jobs (e.g., fast food chains, babysitting). Of those who had worked, 62% of the LD group and 67% of their siblings reported high job success; 6% of the LD group and 1% of the siblings had a history of job failures.

Our experience in a clinical setting suggests that people whose reading achievement levels may be as low as first or second grade, can and do remain successfully employed if they maintain a good work ethic and have good support systems. However, because of their low skill levels, they are often ineligible for promotion. Consequently, some become discouraged. We should not, however, conclude that students with learning disabilities are incapable of learning to read, write, or calculate after they have graduated from high school. Bruck (1985) agrees that they can continue to make progress. Although we can never predict the amount of change these subjects can make, we have observed increases of from one to five grades in reading achievement with some adult dyslexics. Each increase produces more motivation and provides options for job changes.

In a longitudinal study of children who had been in a special school, Rogan and Hartman (1990) found the outcome results were favorable for most in the college and high school groups, whereas results for the other special education group were mixed. They concluded that variables that contributed to a favorable outcome included intensive, effective intervention during the elementary and middle school years, continued supportive tutoring or intervention during mainstream school attendance, counseling when needed, parental support, and the absence of severe neurologic or emotional problems.

## SELF-ESTEEM AND SOCIAL FACTORS

According to Kavale (1988), there is a likelihood for low self-esteem among students with reading and learning disabilities. Because the term *learning disability* indicates that there is a discrepancy between an individual's potential and one or more areas of achievement, the impact of such problems on self-esteem cannot be ignored. The long-lasting and negative effects of school failures may interfere with self-concept. On the other hand, some investigators suggest that the diagnosis of a learning disability may protect children from feelings of low self-esteem and the belief that they are bad, slow, or lazy. For instance, Kistner and Osborne (1987) state that placement in special classes may have a positive impact on self-evaluation because of the more appropriate work level and the assistance. Presumably, these assignments can reduce failure and offer students with learning disabilities an appropriate achievement level peer comparison group. Thus, improved self-evaluations may result.

In the same report, Kistner and Osborne (1987) identified a group of six children who were classified as having negative self image. Although these students did not seem to be more disabled or less well adjusted than the other LD children, they did tend to have higher IQ scores. The authors said their negative feelings may have reflected differences in family background. That is, they may have come from families where there was greater pressure to achieve. Many LD students are realistic about their academic problems, but they continue to maintain relatively positive feelings about themselves.

These observations are somewhat in keeping with those of Smith (1991), who studied self-concept among college students. She found no difference between the LD and non-LD students on a general self-concept scale, but the LD students did rate themselves lower on academic self-esteem.

Hartzell and Compton (1984) studied social success by using a three-point rating scale. High success referred to those people with many friends, leadership qualities, and facility for interpersonal relationships. Low success referred to persons who felt lonely, isolated, and socially awkward. They found significant differences between the LD subjects and their siblings. Only 31% of the LD group reported a high level of social success, whereas 77% of the siblings were rated at this level. Sixteen percent of the LD group were described as lonely, as compared with 8% of the siblings. Lags in interpersonal areas were found in the Spekman, Goldberg, and Herman (1992) study as well.

Bruck (1985) reported that the quality of family relationships of their subjects with learning disabilities were similar to those of the peer control group; however, the former did seem to be at risk for problems with peer relationships and psychological adjustment. Nevertheless, she found no extreme forms of deviance, and only a few had required counseling or psychotherapy. Other studies show a relationship between delinquency and learning disabilities.

These studies and others indicate that support within the home and school is essential. Such support can enhance the child's self-esteem, despite the presence of learning difficulties. As stated above, Kistner and Osborne (1987), found the LD students generally maintained positive feelings about their nonacademic performance; therefore they accepted themselves, despite their school problems. They concluded that parents and teachers should help individuals with learning disabilities develop and maintain positive self-concepts, but not at the expense of motivation for academic learning.

## NEUROLOGICAL STATUS

Although children with severe motor problems are not usually classified as learning disabled, O'Connor and Spreen (1988) found that neurologic status may be related to educational outcome. Students with more gross and observable neurologic signs, in some instances, have a less favorable outcome.

## INTERVENTION RESEARCH

Although many instructional approaches have been developed and implemented with LD children, only a limited number of specific intervention studies have been conducted. In 1989, Lessen et al. conducted a survey of ten years of academic intervention research with learning disabled students by reviewing several journals in the field. Their survey included only data-based and applied studies with school-age children who were classified as learning disabled. Each study had to measure an academic skill as the dependent variable. Less than 4% of the articles they reviewed (119 out of 3,106) addressed the issue of academic intervention. They acknowledged the fact that intervention studies might have appeared in other publications. Nevertheless, their review indicated that from 1978 to 1988, more studies were designed to describe the characteristics of learning-disabled and nondisabled students on one or more variables, than to study the effectiveness of certain instructional procedures.

These authors also noted, as have others, that the intervention studies were often limited to elementary-age students, particularly in the area of reading. Fortunately, in recent years, more studies have been conducted with adolescents across a wider range of problems including written language, mathematics and oral language. However, many studies focus on single aspects of underachievement and provide little information about the breadth of the problems and about the school curriculum.

Kavale (1990) reported that intervention has not been a primary topic in the LD literature. He found that studies pertaining to the characteristics of LD exceed intervention articles by a factor of more than two to one. He says the reason for this discrepancy is not completely clear, but it may be a result of the tension between those in helping professions and those in natural sciences (i.e., the scientific study of LD). A strong emphasis on service and advocacy fostered the development of programs without verification of techniques.

There are other reasons for the lack of intervention research. As the field emerged, it was necessary to conduct studies that provided information about characteristics of the population. Secondly, intervention research is very complex. It requires careful pre-testing to determine each member's deficiency as well as integrities. In addition, well-defined control groups are needed. For example, if we were to conduct a study of intervention on some aspect of reading comprehension, we need to do pretesting, not only in the area of reading, but in oral language and various aspects of reasoning that might be related to reading. Similarly, when conducting studies of written language intervention, one needs to know about oral language and reading skills as well as writing. Given the heterogeneity of the LD population there are not always sufficient numbers of children with similar problems in the same school. Educational intervention requires systematic, controlled instruction and well-designed study of change. Often two or three interventions are needed to be able to compare results. We need to control for (or at least describe) the other types of instruction the children are receiving in school.

Scruggs (1990) presents several relevant issues pertaining to intervention research and highlights the need to differentiate laboratory research from classroom research. In laboratory research, students are generally seen individually in highly controlled situations. Scruggs says such studies are well suited for the evaluation of particular instructional strategies, and quotes Swanson who says they can provide important information on basic research questions and can provide implications for classroom research.

However, as we enter an era of special education in which children will spend more time in the regular classroom, there will be a greater need for classroom-based research. Such studies will be difficult to conduct because of the wide range of achievement levels in classrooms, the differences in experience and skills of teachers, and many other factors. However, all studies should be theory driven. In addition, when controlled studies are conducted, researchers should describe other aspects of a student's overall educational program. The following factors need to be considered in future studies.

## FACTORS TO CONSIDER IN FUTURE STUDIES

### Mental Ability

As stated previously, the heterogeneity of the population is a major factor in all research and LD. If one uses the standard definition, individuals with learning disabilities have normal sensory acuity, no primary physical or emotional handicaps, and at least average mental ability. However, the intelligence levels may vary from one standard deviation below the mean (and sometimes two) up through the superior range. That is, IQ ranges may be 85 and above, or as low as 70 in some states. Thus, the outcomes can be expected to vary with such a wide range of ability, particularly with regard to higher education.

### Type and Severity of Problem

The types of problems and number of areas of underachievement also vary. According to most definitions, students may be classified as having a learning disability if they have a discrepancy between potential and achievement in one or more areas, such as listening comprehension, speaking, reading, written language, mathematics, and reasoning. However, the size of the discrepancy varies. Another factor that may have an impact on outcome is the breadth of the problem. Students with relatively global problems may perform below expectancy in all areas of achievement, whereas others have specific problems. Thus, some individuals have mild, moderate, or severe *specific* problems, while others have mild, moderate, or severe *global* problems.

According to Hartzell and Compton (1984), degree of disability was the most significant contributor to lack of academic and social progress in their LD group. However, this is not always the case. Many severe cases in the Johnson and Blalock (1987) clinic population were not reading above a fourth grade level, yet they were successfully employed, were independent, and had families. Frauenheim and Heckerl (1983) said that the prognosis seems to depend on both the severity of the disability and the available educational interventions.

The *type* of disability must also be considered. For example, many people with learning disabilities have verbal deficits. They have excellent nonverbal and/or mechanical skills, but they have difficulty comprehending or using spoken language. These problems typically interfere with reading, written language, and some aspects of mathematics. Other students have no difficulty with oral communication, but they have specific problems in reading (decoding) and spelling. These are similar to the dyslexic people described by Orton (1937), Rawson (1968), and others.

Individuals with nonverbal disabilities who have high verbal and low performance intelligence scores often have problems that interfere with self-help skills, social perception, interpersonal relationships, and occupations (Johnson and Blalock 1987). Typically, they have good reading ability and verbal skills, but their perceptual motor problems interfere with handwriting, some aspects of mathematics, self-help skills, recreation, and many daily activities. Consequently, they feel less confident outside of school than in the classroom. In a follow-up clinical study, Behrens (1963) found that children made greater gains in verbal than nonverbal skills. He hypothesized that these results might have been related to the type of intervention they had received. That is, emphasis had been given to language, reading, and writing.

Generally, within the LD population, *patterns of problems* tend to co-occur. Rarely do we see isolated areas of underachievement. As a result, many students see more than one professional. For example, students with nonverbal disabilities may be seen by an occupational therapist for correction of visual-motor problems, a learning disabilities specialist for work with handwriting and mathematics, and a psychologist or social worker for improvement of social skills. Similarly, children with language disorders may be seen by both a speech/language pathologist and a learning disabilities specialist. Hartzell and Compton (1984) highlighted the variety of services and reported the numbers of children that had been in public school tutoring programs or special classes, private schools and tutoring, speech therapy, counseling, parent counseling, and motor programs, as well as those who had medication or special diets.

Future studies should describe *specific* interventions that were provided and the degree to which they were integrated. When students are in departmentalized programs, the classroom teachers do not always have the time, or take the time, to discuss how specific problems interfere with course work, nor do they describe the most effective and least effective types of intervention. In addition, when students have multiple problems, it is often necessary to focus on certain critical subjects and spend less time on others. Therefore, it is difficult to determine exactly why some students do or do not make progress in certain areas.

## Age of Identification

Because people with learning disabilities are such a heterogeneous group, the age at which they are identified and begin to receive service varies. Those with severe receptive or expressive language problems, as well as those with severe perceptual-motor problems, may be identified in the preschool years, whereas those with academic problems may not be identified until they have been in school and failed. Students with mild written language disorders may not be detected until the third grade or later. Johnson and Blalock (1987) reported that 10% of the adults in their clinic group had been identified before school entrance, and an additional 35% by the end of first grade. Recently, many adults have been classified as learning disabled for the first time in post-secondary programs or at work. Although most had a history of chronic problems, formal diagnosis was not made until adulthood. Some had received tutoring but had not been in special education. Hartzell and Compton (1984) found that age at diagnosis was not related to academic or social success. Intervention at older ages was effective, even in their upper middle-class population.

## Amount and Duration of Intervention

In the past, and to a certain extent today, students with severe global problems were placed in self-contained classes or in special schools whereas those with specific, mild-to-moderate problems were in resource rooms or in clinical programs outside the school. However, the amount and type of instruction varied.

As more children are identified, case loads in special education increase, so they may be receiving less individualized instruction than in the past. For example, in Illinois, children with learning disabilities were initially seen for one hour every day, and the case loads did not exceed ten. Now the LD teacher may work with 20 or 25 children. Some children in resource rooms are tutored in school subjects, whereas others are given specific remediation. When children are mainstreamed, the integration of special education with regular education varies. Some children are in "pull-out" programs while others are seen by consultants in the regular classroom. Without coordination between the programs there may be minimal transfer of knowledge from one situation to the other. Tutorial programs that provide assistance only with daily homework may be insufficient to help students become independent learners or to develop the skills necessary for independent reading, writing, and computating. On the other hand, training in sub-skills without regard to content may be inadequate.

Many good teachers are often distressed because they cannot

teach as much as they would like. Time limitations, numbers of children, behavior problems, resources, and other factors prevent them from providing maximum instruction. Many special educators also feel pressure to meet the requirements in the classroom while trying to alleviate weaknesses. Often they are overwhelmed by the extent and severity of problems with limited time for intervention. This may result in less job satisfaction and may lead to stress related problems (Olsen 1988).

## Goals and Priorities

Because many students have multiple problems, questions regarding priorities are often raised, particularly in junior and secondary high schools. Teachers must decide whether to help students acquire knowledge in the content areas, irrespective of reading and writing level, or to continue working on basic skills. Ideally, we hope that both can be accomplished. We also hope that early intervention will foster language and reading competence so students can "read to learn" and write well enough to convey what they know. However, because problems persist (albeit progress is reported), special educators, parents, and regular educators are faced with the dilemma of how to master both content and process. For example, if a student has a significant reading problem, sometimes the course content is read to students by parents or volunteers. In other situations, tape recorded books are provided, or students are given books with similar content at lower reading levels. However, high school students with good thinking skills and oral language ability often object to such a practice. They feel they can acquire the content orally and can discuss the material with their peers, but they cannot handle the reading levels of their textbooks.

As stated above, the models for secondary programs have varied over the years. In some, there was a heavy emphasis on basic skills in reading, writing, and mathematics. In others, there was an emphasis on learning strategies (Alley and Deshler 1979), and competencies to help students become more active learners. Other programs concentrated on the academic content. Some programs provided career awareness and counseling for life after high school, and still others included mental health components to foster self-concept and self-esteem.

More recently, with a stronger research base in the field, intervention research has increased and improved (Scruggs and Wong 1990). However, most studies are short term and limited in scope. They do not provide a comprehensive description of curriculum, goals, and procedures used in educational programs. Nor do they include sufficient information about intensity and duration of the services that were provided. While some describe approaches for specific disorders in reading, spelling, written language, or in mathematics, we know little about the total educational plan. Most programs purport to improve some area of achievement, particularly in the elementary grades, whereas others emphasize subject matter and content rather than remediation for reading, spelling, and writing. Many report successful outcomes with specific training in strategies or use of mnemonics for content areas, and use of schema (Scruggs and Wong 1990) but most of these investigations include only a small part of the educational program. Furthermore, we do not know which students made the most or least progress.

### Other Variables

In order to gain a better understanding of the variables that produce the most success, we need much more careful documentation of a students' entire educational program. If we accept the notion that the curriculum includes all school experiences, we need something comparable to marker variables for instruction. For example, Keogh (1982) recommended a marker system for describing LD samples for research studies. The markers include age, grade level, mental ability, SES status, educational level of parents, as well as a description of the child's language, reading, writing, and mathematics achievement levels. Lessen et al. (1989) examined each of the articles they reviewed for sixteen factors that they deemed important to replicate the studies. They found that only three provided information about all sixteen variables that were of interest to them (e.g., sample size, age, gender, identification criteria, placement, academic subject area, new vs. retaught skills, group vs. individualized instruction, length of intervention, instructional materials, follow-up or maintenance, etc.). Thus, they and others have made several recommendations to ensure replicability. Their list included a clear operational description of the sample, evidence that subjects actually needed the intervention provided, specifics related to intervention including number, duration, and frequency of instructional sessions, description of materials, procedures used to foster generalization, and other factors.

If we developed a list of instructional variables, it would include factors such as the general socioeconomic and educational levels of the overall school population, size of school, library facilities, materials, literacy activities at home, type of preschool and/or kindergarten experiences, and plans for transitions across grade levels. In addition, information regarding curriculum scope and sequence would be needed. Conceivably, coding systems could be developed for program descriptions to quantify time and type of content (e.g., phonics, linguistic awareness, contextual reading, comprehension, etc.).

The amount of time spent on each subject, and time spent on

tasks are also relevant. Studies show that even fifteen minutes of read-ing per day yields higher scores. Yet research indicates there is consid-erable variation in the time spent on certain subjects. The serious limi-tations found in the writing of LD adults may reflect lack of time spent writing, as well as persistent processing weakness. However, with the current concerns for early literacy, studies in the 1990s may reveal that more time is spent on writing than in previous years and may reveal more progress.

Given the low scores on mathematics among adults with learn-ing disabilities (Johnson and Blalock 1987; Rogan and Hartman 1990; Spekman, Goldberg, and Herman 1992), researchers need to look care-fully at the time spent on this area. Spekman, Goldberg, and Herman (1992) are among those who hypothesize that mathematics is not given the same emphasis as are language arts. This was the case among ado-lescents in a clinical setting reported by Johnson, Blalock, and Nesbitt (1978) who found that students had received significantly more help in reading and decoding than in written language and mathematics; consequently, many adults were left without the skills needed for independent living. There are now, however, more research studies on mathematics than in the past.

Future researchers should consider programs for social skills. In recent years, a greater emphasis has been placed on this aspect of learn-ing (Bryan and Lee 1990; Hazel and Schumaker 1988). Although not all educators feel this is the responsibility of the school, if we are con-cerned with the whole child, social cognition and interpersonal com-munication cannot be ignored. Vaughn, McIntosh, and Hogan (1990) argue for a social competence and contextualist model, rather than a skills deficit approach. Children also learn from each other. Discussions and collaboration with peers can be instructional and is an area of cur-rent research.

We need more information about the transition programs from school to school, home to school, and school to work. Often people with disabilities find it difficult to make adjustments, particularly into junior high school and departmentalized programs. Initially, they need advocates, but ultimately they need self-advocacy skills. They also need preparation for the world of work. Our studies showed that those who were unemployed needed assistance in learning how to interview for various positions, to understand their strengths and weaknesses, and to learn job maintenance skills. Many needed additional supervision or job coaches in order to master the requirements of their jobs.

The level of commitment of school administrators is important. Some principals make every effort to know all the children in the school and attend Individual Education Program planning sessions for those in special education. In certain instances, the principal serves as a catalyst and leads the discussion. We need to know more about the long term impact of such involvement. Parental support and involvement are crucial in both regular and special education.

The task of measuring teaching effectiveness is not easy. It is particularly difficult to deal with "part-whole" relationships—that is, with the specific intervention practices being investigated, in conjunction with the overall school program. Furthermore, as stated above, laboratory experiments are unlike the natural learning situations children encounter daily. More ethnographic studies are being conducted, but they, too, are difficult to replicate because of the many variables to consider. In the future, it would be helpful if descriptions of well-controlled studies could be combined with a description of other aspects of the educational program. For example, if children are receiving specialized training in phonological awareness, we need good information about other aspects of the reading and writing curriculum.

Future research must focus on the instructional process and the meaning of teaching. The literature on effective teaching is useful and emphasizes the importance of well-defined goals and coordination. However, many of those studies are very general. There are, of course, many forms of instruction including didactic, demonstration, guided inquiry, and so forth, but there is little study on adult–child dyads in special education to determine what forms of instruction facilitate the best outcomes in various content areas with specific types of children. For example, strategy instruction may be beneficial for some aspects of writing, whereas other approaches may be more beneficial for syntax or vocabulary development. Mnemonics of various types are beneficial for certain content areas (Mastropiere and Fulk 1990), but we need to know for whom, and in what contexts they are most and least effective.

We need to examine the "anatomy" of lessons within and across instructional sessions to note how new concepts, rules, and skills are taught initially, then how they are reviewed, applied, and automatized. My own observations of both experienced teachers and students in training is that there is considerable variability. Some teachers have not fully differentiated testing from teaching. For example, reading words from flash cards, or writing words from dictation are ways of collecting data about what a student has learned or needs to be taught. Instruction begins when teachers analyze the successes and errors to determine whether certain rules, generalizations, concepts, and skills require further work. Data collection alone does not constitute teaching. On the other hand, failure to collect data (e.g., checking ability to read or spell words, computation, etc.) may result in children spending time on things they already know, or that are too difficult, or (by chance) are at the correct level. In other words, rather than using a test-teach-test cycle, some educators teach and then test.

The term *education* derives from *educare* which means *to lead*. Our job as educators is to try to *lead* students to higher levels of performance. Some studies reviewed here indicate that many children with LD have had effective interventions and have made excellent progress. We must describe the characteristics of those students and the entire scope of activities within the instructional environment. At the same time we must study those children who make minimal progress and try to identify both intrinsic and extrinsic factors that seem to hold them back. In doing so, we must, of course, recognize that in all fields (e.g., adult aphasia, psychiatry, hearing impairment, etc.) some individuals are resistant to training or have such severe problems that limited progress can be made. We must, however, keep expectations high enough so that students are not understimulated and undertaught.

Studies now show the importance of early intervention, so special education should be available as soon as children with special needs are identified. Therefore, more professional preparation programs are needed for specialists to work with infants and toddlers. At the same time, more specialists are needed to help adults with LD in postsecondary settings.

Future research should also consider the degree to which children are encouraged to become independent learners and self-sufficient. Spekman et al. (1992) reported that few of the adults in their study was completely independent. Thus, in an attempt to reduce the excessive demands of the regular classroom, and to make children with learning disabilities feel more comfortable in school, we must not lose sight of the need to foster independence. Spekman et al. (1992) reported that the most successful individuals were those who demonstrated a high degree of persistence. This persistence was demonstrated in studies of Johnson and Blalock (1987). In their population of 91 adults, only 18 were unemployed, and the authors noted the persistence these people revealed during the interviews. More recently, we identified fourteen adults who were reading below the fourth grade level, despite years of special education. All were employed and most were living independently. Thus, they demonstrated a strong work ethic and a degree of success, despite their relatively severe problems.

## SUMMARY

The outcomes and long-term consequences of learning disabilities vary. According to the view and meta-analysis done by Kavale (1988), students with learning disabilities are apt to have persistent problems in reading and a strong likelihood for low self-esteem. Spekman et al. (1992) reported problems in mathematics and overall independence.

Other studies produced relatively optimistic results, and indicate that students who have good support systems and persistence are more successful than those who do not. We do not know, however, which delivery systems and which educational procedures produce the greatest changes. As we enter a new era of special education, we need more intervention research on specific areas of learning and achievement and much more comprehensive documentation of the total educational program, as well as individual characteristics and family circumstances. More studies on risk and resilience (Werner 1990) are needed. Future prospective studies may provide information about the types of intrinsic and environmental factors, as well as the instructional approaches that predict both long-term needs and successes.

## REFERENCES

Abbot, R. C., and Frank, B. E. 1975. A follow-up of LD children in a private special school. *Academic Therapy* 10:291–98.

Ackerman, P. T., Dykman, R. A., and Peters, J. E. 1977. Learning-disabled boys as adolescents: Cognitive factors and achievement. *Journal of the American Academy of Child Psychiatry* 16:296–313.

Alley, G., and Deshler, D. 1979. *Teaching the Learning Disabled Adolescent: Strategies and Methods.* Denver: Love.

Behrens, T. R. 1963. A study of psychological and electroencephalographic changes in children with learning disorders. An unpublished doctoral dissertation, Northwestern University, Evanston.

Bruck, M. 1985. The adult functioning of children with specific learning disabilities: A follow-up study. In *Advances in Applied Developmental Psychology* Vol. 1, ed. I. E. Sigel. Norwood, NJ: Ablex.

Bryan, T., and Lee, J. 1990. Social skills training with learning disabled children and adolescents: The state of the art. In *Intervention Research in Learning Disabilities*, eds. T. E. Scruggs and B. Y. L. Wong. New York: Springer-Verlag.

Englert, C. S. 1990. Unraveling the mysteries of writing through strategy instruction. In *Intervention Research in Learning Disabilities*, eds. T. E. Scruggs and B. Y. L. Wong. New York: Springer-Verlag.

Fafard, M. B., and Haubrich, P. A. 1981. Vocational and social adjustment of learning disabled young adults: A follow-up study. *Learning Disability Quarterly* 4:122–30.

Fernald, G. M. 1943. *Remedial Techniques in Basic School Subjects.* New York: McGraw-Hill.

Finucci, J. M., Gottfredson, L. S., and Childs, B. 1985. A follow-up study of dyslexic boys. *Annals of Dyslexia* 35:117–36.

Frauenheim, J. G. 1978. Academic achievement characteristics of adult males who were diagnosed as dyslexic in childhood. *Journal of Learning Disabilities* 11:476–83.

Frauenheim, G. J., and Heckerl, J. R. 1983. A longitudinal study of psychological and achievement test performance in severe dyslexic adults. *Journal of Learning Disabilities* 16:339–47.

Frostig, M. 1972. Visual perception, integrative function and academic learning. *Journal of Learning Disabilities* 5:1–15.

Gerber, P., Schneiders, C., Paradise, L., Reiff, H., Ginsberg, R., and Popp, P. 1990. Persisting problems of adults with learning disabilities: Self-reported comparison from their school-age and adult years. *Journal of Learning Disabilities* 23:570–73.

Gottesman, R. L. 1979. Follow-up of learning disabled children. *Learning Disability Quarterly* 2:60–69.

Hartzell, H. E., and Compton, C. 1984. Learning disability: 10-year follow-up. *Pediatrics* 74(6):1058–1064.

Hazazi, S., Johnson, R., Hazazi, J., Gordon, L., and Hill, M. 1989. Employment of youth with and without handicaps following high school: Outcomes and correlates. *Journal of Special Education* 23(3):243–55.

Hazel, J. S., and Schumaker, J. B. 1988. Social skills and learning disabilities: Current issues and recommendations for future research. In *Learning Disabilities: Proceedings of the National Conference*, eds. J. F. Kavanagh and T. J. Truss, Jr. Parkton, MD: York Press.

Hinton, G. G., and Knights, R. M. 1971. Children with learning problems: Academic history, academic prediction, and adjustment three years after assessment. *Exceptional Children* 37:513–19.

Horn, W. F., O'Donnell, J. P., and Vitulano, L. A. 1983. Long-term follow-up studies of learning-disabled persons. *Journal of Learning Disabilities* 16: 542–55.

Ito, H. R. 1980. Long-term effects of resource room programs on learning disabled children's reading. *Journal of Learning Disabilities* 13:322–26.

Johnson, D., and Myklebust, H. R. 1967. *Learning Disabilities: Educational Principles and Practices*. New York: Grune & Stratton.

Johnson, D. J., and Blalock, J. W. Eds. 1987. *Adults with Learning Disabilities: A Clinical Study*. Orlando, FL: Grune & Stratton.

Johnson, D., Blalock, J., and Nesbitt, J. 1978. Adolescents with learning disabilities: Perspectives from an educational clinic. *Learning Disabilities Quarterly* 1(4):24–36.

Kavale, K. A. 1988. The long-term consequences of learning disabilities. In *Handbook of Special Education: Research and Practice*, eds. M. C. Wang, M. C. Reynolds and H. J Walberg. New York: Pergamon Press.

Kavale, K. A. 1990. Variances and verities in learning disability interventions. In *Intervention Research in Learning Disabilities*, eds. T. E. Scruggs and B. Y. L. Wong. New York: Springer-Verlag.

Keogh, B., Major-Kingsley, S., Omori-Gordon, H., and Reid, H. 1982. *A System of Marker Variables for the Field of Learning Disabilities*. Syracuse, NY: Syracuse University Press.

Kephart, N. C. 1971. *The Slow Learner in the Classroom*. Columbus, OH: Merrill.

Kirk, S. A. 1963. Behavioral diagnosis and remediation of learning disabilities. *Proceedings of the Conference on Exploration into the Problems of the Perceptually Handicapped Child*, Vol. 1. Evanston, IL.

Kirk, S. A, McCarthy, J. J., and Kirk, W. D. 1968. *The Illinois Test of Psycholinguist Abilities* (rev. ed.). Urbana: University of Illinois Press.

Kistner, J., and Osborne, M. 1987. A longitudinal study of LD children's self-evaluations. *Learning Disability Quarterly* 10:258–66.

Lessen, E., Dudzinski, M., Karsh, K., and Acker, R. V. 1989. A survey of ten years of academic intervention research with learning disabled students: Implications for research and practice. *Learning Disabilities Focus* 4(2): 106–122.

Levin, E. K., Zigmond, N., and Birch, H. W. 1985. A follow-up study of 52 learning disabled adolescents. *Journal of Learning Disabilities* 18:2–7.

Mastropiere, M. A., and Fulk, B. J. 1990. Enhancing academic performance with mnemonic instruction. In *Intervention Research in Learning Disabilities,* eds. T. E. Scruggs and B. Y. L. Wong. New York: Springer-Verlag.

O'Connor, S. C., and Spreen, O. 1988. The relationship between parents' socioeconomic status and education level, and adult occupational and educational achievement of children with learning disabilities. *Journal of Learning Disabilities* 21(3):148–53.

Olsen, H. 1988. An analysis of stress and burnout in learning disabilities and regular education teachers. An unpublished doctoral dissertation, Northwestern University, Evanston.

Orton, S. 1937. *Reading, Writing and Speech Problems in Children.* New York: W. W. Norton.

Rawson, M. 1968. *Developmental Language Disability: Adult Accomplishments of Dyslexic Boys.* Baltimore: Johns Hopkins Press.

Rogan, L. L., and Hartman, L. D. 1990. Adult outcome of learning disabled students ten years after initial follow-up. *Learning Disabilities Focus* 5(2): 91–102.

Scruggs, T. E. 1990. Foundations of intervention research. In *Intervention Research in Learning Disabilities,* eds. T. E. Scruggs and B. Y. L. Wong,. New York: Springer-Verlag.

Scruggs, T. E., and Wong, B. Y. L. Eds. 1990. *Intervention Research in Learning Disabilities.* New York: Springer-Verlag.

Silver, A., and Hagin, R. 1985. Outcomes of learning disabilities in adolescence. *Annals of the American Society for Adolescent Psychiatry* 12(14):197–213.

Smith, N. 1991. Self-concept in college students with learning disabilities. An unpublished doctoral dissertation, Northwestern University, Evanston.

Spekman, N. H., Goldberg, R. J., and Herman, K. L. 1992. Learning disabled children grow up: A research for factors related to success in the young adults years. *Learning Disabilities Research & Practice* 7(3):161–70.

Spreen, O. 1988. *Learning Disabled Children Growing Up: A Follow-up into Adulthood.* New York: Oxford University Press.

Strauss, A. A., and Lehtinen, L. 1947. *Psychopathology and Education of the Brain-injured Child* (Vol. I). New York: Grune & Stratton.

Vaughn, S., McIntosh, R., and Hogan, A. 1990. Why social skills training doesn't work: An alternative model. In *Intervention Research in Learning Disabilities,* eds. T. E. Scruggs and B. Y. L. Wong. New York: Springer-Verlag.

Vogel, S. A., and Adelman, P. B. 1990. Intervention effectiveness at the postsecondary level for the learning disabled. In *Intervention Research in Learning Disabilities,* eds. T. E. Scruggs and B. Y. L. Wong. New York: Springer-Verlag.

Werner, E. E. 1990. Protective factors and individual resilience. In *Handbook of Early Childhood Intervention,* eds. S. J. Meisels and J. P. Shonkoss. Cambridge: Cambridge University Press.

White, W. J., Schumaker, J. B., Warner, M. M., Alley, G. R., and Deshler, D. D. 1980. *The Current Status of Young Adults Identified as Learning Disabled During their School Career.* Research Report #21. Lawrence: The University of Kansas, Institute for Research in Learning Disabilities.

Zigmond, N., and Thornton, H. 1985. Follow-up of postsecondary age learning disabled graduates and drop-outs. *Learning Disabilities Research* 1(1): 50–55.

# Chapter • 13

# The Establishment of Self-Regulation and Social Understanding in Children and Adolescents with ADHD
## *Family Factors*

*James C. Harris*

The hyperactive child was recognized in the folklore of the late 1800s, as documented in a popular poem about "fidgety Phil who could not sit still." Yet, the associated behavioral aspects were not well described until the beginning of this century, and then by a physician who, strangely enough, was named George Still. In his 1902 Coulstonian lectures, Still, Assistant Physician to the Hospital for Sick Children in London, gave three lectures titled "Some abnormal psychical conditions in children." These addressed a defect in moral self-control in children. Still, commenting on the psychosocial aspects of their attentional problems, wrote: "interesting as these disorders may be as an abstruse problem for the professed psychologist to puzzle over, they have a real practical—shall I say social importance, which I venture to think has been hardly sufficiently recognized" (p. 1008). He goes on to describe their self-control problems in social situations. It is in this area that the child's difficulty has its impact on family functioning.

Still used the term *moral self-control* to refer to "the control of action for the good of all" (p. 1008). He pointed out that moral control can exist only when there is a sufficient cognitive understanding of one's relationship to others. However, Still suggested that intellectual understanding is not enough; volition is also necessary. He went on to describe developmental features in children, emphasizing the inhibitory nature of volition to "overpower" a stimulus, which leads to excessive activity. He referred to the slow and gradual development of inhibitory volition as a child grows older. He noted that inhibitory volition becomes directed toward the most instinctive forms of activity; for example, the expression of emotions. Still intended to describe a morbid defect in volition.

On the other hand, Still viewed moral control as multiply determined; that is, it was the outcome of the cognitive interrelationship with the environment, with moral consciousness, and with volition. In subsequent lectures, he offered examples to demonstrate that mental retardation, a purely cognitive defect, was not the cause of a self-control deficit because nonretarded individuals may show far more severe behavioral defects than those who are mentally retarded. In later lectures, he provided a series of case examples of defects in moral control and categorized them; that is, congenital cases, those acquired following brain injury, those that seemed to have permanent symptoms, those with temporary symptoms, and those where behavioral control was cyclical.

Today we use the terms *socially adapted*, *social competence*, and *prosocial behavior*. We speak of moral development and the emergence of empathy in development rather than "moral control," thereby placing the primary emphasis on a child's self-regulation or self-control. Still's emphasis on volition is reminiscent of the current focus on the motivational aspects of Attention Deficit Hyperactivity Disorder (ADHD) and efforts to understand dysfunction in executive control functions in this disorder. The outcome of defects in moral control are now subsumed under the DSM III-R category, *conduct disorder*, a diagnosis that commonly co-occurs with ADHD.

The long-term goals in the treatment of ADHD and its associated features have not changed since Still's time, that is, to prevent learning failure, antisocial behavior, substance abuse, and other complications of this developmental disability. Current efforts at prevention require an appreciation of the child's relationship with the family and the appropriate use of family-based interventions.

## EXTENDED DEFINITION OF ADHD

Barkley (1990) emphasizes the issue of volition in his extended definition of attention deficit disorder. He proposes a consensus definition of

ADHD that highlights the developmental nature of self-regulatio.. ᴵᴵᵉ adds a functional aspect to the definition by highlighting deficient rule-governed behavior, and difficulties in maintaining work performance.

Barkley's extended definition is:

> Attention-deficit Hyperactivity Disorder is a developmental disorder characterized by developmentally inappropriate degrees of inattention, overactivity, and impulsivity. These often arise in early childhood; are relatively chronic in nature; and are not readily accounted for on the basis of gross neurological, sensory, language, or motor impairment, mental retardation, or severe emotional disturbance. These difficulties are typically associated with deficits in rule-governed behavior and in maintaining a consistent pattern of work performance over time (p. 47).

This definition is particularly important when considering family interaction. Problems with rule-governed behavior are complicated by temperament and personality features associated with ADHD. These include low self-esteem, mood lability, low frustration tolerance, anhedonia (lack of pleasure in accomplishment), and temper outbursts. These personality and temperament features predispose affected children to oppositional behavior and conduct problems and experiences of demoralization, perhaps based on the learned helplessness model of depression.

## SOCIAL COGNITIVE DEFICIT

### Social Cognitive Domain

Social cognition is the processing of information that culminates in accurate perception of the dispositions and intentions of others. Social cognition has an intimate tie to affective or emotional relations with others and has evolved in response to the demands of a complex social environment. The evolutionary basis of social cognition has received new emphasis with the identification of feature recognition cells in the temporal lobe of the brain in primates (Desimone 1991). The linkage of these cells to the prefrontal cortex suggests a selective response of single neurons or groups of neurons to social contact.

The social cognitive system is important to consider in children with ADHD because they demonstrate problems not only in task behavior and distractibility, but also in social perception (interpreting nonverbal cues such as facial expression), role taking (taking another's point of view), social problem solving (generating alternative solutions), and social communication (social pragmatics; e.g., maintaining a conversation).

Although the existence of a specific social cognitive network in the brain has not been demonstrated, deficits in response inhibition have been suggested to be the result of dysfunction in the right frontostriate system. In addition, social emotional learning disability (SELD) has been attributed to right hemispheric dysfunction. Therefore, inattention may extend beyond short attention span to social inattention, potentially a "social" neglect syndrome.

## Dysfunctional Affect Discrimination

In normal development, a variety of affective responses are normally discriminated (Izard 1991). These include joy, anger, fear, sadness, and disgust. Verbal labeling of emotions is a task that follows a developmental sequence. It may be helpful to consider affective discrimination as a pertinent issue in dealing with the social deficit in ADHD.

A recent case report by Damasio, Tranel, and Damasio (1990) may facilitate understanding of the mechanisms of frontal lobe dysfunction that might be pertinent to emotional labeling in cases of ADHD with an associated conduct disorder. Damasio and colleagues (1990) described a patient with sociopathic behavior caused by frontal lobe damage who failed to respond automatically to social stimuli. Damasio has previously pointed out that following damage to the ventromedial frontal cortices, adults with previously normal personalities have developed deficits in decision making and planning that may lead to abnormal social conduct. Damasio now proposes that the defect is due to an inability to activate somatic states linked to punishment and reward. He suggests that, in his previous experience, the patient's somatic states were associated with social situations. In new situations, prior somatic states could be reactivated in connection with anticipated responses from others to provide contextually appropriate options to respond.

Damasio argues that failure to activate somatic (bodily) states deprives an individual of an automatic device to signal the ultimately deleterious consequences of decisions. Although impulsive decisions might bring immediate reward, longer term consequences may go unrecognized. For example, activation of somatic states might lead to the individual's attention being focused on the negative consequences of his or her choices. This awareness might provide the option to inhibit behavior. Here we are speaking of the experience of the body in the mind, commonly referred to as a "gut feeling" about what action to take.

Clinically the automatic response to social stimuli may be an issue in ADHD. It is proposed that children with ADHD may not adequately discriminate bodily feeling states and/or may misperceive social situations. They might experience a faulty, negative, or aversive bodily sensation and have difficulty linking affect to cognition. For example, the child may say to himself (and then to others to justify his behavior), that another child "looked at him the wrong way" to justify fighting.

## EFFECT OF THE CHILD'S DISORDER ON OTHERS

Because of social cognition and affect discrimination difficulties, these children are generally unaware of their effects on others. In fact, the mental disorder described in DSM III-R is the result of perceived effects of children's behavior on others. Children do not complain of a sense of psychological suffering or express ego dystonic symptoms; that is, children generally are not in conflict about their symptoms. This lack of awareness may lead to misunderstanding in their families.

Besides the impact of children's lack of awareness, family relationships are influenced by other associated diagnoses (Munir, Biederman, and Knee 1987), especially diagnoses of oppositional and/or conduct disorder. Children with these other disruptive behavior disorders and/or difficult temperament have a worse prognosis (August and Stewart 1983; Harris et al. 1984) and a greater negative effect on others. In addition to temperament factors and multiple diagnoses, the presence of prosocial behaviors, the capacity for psychological reflectivity, the ability to monitor oneself, the ability to regulate oneself, the capacity to identify and label affect, responsiveness to medication, and concurrent language and learning disabilities are all factors in children that influence family relationships. The recognition and treatment of associated language and learning disabilities is critical to prevent or reduce antisocial behavior (Satterfield, Satterfield, and Cantwell 1981; Harris 1989).

## FAMILY RELATIONSHIPS

The major issue affecting family function involves the interpersonal relationship between parent and child. Adversive or coercive interpersonal exchanges with parents are common as a consequence of the social cognitive and emotional recognition difficulties. The parent-child interaction is marred by poor child compliance, more time off-task, more negative responses to parent request, poorly regulated rule-governed behavior, and less sustained attention to task. A child's negative response to requests leads to a vicious cycle of negativity with adversive and coercive interactions with parents.

Specific family issues that must be considered in addressing the parent/child relationship include parental factors, such as psychosocial background; parental psychiatric and developmental diagnosis (antisocial behavior, depression, alcohol abuse, learning disability); parenting stress, extent of parental acknowledgment of the child's handicap; and parental motivation to participate in a multimodal treatment program. Research findings support the following conclusions about the family of the child with ADHD:

1. *Increased genetic risk.* Genetic factors play a role in the family; the risk of ADHD in first-degree biological relatives is suggested to be 25%–33% (Biederman, Munir, and Knee 1986; Goodman and Stevenson 1989). Studies of identical twins with ADHD show significant concordance between them.

2. *Stressful social interactions.* Social interactions between children with ADHD and their parents have been shown to be different (more stressful and negative) when contrasted to families without an affected child (Breen and Barkley 1988). The sex of the affected child is not at issue; similar family effects are seen for both boys and girls (Breen and Barkley 1988).

3. *Lower levels of parental self-esteem.* Parents and siblings in families with a child with ADHD experience a higher rate of psychological distress. Mothers report lower levels of parental self-esteem and higher levels of depression, especially when the child with ADHD is a preschool child (Barkley 1990).

4. *Increased parental psychiatric disorder.* There is an increased prevalence of antisocial behavior, depression, alcohol abuse, and learning disability in family members. This is especially the case in instances when ADHD is co-morbid with other disruptive behavior disorders (Cantwell 1972, Stewart, deBlois, and Cummings 1980; Barkley 1990).

## ASSESSMENT PROCESS

### Parent as Informant

The social/family context is basic to diagnosis and assessment. Attention deficit-hyperactivity disorder occurs in a family context. It is family members who recognize the condition and initiate referral. Rating scales are particularly important for parents to complete at the time of referral, or as part of the screening procedure, to allow them to designate the child's referral problem. Epidemiological studies use parental ratings such as the CBCL (Achenbach and Edelbrock 1981) to allow identification of the externalizing symptoms of attention deficit disorder and associated co-morbid behavioral disturbances. Structured interviews also may be used. These rely on the parent interview to confirm the diagnosis. Indeed, the DSM III-R criteria for the diagnosis of ADHD are based on others' observations.

The parental assessment interview includes an evaluation of child's behavior, a description of parent/child interaction, ascertainment of parental psychological state, evaluation of marital functioning, and determination of the presence of parental psychiatric disorder.

## Teacher Report

Reports by the teacher of classroom behavior (Connors 1985) may be needed to confirm the diagnosis. These reports are essential because children often will not show symptoms in a one-to-one office setting. Teachers benefit from their experience making age-related comparisons between children and their classroom peers. Teachers' reports may document the effects of a child's behavior on others and responses to that child from peers.

## CONSIDERATIONS IN TREATMENT

The approach to treatment should address the multiple problems of the child and the family. Satterfield, Satterfield, and Cantwell (1981) refer to this approach as multimodal treatment and have reported that multiple interventions offer the best outcome. Treatment may include family systems approaches, focused interventions with the child, adversive/coercive intervention based on the Barkley model (Barkley 1990), drug treatment, and selective couples or individual parental treatment.

The techniques of behavior modification may be applied in the treatment of attention deficit disorder (Christensen and Sprague 1973; Gittelman et al. 1980). However, operant conditioning approaches must be carefully specified. These approaches have been most useful for short-term reduction of off-task behavior. Behavioral reduction strategies need to be balanced with strategies to enhance socially appropriate behavior. Reward-based approaches can be used to reduce over-activity and fidgetiness; however, the reduction of activity is generally not enough to help with a child's adjustment. Children also need to be taught specifically positive skills of learning, particularly of social interaction. Focus on the establishment of prosocial behaviors in addition to reduction of disruptive behavior is essential to treatment (Barkley 1990). These approaches must be combined with appropriate diagnosis and drug treatment.

Cognitive behavior therapy has been used as a tool for teaching techniques of self-control and problem solving. In laboratory tests, cognitive behavioral approaches do reduce impulsiveness. However, longer term effects and changes in real-life performance have not been established adequately. These approaches emphasize self-regulatory intervention, channeling behavioral excess, fostering of a reflective approach, and appreciation of situational social cues. These social cognitive strategies are essential in directly teaching social communicative behavior and affect labeling (Whalen, Henker, and Hinshaw 1985).

Poor child management techniques (handling adversive/coercive interactions), parental psychopathology (especially maternal depression, paternal aggression, and antisocial behavior), and marital discord occur more commonly in these families than in controls and play an important role in behavioral outcome (August and Stewart 1983; Whalen, Henker, and Hinshaw 1985). These family issues lead to a multimodal approach. Often conjoint family therapy is needed. A family approach takes into account parental beliefs and attitudes, psychological distress, strategies for conflict resolution, and other family systems issues. The depressed parent presents a particular dilemma. The depressed mother may rate the child as more defiant, make critical remarks, and show aggressive responses.

Drug treatment is part of a multimodal approach. Pharmacologic intervention affects family function. Pharmacological intervention may lead to improvement in interpersonal compliance and a reduction of negative parent/child interactions (Schachar et al. 1987). However, pharmacotherapy is only one aspect of a treatment and should be carried out with other interventions. Combined drug treatment may be needed that includes augmentation of stimulant medication for comorbid diagnosis, such as intermittent explosive behavior and depression.

## SCHOOL-BASED INTERVENTION

Because failure in school is common, it is important that psychiatric liaison with schools and awareness of special education needs be highlighted in every psychiatric assessment. Furthermore, because of the negative feedback that these children receive, they often think of themselves as stupid and may require counseling to help them deal with problems in self-esteem.

Specific intervention in the classroom is critical for long-term success. One well-developed program is the University of Washington PATHS (Providing Alternative Thinking Strategies) program, wherein educators and counselors facilitate self-control, emotional awareness, and interpersonal problem-solving skills. Its goals are to enhance social competence and social understanding in the classroom.

Cook, Greenberg, and Kusche (1991) used the PATHS program to investigate individual differences in emotional understanding and in children's behavioral responses. They used the curriculum for 69 children (grades 1–4) in special needs classes, who were randomly assigned to intervention and comparison groups by classroom and school. Intervention children used the PATHS program four days a week for seven months. At posttest, the intervention children showed significant improvement in frustration tolerance, improved assertive social skills, better task orientation, enhanced peer social skills, and improved emotional labeling. These findings suggest that PATHS is effective for promoting adaptive classroom behavior and improving emotional understanding in special needs children.

The following specific goals are incorporated in the PATHS curriculum and are goals to address deficits in social cognition and affect regulation. The lessons and their goals are as follows:

1. Increase self-control; the ability to stop and think before acting, especially when upset or coping with a conflict situation. This lesson also includes recognition of upset feelings.
2. Teach attributional processes that lead to an appropriate sense of self-responsibility.
3. Enhance understanding of the vocabulary of logical reasoning and problem solving, e.g., "if . . . then," and "why . . . because."
4. Increase understanding and use of the vocabulary of emotions and emotional states; e.g., excited, disappointed, confused, guilty, etc. and increase use of verbal mediation.
5. Increase ability to recognize and interpret similarities and differences in the feelings, reactions, and points of view of self and others.
6. Increase recognition and understanding of how one's behavior affects others.
7. Increase knowledge of, and skill in, the steps of social problem solving, stopping and thinking, identifying problems and feelings, setting goals, generating alternative solutions, anticipating and evaluating consequences, planning, executing and evaluating a course of action, and trying again if the first solution fails.
8. Increase ability to apply social problem-solving skills to prevent and resolve problems and conflicts in social interactions.

## SUMMARY

The child with ADHD has a disorder that occurs within a family context. The child's difficulty in self-regulation and affect discrimination may have an adverse impact on family functioning. On the other hand, parental difficulties may compound a child's problems and increase the risk for co-morbid diagnoses. Treatment must involve family members in a multimodal treatment paradigm that includes individual, behavioral, social-cognitive, family, drug, and school-based interventions.

## REFERENCES

Achenbach, T. M., and Edelbrock, C. S. 1981. Behavioral problems and competencies reported by parents of normal and disturbed children aged four through sixteen. *Monographs of the Society for Research in Child Development* 466:1–82.

August, G. J., and Stewart, M. A. 1982. Is there a syndrome of pure hyperactivity? *British Journal of Psychiatry* 140:305–311.

August, G. J., and Stewart, M. A. 1983. Family subtypes of childhood hyperactivity. *Journal of Nervous and Mental Disease* 171:362–68.

Barkley, R. A. 1989. Hyperactive boys and girls: Stimulant drug effects in mother child interaction. *Journal of Child Psychology and Psychiatry* 30: 379–90.

Barkley, R. A. 1990. *Attention Deficit Disorder: A Handbook for Diagnosis and Treatment.* New York: Guilford Press.

Biederman, J., Munir, K., Knee, D. 1986. A family study of patients with attention deficit disorder and normal controls. *Journal of Psychiatric Research* 20:263–74.

Breen, M. J., and Barkley, R. A. 1988. Child psychopathology and parenting stress in girls and boys having attention deficit disorder with hyperactivity. *Journal of Pediatric Psychology* 13:165–80.

Cantwell, D. 1972. Psychiatric illness in the families of hyperactive children. *Archives of General Psychiatry* 27:414–27.

Christensen, D., and Sprague, R. 1973. Reduction of hyperactive behavior by conditioning procedures alone and combined with methylphenidate. *Behavior Research and Therapy* 11:331–34.

Connors, C. K. 1985. *The Connors Rating Scales: Instruments for the Assessment of Childhood Psychopathology.* Washington, DC: Children's Hospital National Medical Center.

Cook, R. T., Greenberg, M. T., and Kusche, C. A. 1991. The relationships between emotional understanding, intellectual functioning, and disruptive behavior problems in elementary school aged children. Paper presented at the Annual Meeting of the Society for Research in Child Development, Seattle, WA.

Damasio, A. R., Tranel, D., and Damasio, H. 1990. Individuals with sociopathic behavior caused by frontal damage fail to respond automatically to social stimuli. *Behavioural Brain Research* 41:81–94.

Desimone, R. 1991. Face-selective cells in the temporal cortex of monkeys. *Journal of Cognitive Neuroscience* 3:1–8.

Gittelman, R., Abikoff, H., Pollack, E., Klein, D. F., Katz, S., and Mattes, J. 1980. A controlled trial of behavior modification and methylphenidate. In *Hyperactive Children: The Social Ecology of Identification and Treatment,* eds. C. K. Whalen and B. Henker. New York: Academic Press.

Goodman, R., and Stevenson, J. 1989. A twin study of hyperactivity II. The aetiological role of genes, family relationships and perinatal adversity. *Journal of Child Psychology and Psychiatry* 30:691–709.

Harris, J. C. 1989. Interrelationship of learning and emotional difficulty: Their genesis and treatment. *Ciba Geigy Symposium* 69–77.

Harris, J. C., King, S., Reifler, J., and Rosenberg, L. 1984. Comparison of behavioral and learning disabled children in special schools. *Journal of the American Academy of Child Psychiatry* 23(4):431–37.

Izard, C. 1991. *The Psychology of Emotions.* New York: Plenum.

Kusche, C. A., and Greenberg, M. T. 1991. *Teaching PATHS in your Classroom:*

*The PATHS Curriculum Instructional Manual* (Special Needs Version). Seattle: University of Washington Press.

Munir, K., Biederman, J., and Knee, D. 1987. Psychiatric co-morbidity in patients with attention deficit disorder: A controlled study. *Journal of the American Academy of Child and Adolescent Psychiatry* 26:844–48.

Satterfield, J. H., Satterfield, B. T., and Cantwell, D. P. 1981. Three-year multimodal treatment study in hyperactive boys. *Journal of Pediatrics* 98:650–55.

Schachar, R., Taylor, E., Wiselberg, M, Thorby, G., and Rutter, M. 1987. Changes in family function and relationships in children who respond to methylphenidate. *Journal of the American Academy of Child and Adolescent Psychiatry* 26:728–32.

Stewart, M. A., deBlois, C. S., and Cummings, C. 1980. Psychiatric disorder in the parents of hyperactive boys and those with conduct disorder. *Journal of Child Psychology and Psychiatry* 21:283–92.

Still, G. F. 1902. The Coulstonian lectures on some abnormal psychical conditions in children. *The Lancet* i:1008–1012, 1077–1082, 1163–1168.

Whalen, C. K., Henker, B., and Hinshaw, S. P. 1985. Cognitive behavioral therapies for hyperactive children: Premises, problems, and prospects. *Journal of Abnormal Child Psychology* 13:391–410.

# Chapter • 14

## LEARNING DISABILITIES
### *Beyond the School Years*

*Michael Bender*

Today more individuals with disabilities are becoming part of mainstream society. The passage of the Americans With Disabilities Act in 1992, with provisions that prohibit job discrimination against an otherwise qualified person because of a disability, has been overwhelmingly supported by the public (Harris 1991). Disabled young adults are also entering college at a growing rate. In fact, almost 1 in 11 full-time freshmen attending school in 1991 report having a disability, whereas in 1978 only 1 in 38 disabled young adults reported college attendance (Henderson 1992). Since 1985, individuals with learning disabilities have accounted for the major growth of students with disabilities attending college, and represent approximately 25% of all disabled students.

Although the incidence or inclusion of individuals with disabilities into society seems to be expanding, evaluating the success of these individuals in terms of their daily interactions and working lives remains problematic. Their candid views are often shielded by embarrassment, and only recently have individuals with disabilities become vocal. Some of these young adults' comments are reported in this chapter.

It is important to remember that for young people, high school completion is a period of excitement and great expectations, although many are relieved just to have completed twelve or more years of formal education. Some choose to enter the world of work immediately, and others begin a quest for higher education. Choices as to what type of job or training to pursue, or what course of study to choose, or to which colleges apply, become their major goals.

Individuals with learning disabilities face the same choices. These choices are, however, much more limited in scope, fewer in number, and laden with many more uncertainties. The somewhat safe world of elementary and secondary school is ended. What lies ahead is an unknown world—a world of transition, interpersonal and social relationships, job seeking, job retention, and an abundance of leisure time. Traditionally, little in the way of formal or informal preparation has been made for these major life challenges.

Individuals with learning disabilities are especially anxious during these times, and have many questions. For those seeking the *higher education option*, questions include the following.

—Am I ready for college?
—Should I first try a two-year or community college?
—How do I know a college has resources for students with my disabilities?
—Will it take me longer to graduate from a program than nondisabled students?
—Where do I go first if I need help or counseling?
—Are trained professionals available to help?
—Will I be able to make friends?
—Will there be other students there like me?

For those seeking *entry-level employment*, similar questions and anxieties surface. Specifically they worry about the following.

—Am I ready to enter the world of work?
—Do I possess appropriate work skills?
—Will I have the ability to do a good job?
—Should I tell a perspective employer that I have a learning disability?
—Will I be able to make enough money to support myself?
—What are my chances of being unemployed or underemployed?
—Where do I go and who do I talk to when I have problems?

Whether young adults with learning disabilities choose work or school, they soon find they have additional free or *leisure time*. It quickly becomes apparent that *they* must take the initiative to meet new people and potential friends. For many of these individuals, this is a new facet of independence. They also begin to question whether they should tell new acquaintances that they are learning disabled. Locating leisure or recreational resources and deciding how to budget time and money for extracurricular activities become new areas of anxiety and concern.

A review of their questions reveals that many individuals with learning disabilities experience turmoil upon encountering the "real world." Although most nondisabled individuals at similar stages experience similar feelings, the person with learning disabilities often has fewer positive experiences to build upon and tends to intensify feelings and anxieties. For some, parents or other family members are there to help them through these difficult decision-making times. However, some parents may be overly protective, or take too great a role. A balance of family support and independence is needed if these individuals are to succeed.

### CRITICAL IMPORTANCE OF APPROPRIATE SOCIAL SKILLS

Although the influence and support of significant others such as parents, relatives, or close friends is a major factor in whether young adults with learning disabilities succeed, appropriate use of their interpersonal and social skills plays an equally important role. Ongoing life situations such as the economy, budgeting funds, coping with change, daily stress, and the need for resources, are all essential to successful interaction in society. In short, the ability to use appropriate social skills and to be proficient in demonstrating appropriate social behaviors are major determinants of success.

Figure 1 illustrates the importance of interrelationships, and the close interactions that occur among significant others in terms of life problems, searches for higher education or employment, leisure, and social skills during this critical young adult period. These relationships are highly interactive and, for many individuals with disabilities, must be taught.

In addition to the above interactions are concerns about motivation, job satisfaction, and peer relationships. This complex brew of factors and elements follows the individual through various stages of higher education, employment, and leisure activities.

### HIGHER EDUCATION OPTIONS

Higher education options for individuals with disabilities have expanded significantly during the past few years. As mentioned previously, 1 in 11 full-time freshman entering college in 1991 reported having a disability (Henderson 1992). Aside from those four-year college and university programs that offer special resources for individuals with disabilities, numerous two-year community colleges have expanded their programs to attract these students. Vocational, technical, business, and trade programs have also extended their offerings, often as a means to increase enrollment. When individuals with learning disabilities choose to go to college, many factors come into play.

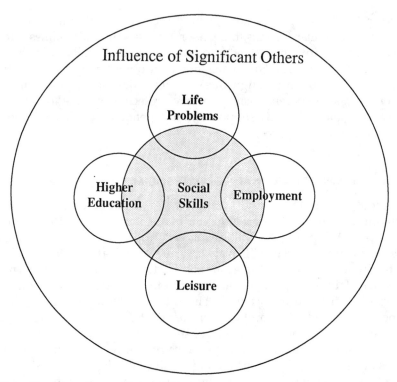

Figure 1.   Importance of interrelationships.

For example, it is widely accepted that parents help to define their child's potential for college and offer advice on career choices at this time (Dowdy, Carter, and Smith 1990). Ironically, special education teachers, vocational rehabilitation counselors, school counselors, and vocational education teachers, by and large, are not credited by students as providing major help during this transition.

Intensive assessment and evaluation often precede formal application to higher education programs. In many instances, results from these costly assessment procedures are sent to potential programs as part of the application process. It is not uncommon for a student's application file to include results from intelligence, achievement, reading and math batteries, interest inventories, aptitude and dexterity tests, personality tests, and countless numbers of academic and behavioral checklists. Because the college application process is confidential, it is not always clear to what extent this information is actually used in the selection process.

Many young people with disabilities, like their nondisabled peers, view college or higher education as a potential escape from routine daily frustrations. Although many may not be sure what to expect emotionally or academically at college, they see it as a chance to "get away" from home, and be with others their age. Unfortunately, after college orientation and transition programs are over, frustrations and problems often surface. The initial problems tend to be academic, but social problems persist also. The students' anguish is reflected in typical comments below.

—I have talked to the instructor several times about my learning disability—I think he is getting tired of me.
—I have trouble keeping up with the assignments.
—I can't figure out what specific information I need to study.
—I panic at taking exams.
—I spend most of my free time studying in my room.
—It's difficult to make friends; I am not sure I belong here.

It must be remembered that individuals with learning disabilities often perceive potential college problems in much the same way as do nondisabled individuals. That is, they view grades, academic deficits, money problems, transportation problems, and personality conflicts as potential sources of difficulty (Dowdy, Carter, and Smith 1990). A major difference, however, is that students with learning disabilities often fail to recognize that *study skills* are critically important to academic success, thus, they rarely list them as areas of concern. This telling omission indicates that individuals with learning disabilities may not understand what is important for academic success. In addition, most realistically predict they will need more time to achieve their educational goals (Henderson 1992), but they often fail to plan how to finance the extra time. Pressure and anxiety build as the financial burden of additional tuition typically falls on their parents. At this time, students often change their major courses of study (sometimes each semester), and the mere completion of school becomes paramount.

Consistently, the anxiety that these young adults experience is exaggerated because they lack appropriate social skills. Social deficits are major determinants to success or failure when other career options are selected. This is especially evident during seeking, finding, and retaining employment.

Although some college or university programs offer counseling or academic support for individuals with learning disabilities, most do not address complex situations or problems that tend to resurface time and again. Unfortunately, only the most persevering student, with strong supports, can survive this initial transition to higher education successfully.

## SEEKING, FINDING, AND RETAINING EMPLOYMENT

Information and follow-up literature on the vocational or work profiles of individuals with learning disabilities are quite limited (Gerber, Ginsberg, and Reiff 1992). Some examples of vocational success exist, but there are also countless numbers of adults who are not successful, are unemployed, or underemployed (President's Committee on the Employment of People with Disabilities 1990). For many young individuals with learning disabilities, it is not lack of opportunity, lack of desire for success, or lack of perseverance that creates failure in the workplace. It is the failure to meet the demands of the working world (Siegel and Gaylord-Ross 1991).

From the 1980s to the 1990s, the discipline of special education, attempting to increase the vocational success of its graduates, heavily emphasized developing a bridge between secondary school and the work world. The concept became known as *transition* and individuals with disabilities began to see such transition plans incorporated into their Individualized Education Programs (IEP). The reauthorization of the Individuals with Disabilities Education Act (IDEA) of 1990 P.L. 101-476 mandated the provision of transition services for students in special education sixteen years of age or older. This specific legislation detailed the process of service provision by providing transition services and: (1) listing the specific set of activities that make up transition services for an individual; (2) explaining the process of inclusion of transition services into a student's IEP; and (3) describing responsibilities of the local education agencies or school systems for monitoring the provided services. Emphasis on transition in the 1980s mainly addressed the bridge from secondary school to the working world and those job skills and training needed to succeed. For the first time, community networks were established that included employers as part of advisory councils. In the early 1990s, emphasis was concentrated on job readiness and employer needs. As a result, many employers looked to school programs to teach the social skills required for successful employment, leaving actual teaching of job skills to "on the job training."

When learning-disabled individuals did enter the job market, it was immediately apparent that they were a *new* resource. In fact, workers with learning disabilities, when compared to nondisabled workers, demonstrated the same or better job performances in terms of "willingness to work hard, reliability, attendance and punctuality, and productivity" (Muklewicz and Bender 1988). In 1991, the National Organization on Disability commissioned Louis Harris and Associates to conduct a national survey of public attitudes toward people with disabilities. The results of this survey revealed that four out of five Americans believed that disabled workers were equally or more productive than nondisabled workers. Knowing that the public now viewed workers with disabilities favorably, the problems remaining for many of them were inability to and lack of knowledge of the means to compete successfully for jobs.

Muklewicz and Bender (1988) began to analyze why so many individuals with learning disabilities had difficulty being hired. After many interviews with employers, they identified several major deficiencies that needed to be taught in transition plans, but often were not. These were: (1) understanding job requirements; (2) knowing how to take part in an interview; and (3) understanding entry-level salaries. They also found that most potential workers did not know how job vacancies occurred, did not understand the concept of competitive job seeking, and did not know how to communicate their employability. Interviews with clients revealed that even when they successfully found a job, they had difficulty with motivation, problem solving, co-worker conflicts, developing friendships, and accepting job changes. In essence, *staying employed* became the major task for them, much the same way as staying in college was for the group who opted for higher education. Ironically, in many instances, barriers to employment were not actively addressed in teaching or training programs.

### Barriers

Often, development of a successful employment plan must address ways or strategies to overcome barriers. For individuals with learning disabilities, these can be grouped into five major barriers: (1) attitudinal; (2) behavioral; (3) educational; (4) external and situation problems; and (5) external employer problems. *Attitudinal* problems for those with learning disabilities can take many forms. For example, it is common to find that individuals with learning disabilities have low vocational self-concepts as well as low self-esteem. Many have poor work histories and some are ambivalent about working. These attitudes must be addressed before workers actively enter the job market, or their stay there will be short and unsuccessful. *Behavioral* problems also assume many forms. Although the major emphasis in this domain must be to develop appropriate social skills, areas such as personal appearance, self-management, and reduction of annoying and inappropriate behaviors must also be addressed.

*Educational Skills* play a critical role in many types of employment. Lack of basic academic skills can be a major disadvantage, especially when one hopes for career advancement. Mastery of functional academic skills is mandatory, not only for job success, but also for understanding related areas of a job, not always detailed in a specific job description. For example, knowledge of safety rules and precautions are required for most jobs, but often are not taught before job placement. There also must be ways to solve problems on the job or to learn alternate strategies when confronted with difficult situations.

Circumventing and avoiding high-risk situations all must be addressed when developing a sound employment plan. There are also many *external and situation* factors that must be considered in the move toward successful employment. For example, problems with public and private transportation may limit the person's ability to seek employment at a specific site. Economic disincentives, such as losing or having existing benefits reduced by increased earnings, may influence the degree to which one may seek employment. A potential source of conflict may also be the degree to which the disabled family member's working may effect the immediate family. Sometimes, families become accustomed to relying upon their disabled family member at home to perform certain chores or errands. Therefore, they may not be positive or encouraging about possible employment or higher education. Because familial support is important, it is wise to anticipate their needs in order to make transition from the family to the work routine as smooth as possible.

*External employer* situations are very difficult to predict and depend upon a specific situation or employer. For example, employers often react in different ways to individuals with disabilities, based on past perceptions. Because employers are in business to make a profit, the state of the economy, and of their business, plays a role. If the potential employee seems to be a poor risk in any way, employment will not be offered.

Employment of persons with "mild" disabilities is one of the most pressing problems in our society (Siegel and Gaylord-Ross 1991). For individuals with severe disabilities, programs such as supported employment where help is provided on the job to clients through job coaches or other arrangements are becoming more readily available. However, for individuals with learning disabilities or other mild disabilities, little supported help exists. This is especially ironic in view of the potential for job success in this population when ongoing, minimal supports are in place. Without these supports, many individuals with learning disabilities are destined for entry-level, nonskilled jobs that are low paying and historically prone to elimination. These jobs offer little chance for advancement.

## SUCCESSFUL CLIENTS

Given equal opportunities for vocational success, why does one client succeed, while another does not? Does a specific program increase the odds for successful job placement? Do school programs curricula provide the prerequisites for success on the job?

Unfortunately, because programs are inconsistent and each learning-disabled individual has unique concerns and strengths, answers to the questions above are difficult to find. A single program or plan is not sufficient to help all clients. Good plans and programs, however, that address major educational areas, such as teaching social and work study skills, certainly increase the odds for vocational success. Gerber, Ginsberg, and Reiff (1992) have suggested that "the adult with learning disabilities must want to succeed, must set achievable goals, and must confront the learning disability so that appropriate measures may be taken to heighten the likelihood of success" (p. 480). They state further that persons must have the desire, the goal orientation, and the ability to reframe or put their disabilities in a positive light. In essence, individuals with learning disabilities must *want to succeed*. A review of the histories of successful individuals shows that they possess not only these traits, but are accustomed to "rolling with the punches." They seem to have extraordinary perseverance and have learned to circumvent or accommodate their problems.

## EMPLOYMENT PERSPECTIVES

Clearly, vocational success depends upon many factors. Among these is the need to understand different employment perspectives associated with job seeking—for example, the perspective of *significant others* in terms of what it might mean to them if their son or daughter finds a job. Loss of companionship, and possibly income, may result if they create a less than supportive environment for the job seeker. The perspective of the *individual* also plays a major role in how aggressively he or she may seek employment. For individuals with learning disabilities who seek to be part of the mainstream and want increased opportunities for advancement and quality of life, the world of work offers them the avenue to these conditions. For others, work in the community might seem overwhelming compared with their heretofore protected home situation. Someone in this latter group should receive more counseling, training time, and preparation before seeking employment .

Finally, there is the perspective of the *employer*, which must be considered in the hiring process. One tends to forget that employers hire individuals based upon their potential to boost productivity and profits. While many are sensitive and understand the needs and concerns of individuals with disabilities, most would not be in business if this were their primary business concern.

Only recently have corporations and small businesses recognized the talents and resources of workers with disabilities. Most now realize that these are individuals who want to work and who represent a potential pool of stable and reliable help. Once the above perspectives are taught and incorporated with the factors of success previously discussed, the chances of a positive and successful work experience are significantly increased.

## LEISURE ACTIVITIES

Perhaps the most misunderstood concept about leisure activities is how to define the leisure categories. Often, leisure is defined narrowly as a sedate and isolated activity, such as watching television, or participation in a sport or game. Actually, leisure has been delineated and classified much more comprehensively, allowing those developing or participating in these programs a variety of choices for leisure activities.

Overs and his colleagues, in 1977, were among the first to develop a leisure classification system, or taxonomy, that grouped avocational activities according to similarities. They divided them into nine major subject categories.

—Games
—Sports
—Nature activities
—Collection activities
—Craft activities
—Art and music activities
—Educational, entertainment, and cultural activities
—Volunteer activities
—Organizational activities

Bender, Brannan, and Verhoven (1984) adapted this model for special populations and individuals with disabilities. Development of their leisure curriculum for handicapped persons marked one of the first times leisure areas were acknowledged specifically to be important for those working with individuals with disabilities.

Leisure also has been incorporated into many career education programs as part of developing comprehensive outcomes for clients. This trend toward environmental and outdoor leisure education underscores the need to be aware of recreational resources as part of the move toward healthy lives and lifelong activities.

Reviews of the stages of individuals' high school completion and subsequent search for higher education or employment shows that free time quickly escalates the necessity for planning leisure activities. This area and its potential to encourage appropriate social skills learning is now receiving attention from those working with individuals with learning disabilities.

Although work, for many, will consume much of their time, one also must consider and plan for time when not working. This leisure, free, or nonwork time, allows for many social skill opportunities as well as opportunities for self-motivation, freedom to make choices, and risk taking (Bender, Brannan, and Verhoven 1984). As one interacts in the community as well as at home, numerous opportunities become available for leisure pursuits. These can include sharing activities with others, joining organizations, experiencing other environments, learning to use unfamiliar equipment, and working with a variety of materials.

For too long the concept of leisure or free time has been associated with skill-type games or activities. Different levels are associated with these activities, as shown in figure 2.

Obviously, many individuals with learning disabilities have shied away from competitive or skill-type games. At best, they may have participated at the spectator level, which offers the least chance for social interaction and may often be confined to television viewing or activities primarily isolated in nature.

Parental support for promoting social interactions and leisure, such as outside activities for their children, has always existed, but has not been very effective. This may be due to parental lack of knowledge of the many leisure resources present in their neighborhoods, as well as their lack of understanding of how to gain access to these resources. Key personnel in the community who are knowledgeable about leisure resources are often difficult to find. When they are identified, most are not trained to work with individuals with disabilities.

Many segments of the population, especially disabled persons, are often underemployed or unemployed to a greater degree than their nondisabled peers. For these individuals, coping with abundant

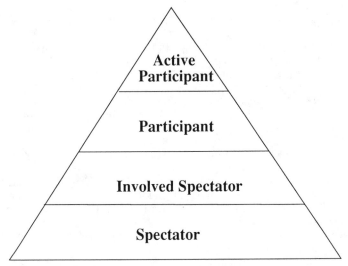

Figure 2. Leisure levels.

free time, most of which is forced upon them, becomes a major area of concern. Bender, Brannan, and Verhoven (1984) have presented the view that appropriate leisure activities can be most beneficial at this time, especially if done in a developmental framework. That is, individuals with disabilities need to be gradually exposed to leisure information and concepts, and supported in making rational, positive choices about how to select and use leisure resources. Then the individual with disabilities can begin to re-examine time-use patterns, and develop the motivation and skills necessary to interact in new leisure experiences.

## SUMMARY

This chapter presents the view that work, higher education, and leisure education provide new and unique opportunities for individuals with learning disabilities when they leave the more narrow confines of secondary school. Interrelationships and choices within these options will become areas of study for those who teach in these disciplines, and new challenges for those people with disabilities, who will find themselves increasingly thrust into these new situations.

The next decade will see more individuals with complex disabilities enter and blend into the competitive worlds of education, work, and leisure. It will be important to document and evaluate the success of these assimilations, in terms of the total inclusion of people with disabilities into all facets of society.

## REFERENCES

Bender, M., Brannan, S., and Verhoven, P. 1984. *Leisure Education for the Handicapped.* Austin, TX: PRO-ED.

Dowdy, C. A., Carter, J. K., and Smith, T. E. C. 1990. Differences in transitional needs of high school students with and without learning disabilities. *Journal of Learning Disabilities* 23 (6):343–48.

Gerber, P. J., Ginsberg, R., and Reiff, H. B. 1992. Identifying alterable patterns in employment success for highly successful adults with learning disabilities. *Journal of Learning Disabilities* 25 (8): 475–87.

Harris, L. 1991. *Public Attitudes Toward People with Disabilities.* New York: Louis Harris and Associates, Inc.

Henderson, C. 1992. *College Freshman with Disabilities: A Statistical Profile.* Washington, DC: American Council on Education, HEATH Resource Center.

IDEA, Individuals with Disabilities Education Act. 1991. Washington: 101st Congress.

Muklewicz, C., and Bender, M. 1988. *Competitive Job-finding Guide for Persons with Handicaps.* Austin, TX: PRO-ED.

Overs, P., Taylor, S., and Atkins, C. 1977. *Avocational Counseling Manual.* Washington: Hawkins and Associates.

President's Committee on the Employment of People with Disabilities. 1990. *From Paternalism to Productivity—Whatever it Takes.* Washington, DC: President's Committee on the Employability of People with Disabilities.

Siegel, S., and Gaylord-Ross, R. 1991 Factors associated with employment success among youths with learning disabilities. *Journal of Learning Disabilities* 23:(4):213–19.

# Subject Index

Crime, intelligence and, 202

DD. *See* Dysthymic disorder
Decision making and planning, damage to ventromedial frontal cortices and, 232
Depression: double, 179; in LD, 58; prevalence of serious (in children and adolescents), 184
Depressive disorders, 177–83; diagnosis of, 183–85; supportive treatment of, 189. *See also* Adjustment disorder with depressed mood (ADDM); Dysthymic disorder (DD); Major depression disorder (MDD)
Developmental dyslexia, 42; inheritance of, 86; possible subtypes of, 87
Developmental language disorders as chronic central nervous system disorders, 196
Disruptive behavior disorders, 196–200; comorbidity with, 200–202; lack of awareness of effect on others of behavior in, 233
Dopamine in brain, 22
Dropout rates, LD and, 211–12
Dunedin longitudinal study, 126, 127
Dyseidetic readers, 41
Dyslexia: attentional disorder with, 19; in boys vs. girls, 9–10; brain anomalies in, 19, 100–102; categorical concept of, 3–5; deep, 45; dimensional (along a continuum) model of, 5–6; direct, 45; emanative influences of models of, 6–7; importance of graduation (vs. discrete) model of, 11–12; phonological, 45; planum temporale and, 100; surface, 44; support for normal distribution model of, 8–9; traditional model of, 3–5; transient system deficit theory of, 99. *See also* Developmental dyslexia; Familial dyslexia; General reading backwardness (GRB); Reading disability
Dyslexics: achievements following special reading instruction, 213; brain lesions in, 18–19; L-type, 43; P-type, 43; residual reading

deficits among compensated, 89
Dysphonetic readers, 41
Dysthymic disorder (DD), 179–80

Educational readiness, tests of, 124
Electroencephalogram analysis, 131
Emotion. *See* Affect discrimination
Employment of LD students and adults, 212–14; dropping out of school and, 211, 212
Executive functions in cognition, 71–72
Eye movements, disturbances of, 27

Familial dyslexia: attention deficit disorders with, 94; brain imaging studies and, 100–102; falsely negative family histories and, 93; genetics and linkage studies of, 88–89, *90, 91*, 92–94, 95–98; immune function and, 94–95; male-female ratio in, 93; mode of inheritance of, 92; neuropsychological studies and, 98; nonpenetrant gene for, 92–93; non-right handedness in, 93; psychophysical studies and, 98–100; severity of, 93–94. *See also* Dyslexia
Family relationships: ADHD and, 233–34; factors in children that influence, 233
Fragile X mutation, factors that influence expression of, 69–70
Fragile X phenotype, 68–69; ascertainment bias in determination of, 70
Fragile X syndrome (fraX), 67; autism and, 73–74; autistic spectrum disorder and, 68, 75–76; cognitive profile in, 70–73; genetics of, 69–70; language and, 72–73; memory and, 73; neuropsychological component of, 71; nonverbal learning disability and, 75–76; social and emotional profile and, 73–75
Frostig School, 209, 212

Gender effects masking disease effects, 101
General reading backwardness (GRB), 3–4

# Author Index